JOHANNESBURG
FROM THE RIVERBANKS
NAVIGATING THE JUKSKEI

Edited by Mehita Iqani and Renugan Raidoo

Published by HSRC Press
Private Bag X9182, Cape Town, 8000, South Africa
www.hsrcpress.ac.za

First published 2025

ISBN (soft cover) 978-0-7969-2688-3
ISBN (pdf) 978-0-7969-2689-0

© 2025 Human Sciences Research Council

This book has undergone a double-blind independent peer-review process overseen by the HSRC Press
Editorial Board.

The views expressed in this publication are those of the authors. They do not necessarily
reflect the views or policies of the Human Sciences Research Council (the Council)
or indicate that the Council endorses the views of the authors. In quoting from this publication,
readers are advised to attribute the source of the information to the individual author concerned
and not to the Council.

The publishers have no responsibility for the continued existence or accuracy of URLs for
external or third-party Internet websites referred to in this book and do not guarantee that any
content on such websites is, or will remain, accurate or appropriate.

Copy-edited by Lou Levine
Typeset by Rina Eksteen
Cover design by Riaan Wilmans
Printed by [Name of printer, city, country]

Distributed in Africa by Blue Weaver
Tel: +27 (021) 701 4477; Fax Local: (021) 701 7302
www.blueweaver.co.za

Distributed worldwide (except central and southern Africa)
by Lynne Rienner Publishers, Inc.
Tel: +1 303-444-6684; Fax: +1 303-444-0824; Email: cservice@rienner.com
www.rienner.com

No part of this publication may be reproduced, stored in a retrieval system, or transmitted by any form or by
any means, electronic, mechanical, photocopying, recording or otherwise, without prior permission from the
copyright owner.

To copy any part of this publication, you may contact DALRO for information and copyright clearance.

Tel: 086 12 DALRO (or 086 12 3256 from within South Africa); +27 (0)11 712-8000
Fax: +27 (0)11 403-9094
Postal Address: P O Box 31627, Braamfontein, 2017, South Africa
www.dalro.co.za

Any unauthorised copying could lead to civil liability and/or criminal sanctions.

Suggested citation: Iqani M & Raidoo R (Eds) (2025) *Johannesburg from the Riverbanks: Navigating the Jukskei.*
Cape Town: HSRC Press

Contents

Figures   v

Tables   viii

Foreword   ix

Acknowledgements   xi

Map of the Jukskei   xiv

1   **Riparian urbanism: Thinking Johannesburg with the Jukskei**   1
Mehita Iqani and Renugan Raidoo

Part 1: Scientific Perspectives   15

2   **The historical Jukskei River valley: A botanical benchmark**   16
Antoinette Bootsma

3   **Macroplastic pollution within the Jukskei River: How much, what kind and why does it matter?**   27
Kyle van Heyde

4   **Bacterial contamination in the Jukskei River in Gauteng Province, South Africa**   37
Kousar Banu Hoorzook and Atheesha Singh

5   **Upper Jukskei Catchment Management Plan**   47
Stuart Dunsmore and Ernita van Wyk

Part 2: Art and the River   61

6   **For the one that dances with jiggling brass: Compositions for the Jukskei**   62
Dunja Herzog

7   **Where water once stood, it shall stand again: Stances on fluvial art practice**   68
Nina Barnett, Refiloe Namise and Abri de Swardt

8   **Radiation and rapture: Images of healing and pollution in the Jukskei River**   88
Landi Raubenheimer

9   **Community engagement at the Jukskei source: A photo essay**   103
Lungile Hlatshwayo

Part 3: River Politics 110

10 **Joburg and the sea: A squalid romance** 111
Sean Christie

11 **Dirty river: Whiteness, pollution and the Jukskei** 121
Nicky Falkof

12 **Reporting on the Jukskei: Behind three headlines** 129
Jamaine Krige

13 **The creaturely life of the Jukskei, and anxious bewilderment of faecal discourse** 141
Jessica Webster

Part 4: River Living 152

14 **On the edge: Riverbank living along a Jukskei tributary** 153
Sarah Charlton

15 **Mamlambo in Waterfall City** 168
Ujithra Ponniah

16 **The river talks** 179
Sibusiso Sangweni

17 **What elites think with the Jukskei: Property, race, and blame in totemic thought** 182
Renugan Raidoo

Part 5: Urban River Management 194

18 **The river is our resource: Alex Water Warriors** 195
Paul Maluleke

19 **Temporary or permanent? The built environment and living conditions in Stjwetla informal settlement** 199
Savory Chikomwe

20 **Converging currents: Urban ecological design strategies towards a resilient river system** 214
Dieter Brandt

21 **The river deserves love: Water for the future** 222
Romy Stander

About the authors 227
Index 233

List of figures

Figure 3.1   Study area   29

Figure 3.2   The river profile of the sites along the Jukskei River   30

Figure 3.3   Perceived environmental or ecological impacts associated with plastic pollution   32

Figure 3.4   The number of macroplastic items moving through sites along the Jukskei River across the four sampling campaigns   33

Figure 4.1   Visual location of the upper Jukskei catchment study area   40

Figure 5.1   Severe flooding in the upper Jukskei catchment, November 2016   48

Figure 5.2   The study catchment location within the quaternary catchment system   49

Figure 5.3   Frequency of storm responses in the Jukskei River natural catchment (black) vs urban catchment (grey)   54

Figure 5.4   The benefits of diverting stormwater runoff to available open spaces (black line) compared to the conventional stormwater network (grey line)   55

Figure 5.5   Water's journey on different surfaces in the catchment area. Planning the stormwater 'load' diverted to an unpaved area of the catchment.   55

Figure 6.1   HUM, 2022, Multimedia installation with seven ceramic beehives and an 8-channel sound installation   67

Figure 7.1   Refiloe Namise, images taken during Episode 1 of *Segopotso sa Gomora*, installation-based performance, 2022, The Point of Order, Johannesburg   70

Figure 7.2   Refiloe Namise, images taken during Episode 3 of *Segopotso sa Gomora*, installation-based performance, 2022, The Point of Order, Johannesburg   71

Figure 7.3   Abri de Swardt, stills from *Ridder Thirst*, 2015-18, HD Projection with double seating structure, 13'38 min   72

Figure 7.4   Nina Barnett, *On Breathing – Vapour* (installation view), 2022, Adler Museum of Medicine, Johannesburg   73

Figure 7.5   Nina Barnett, *Incidental Rift*, 2016 documentation of intervention at Origins Centre, Johannesburg   74

Figure 7.6	Abri de Swardt, *Streams (VI)*, 2021, Giclée Print on Hahnemühle Baryta, 500 X 750 mm 82
Figure 7.7	Refiloe Namise, Installation shots taken from Episode 3 of *Segopotso sa Gomora*, 2022, installation-based performance, The Point of Order, Johannesburg 83
Figure 7.8	Nina Barnett, Vaal water sample in the studio, March 2023 and Nina Barnett, Walking into the flooded dam 2023, documentation of experimentation 84
Figure 7.9	The confluence of the Vaal and the Orange Rivers at Douglas, Northern Cape in 1997 86
Figure 8.1	Gulshan Khan, Plastic and other waste litter the banks of the Jukskei River which runs through the Alexandra Township in Johannesburg on June 3, 2018 92
Figure 8.2	Hannelie Coetzee, still from *Finding the eye of the Jukskei River beneath Joburg* 97
Figure 9.1	A walking tour led by Grant Ngcobo from Dlala Nje in August, 2021 shows local community members from Bertrams at the river at the Victoria Yards culvert. The walking tour was co-created by Water for the Future and Dlala Nje 103
Figure 9.2	A group of women from the local Bertrams community look at the Jukskei headwaters in the culvert near Lang Street, Lorentzville 104
Figure 9.3	On World Water Monitoring Day in September, 2021, visitors to Victoria Yards were invited to come and see the ongoing rejuvenation work at the culvert 104
Figure 9.4	A full moon healing ceremony by the group Exotically Divine, convened for meditation and discussion near artist Io Makandal's land artwork *Extant Rewilding*, 2019-ongoing as part of her MAFA (Wits) practical research 105
Figure 9.5	Children from the community were invited to take part in a collaborative art project about water sustainability in August, 2019. Here they are setting off on a 'droplet treasure hunt' 105
Figure 9.6	One of the children searches for a clue in the droplet treasure hunt, near the Jukskei daylight point near Snake Road 106
Figure 9.7	Community children help Victoria Yards urban farmer Siyabonga Nlangamandla to plant a tree in the EcoSeat designed by Hannelie Coetzee in dialogue with the community. The EcoSeat is an example of a sustainable urban drainage system 106

Figure 9.8   After alien invasive trees are removed from the culvert, one of the ways the wood is repurposed is into aesthetic woven fencing   107

Figure 9.9   The weather station, funded by Campbell Scientific, is located at the Victoria Yards culvert. Along with a Isco sampler sponsored by aquatic ecologist Dr Liz Day in the water at the same location, scientific data is collected   107

Figure 9.10   Local community members from Bertrams assisting with a citizen science data collection activity regarding different types of waste in the area, in Thames Street   108

Figure 9.11   A teenage reclaimer transports her recyclable goods past the Jukskei daylight point. Local businesses have supported recycling and reclaimer self-employment in Bertrams   108

Figure 9.12   An activation took place at the daylight point to invite the community to share ideas about how to clean up the formerly heavily polluted site   109

Figure 9.13   A collaborative effort involving community members who are part of the President Stimulus Fund, Industrial Development Corporation, Johannesburg Inner City Partnership project and local business cleaned up the daylight point on Thames Street. It now features a beautiful mosaic created by artists from the nearby Spaza Gallery   109

Figure 13.1   *Ophidian's Promise* 2024. Artist: Io Makandal (public artwork commission by Alserkal Advisory for A Feral Common, curated by Tairone Bastien). Site: Victoria Yards over the Jukskei River culvert   147

Figure 15.1   Sketch by author   170

Figure 15.2   Mamlambo in Waterfall City   173

Figure 15.3   Interconnected blue pipes of the ozone plant   174

Figure 15.4   Mamlambo's entrance at the city   175

Figure 15.5   Mamlambo charges her rent   176

Figure 17.1   A map of nature trails displayed outside one of the estate's communal spaces   184

Figure 17.2   From the 21st-anniversary commemorative edition of the Dainfern estate magazine, a deck overlooking the river from Willowgrove Village   189

Figure 19.1   The dense Stjwetla settlement sprawling into the off-summer season Jukskei River   201

Figure 19.2   Summary of the basic infrastructure trajectory in Stjwetla   202

Figure 19.3   An 'off-site' sewerage effluent disposal into Jukskei through a white PVC pipe and several trash deposits on the riverbanks   205

List of tables

Table 2.1   A list of indigenous plants known to occur in the Suikerbosrand that are suitable for landscaped environments in Johannesburg   22

Table 2.2   A list of indigenous medicinal plants that grow in the Jukskei River catchment   24

Table 4.1   Glossary of key terms and health implications related to water quality in the Jukskei River   38

Table 5.1   Baseline parameters for the upper Jukskei catchment   50

Table 5.2   Recommended catchment management targets   51

Foreword

Richard Ballard

Professor: Urban Planning | School of Architecture and Planning
University of the Witwatersrand, Johannesburg

When we tell the story of a place, the entry point we use can make a big difference. Many previous accounts of the place described in this book use *the city of Johannesburg* as their subject. The result is an undoubtedly rich historiography of the processes that fuelled the development of the settlement and society at this location. However, when we tell the story of this same place using the Jukskei River as our framing device, important insights are brought into focus.

Firstly, we learn about nature's ambivalent status in the city's culture. We often think of nature as unspoiled wilderness beyond cities. We prefer that nature that does occur within cities should be tamed in the form of treed avenues, manicured gardens and parks, domesticated pets and caged animals in zoos. The Jukskei does not conform to either of these ideals. Its source is now a concrete pipe buried near the most densely populated parts of the city. Once it emerges, its banks are canalised or overgrown by invasive exotic plants. As it threads north through the city, concentrations of harmful refuse, chemicals and sewerage increase. Compared to the river we would have found here before the discovery of gold 140 years ago, it is unrecognisable. Therefore, it is hard for our culture to see it as part of either wilderness or urban nature. Something that should be life-giving, pure, virtuous and beautiful is now dangerous, poisoned and unattractive. It is a source of disgust and shame, an unfortunate anachronism that does not quite belong.

On the other hand, people use and relate to the river extensively. Faith-based communities use it for baptism and prayer. Some people consider the river to have a character, spirit or deity. People derive a sense of place from it, understanding it as part of their heritage. It is a space for recreation and renewal, for walking alongside and looking at. People have created gardens along or near the river. It is a site of, and inspiration for, artistic expression. The urban disenfranchised can derive some income from it, retrieving copper wiring and golf balls or making bricks from river sand. Many have built homes along the river – some with the permission of planners and some without. People who cannot afford rent elsewhere, or who have been hounded from their homes in xenophobic attacks, find refuge by sleeping rough along the river.

And despite its reputation, the river system is full of life. It is a home for birds, insects, amphibians, plants and fish. From time to time, a hippo travels upstream from the Hartbeespoort Dam. The climax ecosystems that would have been present before the city's establishment are no longer present, but the system nevertheless contains wetlands teeming with plants and animals. Therefore, ideal imaginaries of nature – as either wilderness or manicured – rub up against the fact of the river's daily importance to urban communities, human and non-human.

A second insight that comes into focus is how the economy unevenly values both the environment and people. For the most part, the Jukskei is surplus to the needs of capital. As a result, the preservation or integrity of this system does not rise very high on the priority list of most businesses or society at large. The river's source was developed into sports facilities and other concrete commodities because, in Marxist terms, the 'exchange value' of the site trumped its 'use value.' Meanwhile, the 'negative externalities' of economic production and consumption (toxic metals, sewage, discarded items, microplastics, salts and pathogens) are dumped into the river, because the cost of doing so is lower than processing this waste safely. Tellingly, now that large-scale walled estates have begun marketing the river as part of the good life, cleaning it has become a form of investment.

Many humans, too, are surplus to the needs of capital. One in three workers is now unemployed, and many who do have jobs earn below a living wage. Low-income households try to reduce both travel and accommodation costs. Intensive shack building along river banks produces much needed affordable accommodation. Yet these are risky environments, prone to deadly flash floods. In a water-scarce city, consumption of, or contact with, its local water source can lead to gastrointestinal disorders, liver and renal complications, skin and eye infections and endocrine, nervous system and brain problems. Even though enforced apartheid ended decades ago, the ongoing devaluation of environments and people alike reproduces the resultant injustices of environmental racism.

Finally, notwithstanding these harms, the Jukskei teaches us about the relationships of care that people form with the river. Some residents of informal settlements join refuse-clearing teams and lead education programmes to discourage dumping in the river. Scientists monitor water quality and changes to fauna and flora and are exploring ways of revegetating the river environs with endemic species. Urban designers consider the possibility of replacing hard urban surfaces with green infrastructure to reduce flooding, support ecosystems, restore groundwater and allow for local food production. The city of Johannesburg has developed a 'Catchment Management Plan,' signalling the potentially important role of the state in managing our collective relationship with the river. The river has many allies who wish to reduce harm to it.

Telling the story of a place through its non-human features teaches us much about the more-than-human world we inhabit and how we relate to our neighbours, human and non-human. At the time when South Africa was preparing to become a democracy, Bruno Latour posed the following question on the nature of democracy itself: 'Will a different democracy become necessary? A democracy extended to things?'[1] Contemplating the Jukskei shows us that our democratic project has yet to confront this challenge properly.

1   B. Latour, *We have Never been Modern* (Cambridge, MA: Harvard University Press, 1993), p. 12.

Acknowledgements

This book grew out of a symposium that was hosted in October 2022, called *Riparian Urbanism*. This collaboration between the South African Research Chair in Science Communication (SciCom) and Water for the Future was convened by Mehita Iqani, Renugan Raidoo, Jessica Webster and Romy Stander. The symposium took place in Lorentzville, Johannesburg, near Victoria Yards, in a property owned by Gearhouse South Africa, mere meters from the Jukskei's daylight point. Many of the chapters in this book were first presented in some form at this event. The symposium was supported financially and in kind by the SARChI SciCom and Gearhouse (which kindly provided the space for the gathering in Victoria Yards, as well as generously discounted AV services). We could not have organised the symposium without the logistical support of Fumani Jwara and the administrative staff of CREST at Stellenbosch University. We are deeply grateful to Romy Stander for organising all the logistical and community-oriented aspects of the symposium. We are grateful to all presenters at the symposium, and all who attended to listen, discuss and learn.

This book would not have been possible without the inputs of Jessica Webster, who was an original co-editor, before needing to step back from the project. We are grateful to Jess for her intellectual and editorial contributions at the early stage of the book and are so glad that she is still in its pages (as author of Chapter 13).

We thank all the contributors to this book for trusting us with their work and staying with us through the long journey of creating an interdisciplinary publication.

We thank Lloyd Banda and Nakishka Skriker for assistance with finickity formatting.

We are grateful to all the activists and conservations who work to make all rivers, not just Johannesburg's, safer and cleaner for all who live near them. We hope this book can contribute positively to your work.

We are grateful to the HSRC Press for supporting this work and seeing its potential to reach a wide audience.

Mehita:

My first note of thanks goes to Sian Eliot, who did her magic thing of making brilliant connections between friends and sending me to Romy Stander to learn more about her river rejuvenation work. I would never have been able to work on and write about the Jukskei without the support and collaboration of Romy, who is a beacon of positive energy and can-do attitude. Even when faced with seemingly insolvable problems, she is always seeking paths towards a better world for all, something I find perpetually inspiring! I am indebted to Fumani Jwara for his superb support on every SciCom project, but especially this one which came early in our working life together. I am grateful to the National Research Foundation for trusting me with stewarding the SA Research Chair in Science Communication since 2022 and supporting the vision of a research agenda about 'science communication for social justice.' I am deeply grateful to all colleagues at the Department of Journalism at Stellenbosch University for the welcoming and research-supportive environment and for creating an amazing home for the SciCom people. My sincere thanks to Renugan for approaching me with the idea to work on a project together about the river, I hope you enjoyed what emerged from our original brainstorm in the middle of lockdown. This book would not exist without you. The support from home of my partner David du Preez helped make a life where I can create books: thank you Davey. Finally, I want to express my love for the city of Joburg and all the amazing people I was privileged to have met, made friends with, learned from, and partied with during my 11 years of living there. Thank you especially to everyone I ever went on a bike ride with. Maybe one day we can ride together along the Jukskei River.

Renugan:

This book – my first foray into this sort of editing – was a challenge to put together, but such a reward to see come to fruition. I am eternally grateful to the humans and nonhumans who live and work around Dainfern Golf & Residential Estate who introduced me to the river and first got me interested in the various contradictions and possibilities it presented for urban studies. I must also thank the many contributors to this volume for trusting us with their material and attending to the sometimes extensive revisions we suggested in pursuit of our interdisciplinary vision. After presenting a very early version of my chapter at the University of the Witwatersrand's *Faces of the City* seminar in 2021, Nicky Falkof (who also appears in this book) introduced me to Mehita, who at the time was working with Romy Stander and others near the river's daylight point. From the vastly different social worlds that coalesced around our respective inquiries into the same river emerged the idea for this interdisciplinary journey along its course.

I am delighted that Mehita agreed to work with me on this editorial journey! Mehita's Research Chair made it possible for me to travel to the symposium from the US and lightened our workload by funding postdoctoral researchers, research assistants, and media specialists to help with organising.

Over the course of this project, I have lived in Johannesburg, Vermont (US), and Boston (US), only to land at Stellenbosch University next door to where Mehita works. Colleagues at Harvard in Anthropology and in Social Studies were indispensable sources of encouragement and reassurance at moments when I found myself drowning in the project.

During the course of my fieldwork, I held a visiting scholar position at the Wits School of Architecture and Planning in Johannesburg, and was given office space in the South African Research Chair in Spatial Analysis and City Planning. The field research was made possible by an Emslie Horniman Scholarship/Sutasoma Award from the Royal Anthropological Institute, a Fulbright-Hays Doctoral Dissertation Research Abroad grant, and several scholarships from Harvard University. These included a Frank Knox Memorial Travelling Fellowship, a John C. Hansen and Katherine Vogelheim Research and Travel Grant, and a Center for African Studies Summer Grant.

Map of the Jukskei

Original drawing by Io Makandal.

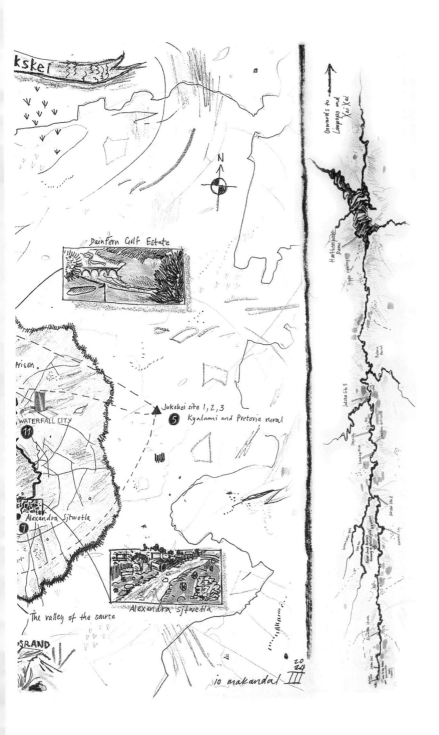

xvi

1 Riparian urbanism: Thinking Johannesburg with the Jukskei

Mehita Iqani and Renugan Raidoo

This chapter offers an overview for the book, by summarising the geography of the Jukskei River in relation to the history and socio-economics of the City of Johannesburg. It presents the notion of 'riparian urbanism' as a preliminary theoretical framework for thinking about Johannesburg in relation to the river, and vice versa.

Introduction

Johannesburg is often referred to as the largest major city that was established with no major water source to serve it. Along with the urban myth of Johannesburg being the largest man-made forest in the world (it isn't)[1] is the myth that the city lacks a notable river, lake, or seafront. To some extent, this characterisation is not unfounded. Drinking water is piped in from the Lesotho Highlands and the Vaal Dam to service the growing population of the city. Although it is true that landlocked Johannesburg has no navigable rivers or lakes that provide connections useful to industry and other capital (the products of the city of gold were moved to market by other means), the small rivers and spruits that run through it are very much a part of the city's past, present, and future. And, from the heart of the city flows the Jukskei, a notable part of the system of spruits and streams that testify to Johannesburg's historical mix of grassland and wetland.

This book takes as its primary object Joburg's biggest river, and its most charismatic (for better or worse): the Jukskei. Prone to violent flooding, emitting unpleasant odours and carrying litter, this river is often in the news for negative reasons (not least the loss of life during summer thunderstorm floods). When it receives media attention in positive ways, it is often due to activist efforts to rejuvenate the river and to integrate it more effectively into the everyday life of the city. Although it is non-navigable until it reaches the Crocodile River and Hartbeespoort Dam, the river runs through or past virtually every kind of urban form Johannesburg has produced. Despite its abundant presence in the city, the Jukskei has attracted scant attention from policymakers, the public at large, and researchers.

There doesn't appear to be a clear origin for the name of this river. Indeed, for many South Africans the term might more readily recall sports. Jukskei is the name of an Afrikaner game still played in some parts of the country that involves throwing a pin at a stake planted in the ground. For fans of more widespread sports, the Trans-Jukskei Derby or Jukskei Derby recalls rugby games between the Blue Bulls and the Lions, or cricket matches between the Titans and the Lions, as the Jukskei historically divided teams into what were formerly called Northern Transvaal and Transvaal. The name itself comes from the Afrikaans words *juk* and *skei*, meaning 'yoke' and 'divide/separate/divorce,' respectively. Indeed, mentions of the river in English from the 19th and early 20th century refer to it as the 'Yokeskei.' Under that name it was mentioned, among other things, for being unpredictable to cross,[2] for the presence of alluvial gold,[3] as home to interesting fauna,[4] and as a site of interethnic violence.[5] A 1917 issue of the *Agricultural Journal of South Africa* notes: 'The name of the Witwatersrand given to this region by the Voortrekkers means in the Dutch tongue the 'Range of White Waters,' and was so-called because the waters flowing from the hills were peculiarly white and clear, owing to the presence of limestone, and also in contrast to the dark waters of the Yokeskei and the Crocodile.'[6] This comparison is perhaps an enduringly apt one, contrasting the ebullient aspirations of the early settlers with the prosaic but enduring 'darkwater' realities of the Jukskei.

Despite the Jukskei's centrality in (and to) the geography of Johannesburg, there has been little sustained effort to document and interpret the river's significance to the city. Such a reckoning is long overdue.

This book offers an interdisciplinary set of conversations from and between those researching, archiving, and analysing the various cultural, social, and scientific aspects of Johannesburg's only perennial river. It is intended as a first step in an ongoing exploration of how the river has made the city, and the city has made the river. It includes, of course, academic contributions from a variety of disciplines, and also the products and reflections of the many activists, journalists, and artists who have grappled with this river. The collection of writings assembled here is diverse, and includes scientific work presented clearly for the lay reader, analysis of fine art, journalistic writing, memoirs of activists, and cultural analysis. This volume collects work on, in, about, and alongside the Jukskei for the benefit of the public and policymakers. It also, we hope, demonstrates a viable example of accessible, interdisciplinary engagement for those who live with rivers (and other natural features) in cities around the world.

There is a wealth of critical urban literature on Johannesburg.[7] This literature explores a wide range of social, cultural and political aspects of this compelling city. These include the ravages of its enduring social inequalities,[8] the social semiotics of its branded skyline,[9] the cultural politics of its gated communities[10] and its emotional landscape,[11] the enduring legacy of apartheid spatial planning on its townships,[12] the boom in luxury malls,[13] the multiple and scattered ways in which its histories have been archived,[14] and the startling, brutal yet often beautiful aesthetics of its architecture.[15] These are just a few key topics that have captured researchers' attention. Although the Johannesburg literature covers many aspects of this enthralling, and enthrallingly unequal, city – from its urban disenfranchised to its urban elites, its joys to its anxieties – to date little scholarship has addressed the place of the Jukskei River in the city. This book changes that.

Johannesburg's river

We commissioned artist Io Makandal to draw a map of the Jukskei River (see pages xiv-xv) for use as a reference for the content of this book. The various locations along the course of the river mentioned in this book are indicated on this map and serve as a visual orientation device for the river and its geographical relation to the city of Johannesburg. The map foregrounds the river, de-emphasising the terrestrial geographies of municipal/provincial boundaries, land use, and relative wealth that dominate discussions of Johannesburg's urban environment. While such geographies remain undeniably important in understanding the city, one argument of this book is that centring the river as an orientating device helps us think urbanity anew. On the right-hand side of Makandal's work appears a 'strip map,' a now-obsolete cartographic form designed to help those navigating roads and rivers by organising other geographical features in relation to the route being navigated. The chapters in this book offer a kind of narrative strip map, re-visioning Johannesburg in relation to the vital artery that is the Jukskei.

The journey of the river was narrated by journalist Sean Christie (whose work also features in this book), who walked its length almost a decade ago.[16] The Jukskei springs most likely from several eyes in the wetlands that used to comprise the eastern valley of what became the city of Johannesburg. The high-density neighbourhoods of Hillbrow and Doornfontein were built on top of these wetlands and eyes, effectively concreting over the natural springs that converged into the river. The source of the Jukskei has thus become integrated – due to environmentally unsound colonial, apartheid, and post-apartheid urban planning – into storm water and sewerage systems that are ageing and poorly maintained. It is now impossible to differentiate the source of the river from the city's sewerage systems. The eco-artist Hannelie Coetzee, exploring underground along with Christie and city officials, located one pure spring deep below street level,[17] but it trickles immediately into the maze of sewerage drains and storm water pipes below Ellis Park and Hillbrow. Her evocative photographs (available on her website, and also discussed in Chapter 8 of this volume) of the source of uncontaminated water, in the dark tangle of sewerage pipes, capture the extent to which the natural resource has become indistinguishable from the concrete realities of modern urban life.

The river then runs under the city for many blocks, through underground sewerage and storm water systems, most of them neglected for decades. The daylight point of the Jukskei is at Queen Street, near the corner with Thames Street, in Lorentzville, a deprived neighbourhood with high unemployment, poor public services, large migrant communities, and limited economic opportunity. Both street names underscore the colonial past of the city, with the Jukskei implied as match, albeit inadequate, to London's Thames. Until very recently this point where the river first enters the above-ground life of the city was identifiable only by a graffitied bridge, piles of dumped refuse, and its use as a shelter for the urban underclass, including the unhoused, those struggling with problematic substance use, and purportedly others engaged in criminal activity. It is now marked by a beautiful mosaic artwork, made collaboratively between the NGO Water for the Future and artists from the Spaza Gallery in Troyeville. The cover of this book features a detail from this mosaic.

From the newly beautified daylight point, the river runs in deep culverts above and below concrete through semi-industrial areas (including through the creative hub of Victoria Yards), before joining a suburban corridor through Bezhuidenhout Valley into Bruma. Although the neighbourhoods along this early stretch are neglected and underserviced, the riverbanks are largely natural and the riparian zones include large, though uncared-for, green spaces, including sports fields and parks. After passing the erstwhile man-made lake (now filled in) at Bruma, the Jukskei River turns northeast to flow past Oriental City China Mall, and the genteel upper class suburbs of Morninghill and Gilloolly's, before following the N3 north, gathering pace, trash, toxins and flooding potential as it works its way past townhouse complexes in Sandringham on its way under London Road into Alexandra, the oldest township in the city. There it flows past many densely populated sections of Alex, including the steep and treacherous banks of the informal settlement at Stjwetla, before finding green space after crossing under Marlboro Road, near the newly built eastern suburbs of greater Sandton.

Passing through patches of open veld and past the high walls of housing complexes, the Jukskei River continues to run northwest, entering elite gated communities like Waterfall Estate. As well as these more prosaic walls, the river also passes those of Leeuwkop Prison where many of Gauteng's prisoners and people awaiting trial are locked away, tucked between Lonehill and Kyalami, the incarceration facility sitting on the upper riverbank. The Jukskei then passes many more lifestyle estates and gated communities, including those in the Dainfern Valley which straddles it, before crossing through the ostentatious Steyn City, and traversing the increasingly built-up quasi-farmlands of Lanseria. By this point, the water carries with it smells, toxins, litter and other jetsam from the city before it merges with the Crocodile River around 50 kilometres away from greater Johannesburg. The Crocodile eventually spills into the Hartbeespoort Dam.

The Jukskei's course betrays the material conditions of diverse socio-economic layers of the city, as well as the complex social relationships implied by the inherent inequality that continues to define Johannesburg life. As much as the existence of the Jukskei River says something about the history of Johannesburg, the Jukskei also flows through the city's future. In 2021 the South African government released its vision for the development of a 'smart city' around Lanseria Airport, in the form of the Greater Lanseria Masterplan,[18] slated for proposed completion by 2030. In the maps illustrating this vision, the blue thread of the Jukskei glows, hinting at urban futures in the greater Johannesburg region that integrate the high-tech with the riparian: indeed, one of the key recommendations for the future development is 'embedding the status of the Crocodile River Nature Reserve.'[19]

River rejuvenation and urban sustainability

The Jukskei has changed Johannesburg as much as Johannesburg has changed it.

What do rivers do for cities, and how do city residents, in turn, make them part of urban life? Rivers used to be seen quite simply as resources that could be exploited to serve economic and urban development, but that thinking has shifted: 'Features that were once considered expendable in order to ensure human assets [...] are now considered assets in their own right. These include stream ecology, stream hydrology, stream geomorphology and water quality.'[20] The health of societies and rivers are connected.[21] Indeed, the South African Human Rights Commission has recently reported that the Vaal River is polluted to unacceptable levels and that this has a direct impact on the human rights of those who live alongside it.[22] Similarly, in a recent study of the social life of the Ganges, as it runs through Varanasi, India (though it should be noted that this study was conducted before the devastating Delta wave of the COVID-19 pandemic in India), the author unsurprisingly concludes that the pollution of the Ganges in that city directly contributes to ill health amongst its population. Similar studies have taken place regarding the Jukskei, with a specific focus on pollution and toxicity levels (see the chapters in the first section of this book).[23] There is no doubt that the Jukskei is terribly polluted, right from its very source. This raises questions not only about how pollution can be eradicated, for the safety of all creatures engaging rivers, including the humans who live alongside them, but also about what that pollution means to cities, and vice versa. Urban rivers produce 'social connectivity', that is, 'the communication and movement of people, goods, ideas, and culture along and across rivers, recognising longitudinal, lateral, and vertical connectivity.'[24] Although in the context of the Jukskei the river does not literally provide transport and trade, there are multiple movements of items, both visible and invisible, along its course, including toxins, pollution and trash, and of course the other, less tangible discourses about the city and the huge diversity of people who live in it.

There is growing concern about the pollution of urban rivers, especially in the Global South.[25] Evidence from around the world shows that rivers can add significant value to the urban economy[26] when they are not poisoned and polluted. In other words, investment in rejuvenation pays off.

> Healthy and functioning river systems are appealing and attractive to residents and businesses. A society engaged in enjoying riverfront features and activities also cares about the long-term sustainability of river systems. Communities have started to understand the appeal of a more natural riverfront for residents and visitors. Apart from touristic advantages, there are some other benefits as well, including cost-effective flood control, improved water quality, reduced infrastructure costs and increased property values and tax base.[27]

River rejuvenation is a complex, interdisciplinary scientific field.[28] One key challenge that has been identified by experts in the science of river restoration is:

> a lack of scientific knowledge of watershed-scale process dynamics, institutional structures that are poorly suited to large-scale adaptive management, and a lack of political support to re-establish delivery of the ecosystem amenities lost through river degradation.[29]

Public engagement, and the nurturing of a deliberative process, is central to effective river rejuvenation attempts. Communities living with and along rivers need to have the chance to learn through engagement, and have their own perspectives integrated into policymaking and the implementation of the scientific recommendations.[30] This holds true for Johannesburg as much as any other city.

At the Jukskei's source, a project to rejuvenate and remediate the Jukskei River at its daylight point is being driven by a public-private partnership forged by the NGO Water for the Future (WFTF) (discussed in Chapter 21). Original Soweto Highveld Grassland (a vegetation type native to the highveld and able to contribute positively to rejuvenating areas overrun with alien species, including along the banks of the Jukskei), that thrived before urbanisation, is being reintroduced to try and create a green corridor from the daylight point through to the borders of the City of Johannesburg. The aim is to build a resilient infrastructure along with an informed pro-active community, and to offer replicable rejuvenation models that can be scaled up all along the pathway of the river. Along the course of the river, specifically in Alexandra, crucial work is being done by the Alexandra Water Warriors (see Chapters 16 and 18), who are creating jobs through river cleanup efforts. These types of community organisation are increasingly being recognised as a leading resource on river cleanups, and deserve ongoing public and private sector support.

Climate change is a major global challenge, with specific implications for South Africa[31] in general and water security specifically.[32] One key framework for humanities-driven research into climate change is to consider how cities can be more resilient, as they are likely to face an influx of migration when climate change-related disasters force people away from coastal areas and other areas negatively affected by anthropogenic climate change.[33] Environmental communication[34] is one way to explore the question of how the science of climate change and river rejuvenation and their social consequences come into public discourse in South Africa. Water security, including the health of perennial rivers, is a key part of this bigger picture. Building climate resilience needs to be based on a dialogic and collaborative ethic, seeking to push forward an agenda that moves from ' "deficit" to "dialogue" ' by bringing relevant, issues-driven science into 'greater proximity to the public' through a 'democratised relationship.'[35] This is just as true for the bigger picture issues (climate change in general) and more focused areas of ecological rejuvenation, such as work on the Jukskei. New forms of climate resilient sustainable development in urban settings, particularly in South Africa's economic hub and most densely populated city, Johannesburg, are needed to gain deeper insight into narratives about urbanism and the climate emergency.

Riparian urbanism

In ecology, the term 'riparian' most simply refers to 'the ecosystems adjacent to the river.'[36] Riparian areas are those that are situated at the interface of terrestrial and aquatic ecosystems, most obviously along the banks of rivers,[37] which expand and contract when flooding or during droughts, but also around the edges of other bodies of water. The riparian zone includes more than just a river's floodplain. It also includes narrow strips along river courses that cut deeply into landscapes, and islands in river courses, thereby integrating multiple ecosystems and landscapes.[38] Ecologists and hydrologists who study riparian zones are typically interested in water flow, hydrologic linkages, sediment movement, channel dynamics, soil characteristics and ecosystem functioning[39] – all of which can be affected by human activity.

In the Anthropocene,[40] there is barely any natural feature on the earth that has not been touched or affected by human activity, usually to the detriment of the other species living there. Almost every landscape and body of water has been irrevocably changed for the worse, directly or indirectly, by humanity. For the rivers that have historically hosted human settlement and facilitated human development, that influence is as old as history. The centrality of big rivers to the economic and cultural life of many major cities is testament to this. Many rivers have been urbanised and are integrated into the complexities and lived experiences of the cities and towns through which they flow. It is to this complex relation between the urban and the riparian that we gesture with the term, 'riparian urbanism.' As a working definition for the concept of riparian urbanism, we point out that it is impossible to imagine certain cities without their rivers, or fully restore the same rivers to their pre-citied condition. Riparian urbanism describes the inseparable condition of rivers and cities, where the human and the non-human have co-created, and continue to co-create, the urban condition. Humans, other-than-human life, and nonliving elements of the environment all depend on one another. If we are to imagine a viable place for humans on a future Earth, it can only be as part of an interconnected more-than-human social.

In Johannesburg, we argue that there is a uniquely complex relationship between ecology and economy, hydrology and sociology, that is attendant to the riparian urbanism of the Jukskei River. Because the source of the river has been subsumed into the underbelly of the city itself and has been largely ignored by the majority of the populace as well as the city and provincial governments, the Jukskei has been urbanised (in a pejorative sense poisoned and polluted) more thoroughly than many other rivers, for example those that arise in remote mountain headwaters before flowing through or past towns and cities. Johannesburg is beset with multiple social challenges, already acute in this dense urban setting, and heightened by the COVID-19 pandemic, the looting of 2021, and the persistently devastating socio-economic legacies of apartheid. But so too does Johannesburg always find a way to thrive and live up to its moniker as a city of gold, where many flock to seek their fortunes, and creative entrepreneurs and business tycoons rub shoulders with the destitute, where glittering skyscrapers keep being built even while inner-city buildings crumble, or burn, out of neglect by both property owners and city managers.

That the river's significance is primarily *not* as conduit for or generator of capital further stresses our riparian framing, drawing attention to those humans and non-humans who live on and near its banks, whether by choice or necessity. These riparian citizens' wellbeing depends in part on the behaviours of other riparian citizens upstream (historically and geographically), with the waters of the river serving to connect the citizenry of a famously divided city.

The confluence of the terms *riparian* and *urbanism* offers an assessment of Johannesburg's history, development, and culture from the banks of the river that runs through it. Riparian refers to the interface between the river and the banks that define, direct and are eroded by it. Urbanism calls attention to those beings – human and non-human – who live at the aquatic-terrestrial boundary, how they use and manage the capricious river, and the city and urban landscapes that frame those interactions.

The river travels through, and carries with it, many of the features of the city and its socio-economic contradictions. Johannesburg's fractured and fractious urbanity has been forced into the Jukskei's riparian condition. Before the city was built, the river was there, bubbling up from the Highveld wetlands and winding its way to join other rivers until the Indian Ocean. Yet, now that the city is here, exhibiting both an inertial permanence and entropic signs of deterioration, deeply unequal yet still the throbbing economic heart of the country, unsound development at the source of the river means that it now emerges into fresh air and daylight from a storm drain. While it is entirely changed by the presence of the city and its people, the river also does something to the urbanity of the city.

It starts in, runs past, and flows through parts of Johannesburg that although in the same city are worlds apart. What does it tell us about this metropolis? How does the urbanism of Johannesburg affect the Jukskei, and how can the pollution and other ecological damage caused by the city to the river be better understood, and even reversed, with the help of multidisciplinary research? How, in turn, does the river affect the city in specific ways, offering both challenges and opportunities for linking spaces and communities that were intentionally segregated by apartheid spatial planning? This book offers some answers to these questions, and a starting point for future multi- and interdisciplinary research into the urban environment.

Structure of the book

This book brings together knowledge about the Jukskei from multiple perspectives for readers interested in Johannesburg and its river.

In the chapters that follow, you will read work by people who have worked with, on, and in the Jukskei's riparian biome – including artists, activists, natural scientists, hydrologists, ecologists, urbanists, designers, historians, anthropologists, policy-makers and social scientists. They describe, analyse and theorise how Johannesburg and its residents relate to the temperamental Jukskei. It is important to note that there is a great diversity in the contributors to this book. Some are seasoned writers, either academics in the humanities or journalists with long careers behind them, while others are less accustomed to writing, and spend more time in the field or laboratory gathering and analysing data, in the art studio (and beyond) conceptualising and making creative work, or networking on the ground with communities organising and implementing collaborative action. As such, you will find that there are very different writing styles that lie ahead. While some of the chapters try to present scientific data in such a way that non-experts can understand them, others offer reflections into creative practice or activism, while yet others deploy academic tools to make theoretical contributions to our understandings of the world. Although diverse in these ways, the chapters are still united by an interest in, and work upon, the Jukskei. We invite readers to explore the book in any order that they like, and to engage with each chapter for the insight that it offers about what the Jukskei means to Johannesburg, and Johannesburg to the Jukskei.

Nevertheless, the format of a book requires that it is ordered, somehow, and we have done so thematically, by grouping contributions roughly according to whether they offer scientific, artistic, social, or political insights to the river.

Right before this Introduction, you will find Io Makandal's hand drawn map of the Jukskei, which offers a visual guide to orientate readers towards the specific riparian locations explored in each chapter.

Part 1 presents scientific evidence, translated for the lay reader, of studies into the condition of the river. **Antoinette Bootsma** offers a botanical view of what the Jukskei valley looked like before the city was built on top of it. As an alternative vision, she considers a valley in Suikerbosrand with similar altitude, aspect, climate and geology. The endemic flora, and their medicinal and cultural affordances, provide a vision of what the Jukskei's valleys might have been. **Kyle van Heyde** reports the findings of an extensive study that mapped the presence of macroplastic pollution in the river. **Kousar Hoorzook and Atheesha Singh** report the findings of an analysis of pathogens in the waters at the daylight point of the Jukskei and offer advice about how to stay safe after coming into contact with the water. **Stuart Dunsmore** and **Ernita van Wyk** summarise the key take-home policy recommendations emerging from an extensive survey assessing the hydrological aspects of the upper Jukskei. Key challenges and opportunities related to water catchment management in Johannesburg are outlined. While presenting important information, these contributions should also be read as examples of how technical information can be re-packaged for a general audience in order to encourage a responsible and informed riparian citizenry.

Part 2 offers a range of chapters discussing artistic practice with, at or in relation to the river. **Dunja Herzog** offers a discussion of a sound art installation using brass instruments that she created on the banks of the Jukskei. It considers the relation of sound vibration to the river. The artists **Nina Barnett, Refiloe Namise** and **Abri de Swardt**, all of whom have worked with the Jukskei in some aspect of their performance, installation, or video art, reflect on one another's work, and discuss the role of the river in their artistic practice. **Landi Raubenheimer** writes on recent photographs of the river by two artists: Gulshan Khan and Hannelie Coetzee. Both portray the contradictory qualities of the Jukskei by focusing both on its material qualities which point to urban decay and pollution, and on its healing qualities which, in spite of its physical demise, renders spell-binding images. A photo essay by **Lungi Hlatshwayo,** who was a community activist and a director of the NGO Water for the Future until her untimely passing in 2023, documents various creative community engagements linked to the river rejuvenation efforts.

Part 3 examines the relation of the river to local and national politics. **Sean Christie**, a seasoned journalist who has written extensively about the Jukskei and the city of Johannesburg, reflects on the strange relationship that Johannesburg has with the idea of the sea (to which it is very materially connected through its river). **Nicky Falkof** critically analyses a strange event, in which right wing public figure Steve Hofmeyr threw several U2 concert tickets in the Jukskei, purportedly in protest against what he perceived to be the band's anti-Afrikaner statements. **Jamaine Krige** offers a behind-the-scenes glimpse into the emotional world of a journalist whose beat covers ecological aspects of the city of Johannesburg. She writes about the backstory of three Jukskei news pieces (a drowned child, a wandering hippo, and a fire in Stjwetla) in vignettes. **Jessica Webster** explores the affective tension between the real and symbolic death of the Jukskei, characterising this condition as neither dead nor alive. She argues that this river as site of disuse, of violent poverty, and excrement, is also where a peculiar form of creaturely life might be elaborated.

Part 4 collects work that reveals the wide variety of lived experiences of people who inhabit the riverbanks. **Sarah Charlton** reports on a research project that aimed to better understand the lives of those who live along one of the tributaries to the Jukskei, the Braamfontein Spruit. The chapter presents the statements of several interview participants to argue that although they are labelled homeless, they are in fact making strategic choices about where and how to survive economically in Johannesburg. **Ujithra Ponniah** offers fieldnotes from an extensive ethnography of high-end luxury estates in the north of Johannesburg. Her chapter shows how wealth and power relate problematically to the river, and how elite estates have lost touch with the politics of water. **Sibusiso Sangweni**, a key member of the Alex Water Warriors, who worked hard every week to clean up the river until his untimely passing in 2023, shares his life story and muses on his relationship with the river. **Renugan Raidoo**, drawing on an ethnography of Dainfern, one of Johannesburg's elite gated communities straddling the Jukskei, explores the multiple emotional relations that Dainfern residents have with the river, from adulating it for its natural beauty, to despising it for the litter and foul smells it carries. He theorises how – and why – it occasions a wide range of affective attachments, and how those attachments are embroiled in contemporary politics of property, race, and conservation.

Part 5 focuses on urban river management. **Paul Maluleke**, the founder of Alex Water Warriors offers a compelling rationale for ongoing support of community clean up efforts in Alexandra. **Savory Chikomwe** draws on an extensive study of the urban planning challenges and opportunities related to the 'informal' settlement of Stjwetla, in Alexandra, which borders the river. His chapter shows how a condition of permanent impermanence has been forced on the settlement by government policy, and outlines living conditions in relation to the river. **Dieter Brandt** reflects on his extensive experience in eco-urban river management, to explore the potential for the proper management of river systems. This is his foundation to outline important lessons for the Jukskei and state what benefits might accrue as a result of proper management. **Romy Stander**, one of the founders of the NGO Water for the Future, which is working to rejuvenate the upper Jukskei in Bertrams through community engagement and public-private partnerships, reflects on the journey towards becoming an activist and the work that lies ahead.

Conclusion

Together, the contributions in this book illustrate the potential of critical interdisciplinary studies of Johannesburg to deepen social and scientific understandings of and interactions with the river. We hope that these will serve as a useful and thought-provoking collection for ongoing research and activism in service of river rejuvenation, critical thinking about Johannesburg and the Jukskei, and the work of theorising riparian urbanism in cities around the world during the age of the Anthropocene. We also hope that the book will inspire those who live in Johannesburg to turn towards their river, to appreciate it and to invest in it, and to treasure it as a resource that, if loved, respected, rejuvenated and protected, could help to produce better forms of riparian urbanism for future human and other-than-human riparian citizens.

Notes

1   Africa Check, 'Is Johannesburg the World's Largest Man-Made Forest? The Claim Is a Myth,' Africa Check, 0505-2323 2013, http://africacheck.org/fact-checks/reports/johannesburg-worlds-largest-man-made-forest-claim-myth.

2   T. Gutsche, *There Was a Man: The Life and Times of Sir Arnold Theiler K.C.M.G. of Onderstepoort* (Cape Town: Howard Timmins, 1979), p. 36.

3   K. J. de Kok, *Empires of the Veld* (Durban: J. C. Juta & Co., 1904), 51; E. H. L. Schwarz, *The Discoveries of Economic Importance Made by the Albany Pioneers* (Grahamstown: African Book Company, Ltd., 1908), 9, https://hdl.handle.net/2027/mdp.39015067336977?urlappend=%3Bseq=3.

4   For example B. de Meillon, 'The Early Stages and Male Hypopygium of Anopheles Argenteolobatus, Gough,' *Bulletin of Entomological Research* 19, no. 4 (1928): 401–404, https://doi.org/10.1017/S0007485300020770; 'Correspondence,' *Ostrich* 14, no. 3 (1 November 1943): 183–196, https://doi.org/10.1080/00306525.1943.9634692.

5   'The Transvaal: Danger of a Native War,' *The Manchester Guardian*, 30 April 1881, https://www.proquest.com/docview/478877202?parentSessionId=PxvGFNnB5E97MC5RTVE lKgZuVFTiqh2sooHijGNDY8A%3D&pq-origsite=primo&accountid=11311.

6   'Makers of Johannesburg,' *Agricultural Journal of South Africa*, 1917, 326–330.

7   Philip Harrison et al. (eds), *Changing Space, Changing City: Johannesburg after Apartheid* (Johannesburg: Wits University Press, 2014).

8   Jo Beall, Owen Crankshaw, and Sue Parnell, *Uniting a Divided City: Governance and Social Exclusion in Johannesburg* (Earthscan, 2013); Martin J. Murray, *City of Extremes: The Spatial Politics of Johannesburg* (Duke University Press, 2011).

9   Gilles Baro, 'The Language of Post-Apartheid Urban Development: The Semiotic Landscape of Marshalltown in Johannesburg' (Johannesburg, University of the Witwatersrand, 2017); Mehita Iqani and Gilles Baro, 'The Branded Skyline? A Socio-Semiotic Critique of Johannesburg's Architectural Adverts,' *African Studies* 76, no. 1 (2 January 2017): 102–120, https://doi.org/10.1080/00020184.2017.1285670.

10   Derek Hook and Michele Vrdoljak, 'Gated Communities, Heterotopia and a "Rights" of Privilege: A "heterotopology" of the South African Security-Park,' *Geoforum* 33, no. 2 (2002): 195–219; Ulrich Jürgens and Martin Gnad, 'Gated Communities in South Africa – Experiences from Johannesburg,' *Environment and Planning B: Planning and Design* 29, no. 3 (1 June 2002): 337–353, https://doi.org/10.1068/b2756; Martin J Murray, 'Waterfall City (Johannesburg): Privatized Urbanism in Extremis,' *Environment and Planning A: Economy and Space* 47, no. 3 (1 March 2015): 503–520, https://doi.org/10.1068/a140038p.

11   Nicky Falkof, 'Ugly Noo-Noos and Suburban Nightmares,' in *Anxious Joburg: The Inner Lives of a Global South City*, ed. Nicky Falkof and Cobus van Staden (New York: NYU Press, 2020).

12   P. L. Bonner and Lauren Segal, *Soweto: A History* (Johannesburg: Maskew Miller Longman, 1998); Jennifer Briedenhann and Pranill Ramchander, 'Township Tourism: Blessing or Blight? The Case of Soweto in South Africa,' in *Cultural Tourism in a Changing World*, ed. Melanie K. Smith and Mike Robinson (Channel View Publications, 2006); Paul Friedrich Detlev Krige, 'Power, Identity and Agency at Work in the Popular Economies of Soweto and Black Johannesburg.' (Thesis, 2011), http://wiredspace.wits.ac.za/handle/10539/10143.

13   Ana Aceska and Barbara Heer, 'Everyday Encounters in the Shopping Mall: (Un)Making Boundaries in the Divided Cities of Johannesburg and Mostar,' *Anthropological Forum* 29, no. 1 (2 January 2019): 47–461, https://doi.org/10.1080/00664677.2019.1585751; Bridget Kenny, 'The Sprawl of Malls: Financialisation, Service Work and Inequality in Johannesburg's Urban Geography,' *Transformation: Critical Perspectives on Southern Africa* 101, no. 1 (2019): 36–60, https://doi.org/10.1353/trn.2019.0036; J.-A. Mbembe, 'Aesthetics of Superfluity,' *Public Culture* 16, no. 3 (2004): 373–405.

14   Bettina Malcomess and Dorothee Kreutzfeldt, *Not No Place: Johannesburg, Fragments of Spaces and Times* (Johannesburg: Jacana Media, 2013).

15   Clive M. Chipkin, *Johannesburg Style: Architecture & Society, 1880s-1960s* (Cape Town; Johannesburg: D. Philip Publishers: Thorold's Africana Books, 1993); Gerald Garner, *Spaces & Places: Johannesburg* (Johannesburg: Double G Media, 2010).

16   Sean Christie, 'Searching for the Soul of the Jukskei,' *Mail & Guardian*, 2 January 2014, Online edition, https://mg.co.za/article/2014-01-02-searching-for-the-soul-of-the-jukskei/.

17   Hannelie Coetzee, *Finding the eye of Jukskei River beneath Joburg*, 2020, Video, 2020, https://www.hanneliecoetzee.com/portfolios/2020-finding-the-eye-of-jukskei-river-beneath-joburg/.

18   Gauteng Premier's Office, 'Greater Lanseria Master Plan: Tomorrow's Sustainable City Today,' 26 July 2021, https://storymaps.arcgis.com/stories/cbc7678cb3e44748b0d9089e39248368.

19   Gauteng Premier's Office.

20   Sophia Jane Findlay and Mark Patrick Taylor, 'Why Rehabilitate Urban River Systems?' *Area* 38, no. 3 (September 2006): 314, https://doi.org/10.1111/j.1475-4762.2006.00696.x.

21   Suhani Shah, 'The Social Life of Rivers – Assessing correlations between societal stability and river health,' *International Journal of Social Science and Economic Research* 05, no. 03 (30 March 2020): 816–821, https://doi.org/10.46609/IJSSER.2020.v05i03.017.

22   Jonas Ben Sibanyoni, 'Final Report of the Gauteng Provincial Inquiry Into the Sewage Problem of the Vaal River' (SA Human Rights Commission, 17 February 2021).

23   Wadzanai Matowanyika, 'Impact of Alexandra Township on The Water Quality of the Jukskei River' (Masters Dissertation, Johannesburg, University of the Witwatersrand, 2010); M van Veelen and F. C. van Zyl, 'Integrated Water Quality Management: Getting People Involved in the Jukskei River,' *Water Science and Technology* 32, no. 5–6 (1995), https://doi.org/10.1016/0273-1223(95)00658-3.

24   G. Mathias Kondolf and Pedro J. Pinto, 'The Social Connectivity of Urban Rivers,' *Geomorphology* 277 (January 2017): 182–196, https://doi.org/10.1016/j.geomorph.2016.09.028.

25   Zuxin Xu et al., 'Urban River Pollution Control in Developing Countries,' *Nature Sustainability* 2, no. 3 (March 2019): 158–160, https://doi.org/10.1038/s41893-019-0249-7.

26   Mekala Gayathri Devi et al., 'Valuing a Clean River: A Case Study of Musi River, Hyderabad, India,' 2009, https://doi.org/10.22004/AG.ECON.48164; Gerald J. Kauffman, 'Economic Value of Nature and Ecosystems in the Delaware River Basin,' *Journal of Contemporary Water Research & Education* 158, no. 1 (August 2016): 98–119, https://doi.org/10.1111/j.1936-704X.2016.03222.x.

27   Bulent Cengiz, 'Urban River Landscapes,' in *Advances in Landscape Architecture*, ed. Murat Ozyavuz (InTech, 2013), sec. 3.1, https://doi.org/10.5772/56156.

28 M. A. Palmer et al., 'Standards for Ecologically Successful River Restoration: Ecological Success in River Restoration,' *Journal of Applied Ecology* 42, no. 2 (14 March 2005): 208–217, https://doi.org/10.1111/j.1365-2664.2005.01004.x; Margaret A. Palmer and Emily S. Bernhardt, 'Hydroecology and River Restoration: Ripe for Research and Synthesis,' *Water Resources Research* 42, no. 3 (March 2006), https://doi.org/10.1029/2005WR004354; Judith Petts, 'Learning about Learning: Lessons from Public Engagement and Deliberation on Urban River Restoration,' *The Geographical Journal* 173, no. 4 (December 2007): 300–311, https://doi.org/10.1111/j.1475-4959.2007.00254.x; Ellen Wohl et al., 'River Restoration: OPINION,' *Water Resources Research* 41, no. 10 (October 2005), https://doi.org/10.1029/2005WR003985; Ellen Wohl, Stuart N. Lane, and Andrew C. Wilcox, 'The Science and Practice of River Restoration,' *Water Resources Research* 51, no. 8 (August 2015): 5974–5997, https://doi.org/10.1002/2014WR016874.

29 Wohl et al., 'River Restoration,' 1.

30 Petts, 'Learning about Learning.'

31 R. J. Scholes, Mary Scholes, and Mike Lucas, *Climate Change: Briefings from Southern Africa* (Johannesburg: Wits University Press, 2015).

32 DSI, 'White Paper on Science, Technology and Innovation' (Department of Science and Innovation, 2019), 15.

33 Scholes, Scholes, and Lucas, *Climate Change*.

34 Daniela Mahl et al., 'We Are a Bit Blind About It': A Qualitative Analysis of Climate Change-Related Perceptions and Communication Across South African Communities,' *Environmental Communication* 14, no. 6 (17 August 2020): 802–815, https://doi.org/10.1080/17524032.2 020.1736116; Corlia Meyer, 'Perceptions of the Environment and Environmental Issues in Stellenbosch, South Africa: A Mixed-Methods Approach' (Thesis, Stellenbosch : Stellenbosch University, 2018), https://scholar.sun.ac.za:443/handle/10019.1/104937.

35 Peter Weingart, Marina Joubert, and Bankole Falade, *Science Communication in South Africa: Reflections on Current Issues* (African Minds, 2020), 4.

36 George P. Malanson, *Riparian Landscapes* (Cambridge: Cambridge University Press, 1996), 9.

37 Malchus B. Baker, *Riparian Areas of the Southwestern United States: Hydrology, Ecology, and Management* (Boca Raton, Fla.: Lewis Publishers, 2004), 1.

38 Malanson, *Riparian Landscapes*, 9.1.

39 Baker, *Riparian Areas of the Southwestern United States*, 3.

40 Timothy Clark, *Ecocriticism on the Edge: The Anthropocene as a Threshold Concept*. (Bloomsbury Publishing, 2015).We use the term 'Anthropocene' in an inclusive sense that acknowledges the unequal effects that different types of humans have had on climate change, critiques that have led others to coin terms like inter alia Plantationocene and Capitalocene.

PART 1
SCIENTIFIC PERSPECTIVES

2 The historical Jukskei River valley: A botanical benchmark

Antoinette Bootsma

The Jukskei River is in a terrible state, smothered with toxic pollutants, forever changed from a once beautiful river to a concrete canal in a hot, busy city. What can we realistically do to improve the river's condition? In the context of our frame of reference of disturbed urban environments as 'normal,' botanical research from a protected valley with similar geological characteristics gives us an idea of what the river looked like before the city of Johannesburg was built. This journey back in botanical time frames an alternative view of what a river should look like. While it is not realistic to return the Jukskei River valley to this benchmark, this chapter suggests that nurturing a love for this environment may be useful both to activist measures to rejuvenate the river, as well as socially and culturally relevant to city inhabitants who might lack a tangible reference point for what an unpolluted river looks and feels like.

Introduction: A new normal on the banks of a toxic river?

Towards the end of a series of talks focused on the Jukskei River, hosted by Water for the Future at a local venue in Bertrams, in the heart of old Johannesburg, a community elder raised her hand and asked, 'So what can we do? How can we make our environment better? We know how bad the river water is, but what do we do?'

This searing question came after two days of presentations that painted an utterly bleak picture of the state of this urban river, which is heavily polluted and toxic to anyone who touches its water. Two weeks earlier, at a symposium focused on the similarly polluted Hennops River that lies north of Johannesburg, a picture flashed onto the screen of a river choked with plastic. The caption read, 'Is this the new normal?' If desperately degraded environments are where urban children spend their youth, how can the perception that watercourses are 'normally' filled with sewage and waste, be shifted? This is necessary if people living in cities are to become effective partners in managing urban rivers and wetlands in service of making them healthy environments again.

Most people who grew up in a city lack memories of unspoiled natural environments. City dwellers might not have lived experience of stepping through thigh-high mats of (invasive) kikuyu grass, or being warned by parents not to eat (also invasive) 'gifappeltjies' (various *Solanum* species produce small yellow apple-like fruit, referred to as Poison Apple in English, umthuma or itunga in isiXhosa and mtuma in isiZulu) or 'malpitte' (*Datura stramonium,* also called iloqi in isiZulu; lechoe in Sesotho and umhlavuthwa in isiXhosa, which can cause a hallucinogenic condition or death).[1] Few urban children today will grow up with memories of catching tadpoles in a stream. Urban development and the relentless pressure of alien invasive species such as black wattles, pompom weed, global trends of bush encroachment and too frequent fires have forever changed much of the environment around South African cities and towns. In many countries, the ecological landscape has been so far removed from its natural state that environmental regulations and policies don't even attempt to propose returning areas to their previous, natural state. Revegetation (replanting), dominated by common indigenous species is the best that rejuvenation efforts can hope to achieve. In considering how to rejuvenate the extremely polluted Jukskei River, it is worth spending a little effort to find out how its source valley might have looked before Johannesburg was built. This is not to suggest that it would be possible, or preferable, to try to return it to that condition, but to help guide policies about how to bring back some of the indigenous species that used to grow here, to restore some of the natural features that used to exist, for the benefit of all who live in the area.

Travelling to the past: Pre-colonisation Highveld

People who live in cities are less likely to care about their environments if they don't have positive experiences and memories of those environments. To help people who don't have their own positive memories and associations of nature, we can try to create a bit of 'time travel' through historical botany. Descriptions of landscapes before they were disturbed by humans are found in many guises. Studies of palynology, for example, give a glimpse of what plant species used to grow in a particular landscape, based on a study of pollen grains in deep soil layers, sometimes even in fossilised forms. Through their grazing habits, large herbivores selected specific species to graze on, hereby balancing these species numbers. This changed when these large creatures were hunted to extinction in paleo and neolithic times.

The Highveld region may well be a key location where our ancestors first took stones in hand and chipped off flakes to make a tool.[2] Concentrations of Early Stone Age sites are usually present on the flood-plains of perennial rivers and may date to over two million years ago.[3] These early human ancestors, including the Australopithecines, Little Foot and others from the Cradle of Humankind area, well knew the value of the plants that were common to the Highveld. Apart from the veld's value to grazing animals, people knew how to use plants to treat common ailments, stop bleeding or draw out an infection using plant poultices. They probably knew which herbs would ease childbearing and which ones would cure cancer. Their distant descendants, the San people who lived in Southern Africa since the middle of the last millennium, have an extensive knowledge of herbal pharmacology (the science of drugs and medications).[4] They knew how to prepare glue to trap birds and poison to arm their arrows. They knew which fragrant herbs would attract suitors or please their mates. It is certain that people who lived in and around the Jukskei valley used the local plants for a wide variety of known magical and medicinal uses, many of which are lost to time.

Many animals likely roamed the Highveld, including baboons, leopards, and brown hyena. The existence of large herds comprising up to eight species of grazers is inferred from the written record from the 19th and early 20th century.[5] The relationship between human ancestors, predators, and grazers, together with natural processes of frost and fire, shaped the ecological landscape of the early Highveld grassland.

Finding an ecological benchmark for the Jukskei River

Without doubt, long before colonisation and the establishment of the city of Johannesburg, the river that came to be called the Jukskei was once unpolluted and clean. We can never know the full detail of biodiversity (the understanding of the variety of plant and animal life in a particular habitat), nor the stories and lives of the people who walked its banks. But there are clues for us to follow. Some pictures of the parks and early recreational activities along the Jukskei headwaters of the first settlers of this part of Johannesburg still exist. Areas where it flows that are outside the city still exist which it has not been completely transformed.

An integral premise in ecology is the use of benchmark sites from which to evaluate the degree of change that habitats have undergone. This is well described in the literature. (The WET-Health method of assessing wetland integrity as set out in the WET-Health assessment method[6] is a good example). An accurate description of habitats and species in the benchmark sites forms a platform from which to measure change and determine auditable or measurable targets in sites that are polluted or compromised. Ecological assessments of species cover, abundance, richness and the distribution and extent of common and rare species are often used to describe benchmark and target sites.

To find a benchmark site that shows what an area looked like before transformation by the industrialisation of the last century, a site needs to be identified with similar environmental *drivers*. These are aspects that determine what habitats (*responders*) develop. Climate and soil type support specific plants adapted to those conditions. The plant diversity and structure in turn determine which animals frequent these habitats. Granitic, sandy, well-drained soil supports species different from those that flourish on waterlogged, clay soil resting on shale. Millions of years of shifts in drivers, sometimes subtle, sometimes dramatic, give us assemblages of species that are, often predictably, found together in ecosystems.

The uppermost section of the Jukskei River falls roughly in the Ventersdorp Supergroup (including the Klipriviersberg Group) in the Witwatersrand Basin. Just north of Lorentzville the geology changes with the formation of the Johannesburg dome, comprised of andesite shale and granites. According to the vegetation types, this geology (where it remains untransformed by agriculture, urbanisation or other human activities) supports Soweto Highveld Grassland.[7] This vegetation type is characterised by common and rare plants that thrive on the soils formed by sedimentary rocks laid down over a period which ended about 2 700 million years ago, when widespread faulting resulted in extensive lava flows. There has been plenty of time for this landscape to develop intricate networks of species assemblages, specialised into units that prefer specific slopes, light intensity, soil moisture gradients and so many other nuanced aspects of the land. In turn, these niches support creatures of all sorts, invertebrates, insects, mammals and birds.

All of these factors need to match, in identifying a suitable benchmark for the Jukskei catchment. There is a pocket of land which has not been transformed, where conservation has intervened to make sure it is somewhat protected from the march of time, from development, grazing, ploughing and invasion of weeds: the Suikerbosrand Nature Reserve.

An undisturbed reference in Suikerbosrand

In 1980, Prof. George J. Bredenkamp and Dr G.K. Theron published a detailed assessment of plant assemblages of the Ventersdorp Geological System of the Suikerbosrand Nature Reserve. They describe the environment as follows:

> The plateaux are drained by a number of kloofs, some of which cut deeply into the mountains resulting in steep slopes, characteristically covered with woody vegetation. The lower valleys in the bigger kloofs are sheltered and contain deep, fertile clayey soils of alluvial and colluvial origin. The soils of the study area however, are, mostly fairly shallow with a sandy clay or sandy clay loam texture.

The survey for their study included delineation of thirteen different physiographic (another term for physical geography) and physiognomic (the general form or appearance of the landscape) units on which one hundred and ninety three sample plots were divided, and in which cover abundance was recorded.[8] Cover abundance is a measure of plant cover, used in vegetation science. It is based on percentages, but uses abundance estimates for species with a low plant cover. The floristic composition of plant communities is represented in the composition of two main vegetation communities, *Euclea crispa – Rhoicissus tridentata* Bush and Savanna Communities and *Trachypogon spicatus – Themeda triandra* Grassland Communities. A variant of the *Euclea crispa – Rhoicissus tridentata* community is the *Rhus pyroides – Rhamnus prinoides – Cassinopsis ilicifolia community*. This group of plants is described as favouring sheltered, moist kloofs on sandy loam soils at an altitude of 1 740–1 770 m,[9] similar to the Jukskei River valley. These conditions are similar to what we would find if we travelled back to around 1850, before the establishment of townships and reservoirs in Johannesburg. This is when natural processes of ecological succession, or the process by which the structure of a biological community evolves over time, chose groups of species with close ties to the specific characteristics of the soil, slopes, frost, moisture, dispersers and grazers on the Highveld.

Urbanisation of the Jukskei River catchment valley

Since the early 1900s, the upper reach of the Jukskei River has been confined to a canal. But what did it look like before it was transformed, well before the establishment of the township of Doornfontein in 1887? No images are available from this time, though descriptions of the area are reported. Marion Laserson reports that the first reservoir was constructed over one of the springs of the Jukskei River in 1888. A storage reservoir was constructed over another spring of the Jukskei close to Joe Slovo Drive (then called Harrow Road). This reservoir is still in use today and has a capacity of 4,5 megalitres. At the current Ellis Park tennis courts, another reservoir was constructed in 1894. Several other smaller reservoirs were reportedly constructed around this area.[10]

About 500 m east of Joe Slovo Drive is the swimming pool at the Ellis Park Stadium. This area was reported as originally being a marsh with reeds and open water, and numerous trees that appear to be planted such as eucalyptus and pines on the hills to the north and west, as shown in a drawing in Laserson (2018). This marsh or wetland (both terms refer to an area where wet soil supports plants adapted to grow in waterlogged areas), where water welled up from the surrounding ridges, was deepened and excavated to form a lake. The eye of the Jukskei at Ellis Park was fitted with pipes to supply the increasing demands of the town in June 1888. The uncovered lake had a capacity of 98 megalitres and was used for rowing and leisure activities when Ellis Park was proclaimed in 1905.[11]

Reference to springs, marshes, lakes, ridges and rivers in historical accounts of early Johannesburg are the most important clues from which to form a setting for a picture of what the Jukskei River looked like before it was confined to a canal. A 'spring' is defined as follows:

> An opening at or near the surface of the Earth for the discharge of water from underground sources. A spring is a natural discharge point of subterranean water at the surface of the ground or directly into the bed of a stream, lake, or sea. Water in springs generally originates as rainfall that has soaked into the soil and percolated into underlying rocks. Permeable rocks (those containing interconnected pore spaces through which water can migrate). If the pressure is sufficiently high and the water will rise to the surface without pumping. This is called an artesian spring. (sic)[12]

The quartzite ridges around the Jukskei River valley form an ideal environment for water to percolate slowly and then decant from artesian springs, which can give rise to wetland systems that can range in size from a puddle to a hectare, or more.

Sometimes water is confined to a seep and is somewhat isolated from streams or rivers. Some wetlands can provide enough groundwater to sustain baseflow in a stream. Many springs can form pools when grazing animals trample the soft soil

THE HISTORICAL JUKSKEI RIVER VALLEY

when they graze on the rich plants that grow in the constant moisture. Wetlands support specialised plants such as sedges, reeds, grasses, herbs and algae, and provide habitat for fauna, including an array of unique crustaceans, fish and macroinvertebrates (animals without backbones).

A classification of watercourses currently in use[13] explains the characteristics and mechanisms of a river or stream and a marsh or wetland. From historic descriptions of the source of the Jukskei, it appears that the water decanting from the spring resulted in a fair-sized wetland (sufficiently large to be altered into a lake used for boating and the supply of water to several reservoirs). It is likely that the landscape supported the springs which formed large wetlands that then narrowed into a stream. Looking at the depressions at the location of Joe Slovo Drive, where the swimming pool and tennis course now are, one can imagine how springs here may have seeped water and formed wetlands. The steep slope below the tennis courts may well have formed the upper reaches of a stream.

The difference between a stream or river and a wetland are not always well defined, although the two systems are fundamentally different in their hydrological characteristics.

Wetlands are low energy, fluvial, net depositional systems, where slow moving water creates soils that are sufficiently saturated to support plants specially adapted to grow in these conditions, and where oxidation and reduction of iron elements in the soil can occur. Wetland types that likely occurred at the source of the Jukskei River likely included seeps and valley bottom hydrogeomorphic units (hydrologically linked landform units). Springs at the source of the Jukskei River valley likely formed seepage wetlands. Seepages occur where springs are decanting into the soil profile near the surface, causing hydric conditions to develop; or where throughflow in the soil profile is forced close to the surface due to impervious layers, such as plinthite layers; or where large outcrops of impervious rock force subsurface water up to the surface.[14]

Streams and rivers are considered to be riparian systems. Here, fast flowing water forms conditions where alluvial deposits of transported sediment occur and distinct channels with specific structural components are visible. Rivers are linear fluvial, eroded landforms which carry channelised flow on a permanent, seasonal or ephemeral/episodic basis. The river channel flows within a confined valley (gorge) or within an incised macro-channel.[15]

The Jukskei River likely flowed from wetlands that grew from springs on the slopes of the ridges. A wetland-riparian mosaic probably gave way to a river as the slope flattened on the floor of the valley, where permanent flow was contained between rocky banks. Along the banks of streams in our ecological benchmark, the Suikerbosrand, pale grey-green shrubs and trees, aloes and golden grass mark the thread of water in the valley. This is how it was with the Jukskei.

Integrating historical clues into a botanical rejuvenation plan

Now, the Jukskei River headwaters run through a concrete channel. This has come to be seen as 'normal', but as the historical clues show, it is not at all normal for a marshy wetland, featuring many springs and streams which then naturally congregated into a river, to be covered over with concrete and forced into a single culvert.

The Jukskei River cannot be returned to the wetland-riparian complex that it once was, sprung from the folds of surrounding ridges, and guardian of a rich diversity of plants and animals. This would be an unrealistic aim. The golden plains and green valleys of the Highveld have given way to the birth of a commercial giant: the city of Johannesburg. A new balance needs to be found, for the river. However, there is value in grounding a rejuvenation plan in knowledge of the past and looking to the pre-urbanisation river for guidance and ideas on how to improve it now. One key strategy can be choosing to reintroduce plant species that were once endemic to the riparian zone.

The Suikerbosrand provides many examples of plant species that can be used in urban landscaping around the Jukskei River. Many of these species are common to the Highveld and are referred to in folk tales, seen in city streetscapes, and indigenous gardens in Johannesburg. Some of these plant species are listed below.

Plants suitable for reintroduction to the Jukskei River valley

The golden grass is the Highveld's most striking feature. However, pockets of trees and shrubs form important habitat. This mass of vegetation forms a collective unit. Yet the patterns of diversity are intimately linked to biophysical gradients, such as those created by moisture, soil chemistry, slope, frost or burning. The species below are recorded from the Suikerbosrand but are ideal for reintroduction to landscaped environments in Johannesburg.

Table 2.1 *A list of indigenous plants known to occur in the Suikerbosrand that are suitable for landscaped environments in Johannesburg*

Latin name	Common name (English)	African language names	Interesting fact[16]
Budleja salviifolia	Sagebush, butterfly bush	ewanci (isiXhosa), igwangi, iloshane (isiZulu), chipambati (Shona), lelothwane (S. Sotho)	The wood is hard and heavy and has traditionally been used for assegais and fishing rods, or as fuel or hedging.
Celtis africana	White stinkwood	uSinga Iwesalukazi (isiZulu), umVumvu (isiXhosa), Modutu (Sotho & Tswana)	This wood is a good general timber suitable for making planks, shelving, yokes, tent-bows and furniture. Culturally, it was mixed with crocodile fat as a charm against lightning, and many people believe that it has power over evil and that pegs of wood driven into the ground will keep witches away.

Latin name	Common name (English)	African language names	Interesting fact[16]
Leucosidea sericea	Oldwood	umtsitshi (isiZulu), isidwaswa (isiXhosa), mosino (N. Sotho)	The wood makes good, durable fence posts in permanently wet soil. Culturally the tree is used as a charm to protect the inhabitants of homesteads.
Searcia (previously known as *Rhus*) *pyroides*	Common currant	Gewone taaibos (Afrikaans), nhlokoshiyane (isiZulu)	This small tree attracts multitudes of birds and insects and can be grown as a hedge.
Senegalia (previously known as *Acacia*) *caffra*	Common hook thorn	umTholo (isiZulu), katdoring (Afrikaans), Motholo (N. Sotho), Mbvhinya-xihloka (Tsonga)	The wood is dense and hard and beautifully grained. The foliage is enjoyed by game and stock. The common hook-thorn is used traditionally for many purposes, such as fencing posts.
Vachelia (previously known as *Acacia*) *karoo*	Sweet thorn	mookana (N. Sotho), mooka (Tswana, umuNga (isiZulu and isiXhosa), soetdoring (Afrikaans)	The tree produces a pleasant tasting gum, eaten by people and animals. It is a particularly good fodder tree; stock and game feed on the leaves, flowers and pods.
Euclea crispa	Blue guarri	iyeza-lokuxaxazisa (isiXhosa), motlhaletsongane (Setswana), idungamuzi (isiZulu)	The wood from this tree is used for timber, producing a hard, dark heartwood timber, similar to ebony. It has edible fruit, and the chewed ends of the twigs serve as toothbrushes.
Ziziphus muconata	Buffalo thorn	blinkblaar-wag-'n-bietjie (Afrikaans), umphafa (isiXhosa and isiZulu), moonaona (N. Sotho)	The fruits of *Ziziphus* species are an important source of food for birds. This species and its relatives have many cultural and spiritual uses.

Magical and medicinal plants

South Africa has a very rich and diverse culture of using plants magically and medicinally. Herbs used by our ancestors are still to be found in the Jukskei catchment. This knowledge is in many cases well captured and researched.[17,18,19] Anecdotal evidence indicates that plants used medicinally may not always have active chemical compounds. They can be used simply to lift the spirits of a depressed person because they have a particular rugged beauty, or to win the heart of a lover by finding a stem from a plant that grows in dangerously inaccessible places. Many medicinal plants do have well researched phytochemicals, or biologically active compounds. [20,21]

Table 2.2 *A list of indigenous medicinal plants that grow in the Jukskei River catchment*

Latin name	Common name (English)	African language names	Interesting fact
Artemisia afra	African wormwood	lengana (Sotho, Tswana), umhlonyane (isiXhosa and isiZulu).	This highly aromatic plant is one of the most widely used traditional medicines in South Africa. It is used to treat coughs, colds, fevers, headaches, earaches, and intestinal worms, amongst others). There is significant geographical variability in chemical compounds.
Catha edulis	Bushman's tea	Boesmantee (Afrikaans), Igqwaka (isiXhosa), Inandinandi (Ndebele), Luthadzi (Venda), Mohlatse (North Sotho), Umhlwazi (isiZulu),	The active ingredient, cathinone, reduces fatigue and increases mental power and generally has a stimulating effect.
Centella asiatica	Marsh pennywort	Bolila-balinku (South Sotho), Icudwane (isiZulu),	The leaves of this moisture-loving plant smell like carrots when crushed. It is traditionally used to treat wounds, and as a purgative and diuretic. Its wound-healing, antifungal and anti-inflammatory activity is associated with a titerpenoid saponon, aglycone with a trisaccharide bonded to it. Extracts from plant are used commercially in various commercial products.
Cotyledon orbiculata	Pig's ear	Plakkie (Afrikaans), imphewula (isiXhosa), seredile (Sotho, Tswana)	This plant is an excellent garden succulent and is widely used to soften and treat corns and warts. The leaf is sometimes eaten as a vermifuge, and juice may be used for earache and toothache. The plant contains several cardiac glycosides of a bufadienolide type, which may be poisonous.
Lippia javanica	Fever tea	mumara (Shona), musukudu (Tswana), umsuzwane (isiZulu)	Tea made from this plant is used to treat coughs, colds, and fever. Poultices are used to treat lice and scabies. *Lippia javanica* is rich in volatile oil and numerous monoterpenoids that have decongestant and anti-inflammatory properties.
Scabiosa columbaria	Wild Scabious	Bitterwortel (Afrikaans), makgha (isiXhosa), ibheka (isiZulu)	This plant is a remedy for colic and heartburn, amongst several traditional uses. Powdered roots are sometimes used as an aromatic baby powder. Rootstock yields two iridoid glycosides, loganin and sweroside. Sweroside has moderate antibacterial activity.
Scadoxis puniceus	Red paintbrush	umphompho (isiZulu)	This magnificent bulbous plant is traditionally used to treat coughs and gastrointestinal problems. It is rich in isoquinoline alkaloids which are highly toxic.
Warburgia salutaris	Pepper bark tree	mulanga (Venda), isibhaha (isiZulu)	This medium sized tree provides a popular and widely-used remedy for coughs, colds and chest complaints. The bark contains numerous drimane sesquiterpenoids which are antibacterial.

The plants listed above (and many others that are known to have grown in this region, that have not been listed) are easy to grow and their medicinal, cultural and aesthetic values are well described. They are a tangible link between our past and a future that we can shape into a beautiful, achievable environment. Growing these plants in streetscapes, containers, gardens and public spaces along the Jukskei River canal, provides for a host of inexpensive projects that draw together people who love this space.

Lessons for the Jukskei from the Suikerbosrand

Remaining natural places such as the Suikerbosrand are protected time capsules, lovingly managed by scientists, managers and a host of support staff, who base their conservation decisions on sound ecological principles. Many generations of children have walked in nature reserves like this and have learned to love these environments.

They offer a vision for how efforts to restore pockets of nature in urban environments can bear results, so that everyone who lives there can enjoy the spirit of the Highveld, in the city, as well as in nature reserves. While all children may not get the opportunity to go hiking in a nature reserve, we can expose them to the empty vistas of unspoilt nature through our stories and art, so that this benchmark may enter their psyches and become part of their world view. This could hopefully contribute to replacing the idea that toxic streams bordered by weeds are what the environment 'normally' looks like. Nurturing a love for our environment will help them to grow into loving, pragmatic managers, activists, designers, artists, writers and custodians of the magically urban Jukskei River valley.

Notes

1   See https://www.plantzafrica.com/.

2   Revil Mason, *Prehistory of the Transvaal: A Record of Human Activity (1962)*: 498.

3   Faye Lander and Thembi Russell, '*The Archaeological Evidence for the Appearance of Pastoralism and Farming in Southern Africa*' (2018).

4   S. Erik Holm, *Bibliography of South African Pre- and Protohistoric Archaeology* (1966).

5   André F. Boshoff and Graham I. H. Kerley, 'Lost Herds of the Highveld: Evidence from the Written, Historical Record,' *African Journal of Wildlife Research* 45, no. 3 (October 1, 2015): 287-300. https://doi.org/10.3957/056.045.02870.

6   M. Douglas Macfarlane, D. J. Edwards Ollis, and D. C. Kotze, *WET-Health (Version 2.0): A Refined Suite of Tools for Assessing the Present Ecological State of Wetland Ecosystems* (2020).

7   L. Mucina and M. C. Rutherford, *Vegetation Map of South Africa, Lesotho and Swaziland* (2006).

8   V. Westhoff and E. van der Maarel, *The Braun-Blanquet Approach* (1978).

9   G. J. Bredenkamp and G. K. Theron, 'A Synecological Account of the Suikerbosrand Nature Reserve II' (1980).

10 M. Laserson, *Renovation of The Jukskei River Canal in Bertrams, Lorentzville, Judith's Paarl to Bezuidenhout Valley* (2018).

11 M. Laserson, *Renovation of The Jukskei River Canal in Bertrams, Lorentzville, Judith's Paarl to Bezuidenhout Valley* (2018).

12 Britannica, T. Editors of Encyclopaedia. 'spring.' *Encyclopaedia Britannica*, January 16, 2020. https://www.britannica.com/science/spring-water.

13 D. J. Ollis, C. D. Snaddon, N. M. Job, and N. Mbona, *Classification System for Wetlands and Other Aquatic Ecosystems in South Africa* (2013).

14 D. J. Ollis, C. D. Snaddon, N. M. Job, and N. Mbona, *Classification System for Wetlands and Other Aquatic Ecosystems in South Africa: User Manual: Inland System* (2013).

15 D. J. Ollis, C. D. Snaddon, N. M. Job, and N. Mbona, *Classification System for Wetlands and Other Aquatic Ecosystems in South Africa: User Manual: Inland System* (2013).

16 See https://www.plantzafrica.com/.

17 B. van Wyk and N. Gericke, *People's Plants: A Guide to Useful Plants of Southern Africa* (2007).

18 B. van Wyk, B. van Oudtshoorn, and N. Gericke, *Medicinal Plants of South Africa* (2009).

19 T. H. Arnold, C. A. Prentice, E. E. Snyman, M. Tomalin, N. R. Crouch, and C. Pottas-Bircher, *Medicinal and Magical Plants of Southern Africa: An Annotated Checklist* (2002).

20 B. van Wyk and N. Gericke, *People's Plants: A Guide to Useful Plants of Southern Africa* (2007).

21 Important disclaimer: The information offered is based on a literature review and should not be considered as a recommendation or an endorsement of any particular medical or health treatment.

3 Macroplastic pollution within the Jukskei River: How much, what kind and why does it matter?

Kyle van Heyde

From source to sink, plastic items interact with the environment on land, in our freshwater resources and oceans. Understanding the sources of macroplastic pollution within rivers, their quantity and characteristics, and the mechanisms which control their fate and transport, is crucial for solutions to reduce global plastic pollution. Plastic pollution has become a prevalent problem in South Africa, along the coastline and within terrestrial ecosystems. The Jukskei River is severely polluted with harmful organic materials, sewage, and abundant plastic waste. This study investigated community perceptions and macroplastic pollution within the Jukskei River. Macroplastic pollution is evident throughout the Jukskei River, with the frequency of items ranging from 3 012 items per day at the headwaters of the Jukskei to 517 679 items per day prior to its confluence with the Crocodile River. The most common types of plastic pollution present across sites were Low-Density Polyethylene and Polystyrene, commonly used for single-use plastics. Plastic pollution threatens the ecosystem services, aquatic fauna and flora, water infrastructure and the cultural significance of the Jukskei River.

Introduction: A background to plastic pollution

Plastic has changed our world for the better, enabling advances in manufacturing, technology and healthcare[1] – and, as we are all bound to have heard, for worse. No environment is free of plastic pollution, nor is there a clear idea of its long-term effects on living organisms.[2] Once plastic items enter the environment, they become degraded or broken down by physical, chemical and biological processes, rendering the materials brittle, fragmented and discoloured.[3] New research has found micro and nano plastic particles in human lungs, blood and the digestive system.[4] Further, plastic waste has been shown to harbour diseases such as malaria, a novel transport platform for waterborne pathogens, and it poses a flood risk and economic burden on communities.[5] Plastic pollution has been separated into three categories, according to their size: nanoplastics (1 to <1 000 nm), microplastics (1 µm to 5 mm) and macroplastics (>5 mm). The size of plastic debris affects mitigation strategies for their removal, the transport of pathogens and invasive species, and their effect on humans, flora and fauna from entanglement to endocrine disruption.[6]

Riverine plastic pollution is a relatively young research field, with the first efforts to quantify riverine plastic debris published in the early 2010s.[7] Riverine plastic pollution refers to the contamination of rivers and their surrounding environments with plastic waste. The first sites of inquiry into riverine plastic pollution were undertaken by sampling waterways in Europe and North America.[8] There is a limited but growing body of work in developing countries, despite the significant challenge facing both developed and developing countries in controlling the leakage of plastic waste into the environment.[9]

Within South Africa, as is true globally, there is a need to understand the sources, movement and perceptions of plastic materials to mitigate their increasing occurrence in water resources.[10] Ecosystem services, the benefits that humans derive from natural ecosystems provided by inland water sources, are fraught with deteriorating water quality brought about by plastic pollution, while water and waste infrastructure are placed under increasing pressure through the large volumes of plastic pollution present.[11] As awareness of plastic pollution increases and gains traction, citizens, communities, the private sector and the government are organising cleanups in public and natural spaces to remove these items from the environment.[12] The ubiquity and abundance of plastic pollution in the environment cannot be overstated. South Africa ranks among the top 20 countries contributing to marine plastic debris annually.[13] Plastic pollution is common along highways, rivers and lakes, in rural and agricultural areas, along the coastline and out at sea.[14] Beyond economic, aesthetic and ecosystem service value, riverine ecosystems play an important role in South African ritual and cultural life.[15] Especially near urban centres, South Africa's riverine ecosystems are increasingly threatened by plastic pollution, hampering their societal and natural value.[16]

The Jukskei River is one of the most polluted rivers within the Gauteng region, and numerous NGOs are working within this system to remove pollution.[17] Along the course of the Jukskei River, the quality and availability of waste management and infrastructure varies drastically, leading some communities to use the rivers as a waste stream.[18] This study investigated macroplastic pollution within the Jukskei River, quantifying and characterising the plastic items captured along the riparian zone and in the water column. The study further investigated perceptions of plastic pollution in rivers among communities that reside near the Jukskei River.

Methods used in this study

The Jukskei River flows for approximately 66 km from a series of springs in Ellis Park, Johannesburg, to its confluence with the Crocodile River in Pretoria Rural. At its headwaters, the Jukskei River flows through a diverse range of highly urbanised areas, from the outskirts of Johannesburg CBD to high-income regions such as Bedfordview and low-income areas such as Alexandra. Continuing its journey, the Jukskei River flows toward Midrand, passing through schools and industrial and residential areas. As the Jukskei River approaches its confluence, the highly urbanised city landscape gives way to less developed agricultural and rural land. Along this final leg, the Jukskei River accommodates a variety of weekend getaway

Figure 3.1 *Study area*

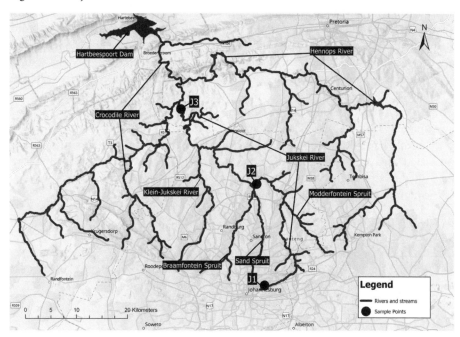

Map redrawn by Enathi Motolwana, HSRC

resorts, adventure camps and private game farms. Three sites were selected along the Jukskei River for this study (Figure 3.1).

To assess perceptions of plastic pollution within riverine ecosystems and how they relate to the issues within the Jukskei River, a survey was developed and deployed using Google Forms. The first batch of surveys was sent out on the 17th of January 2022, for online participation. Over nine months, 227 community organisations, Facebook groups, scout societies, river cleanup initiatives and environmental groups were contacted for participation in the survey. Of the 227 groups contacted, 142 people participated in the online survey, with high response levels throughout the survey. Although the survey was offered in a hardcopy and online format, all respondents completed the online version. This survey aimed to investigate and compare awareness and knowledge of plastic pollution, explore connotations associated with plastic pollution and how these are formed, explore perceptions and ideas on reducing the plastic pollution load, and incite pro-environmental behaviour within river networks.

The first site along the Jukskei River was located where the waters of the Jukskei from the springs under Johannesburg meet daylight – at a culvert in Victoria Yards in Lorentzville (on the eastern edge of the CBD). This site is in a highly urbanised area of Johannesburg and faces issues relating to waste management services, illegal dumping and a lack of basic municipal waste and water infrastructure. At this point in its journey, the river is confined to a narrow, deep culvert with little to no riparian zone present. The second sample site along the Jukskei River is located in Kyalami, approximately 30 km downstream of the first sample site. The river has evolved from confinement in the Bezuidenhout Valley culvert to a broader, free-flowing river with a dense riparian zone. The third sample site along the Jukskei River is in Pretoria Rural, which lies approximately 250 m upstream of the confluence between the Jukskei and Crocodile Rivers. When the waters of the Jukskei River reach this site, they have meandered through approximately 41 km of urban landscape, followed by approximately 25 km of mixed land usage and open land. This sample site lies within the Crocodile River Reserve (CRR), a partnership between landowners to establish a protected area to preserve this region's natural biodiversity and landscape. The Jukskei River has widened substantially at the final site and lies within a relatively pristine natural landscape, with a dense riparian zone (Figure 3.2).

Figure 3.2 *The river profile of the sites along the Jukskei River*

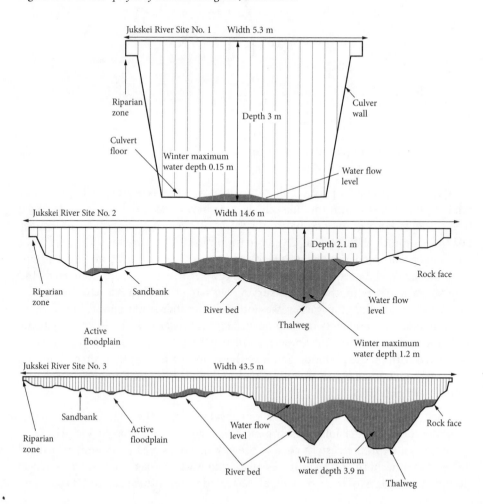

Sampling for macroplastic pollution took place over 12 months, once per quarter. The first sampling campaign occurred in November 2021, followed by the second in February 2022, the third in May and the fourth in August. These months were selected to capture seasonal variations. A custom-made steel frame was deployed across all nine sample sites over the four sampling campaigns. Sampling took place within the mainstream or section of flow within the river. A grid was used along the banks at each sample site, the grid size and placement were standardised across sites to ensure comparability of plastic pollution within the riparian zone. Quantifying plastic pollution within these river networks was done by capturing, identifying and measuring the plastic waste. Statistics and spatial analysis were used to gain insight into macroplastic pollution in the Jukskei River.

A brief review of results from this study

Perceptions

A small but diverse sample participated in the survey. The largest demographic group for this survey consisted of women aged 45–54, white, with an undergraduate degree, residing in the City of Johannesburg, identifying their stakeholder group as a local community member. The survey results of this study reveal that the Jukskei River is an essential site for cultural, religious and recreational activities. However, these sites have come under increasing pressure from macroplastic pollution.

Respondents were asked how long they had interacted with the Jukskei River to better understand their relationship with it. More than half of the respondents (54%) had interacted with the Jukskei River for over ten years, which resulted in most respondents having a deep knowledge of this system. Furthermore, 20% of respondents had interacted with this river for five to ten years, while 25% had interacted for less than five years.

To understand respondents' awareness of pollution in riverine environments, they were asked whether they notice pollution along and within rivers and streams. Most respondents, 67%, always saw pollution, followed by 24% of respondents who often notice pollution and 6% who sometimes note it. Only 3% of respondents rarely and never notice pollution. The respondents who saw pollution in rivers and streams were then asked if they had ever noticed plastic pollution in these environments. All respondents had noticed plastic pollution; 88% said they saw it all the time, while 12% noticed it sometimes. Plastic pollution was the most common pollutant that respondents noticed – followed by rubble and building debris, glass and organic waste (sewerage). Respondents were asked whether they believe plastic pollution is bad for the environment. Most respondents, 93%, felt plastic pollution was a problem, while 7% thought it was not.

To gain better insight into respondents' perceived issues with plastic pollution, they were asked to explain the major environmental or ecological impacts they

Figure 3.3 *Perceived environmental or ecological impacts associated with plastic pollution*

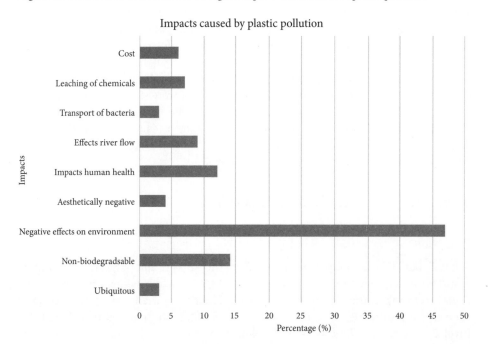

associated with plastic pollution. Respondents gave various reasons why plastic is a problem, ranging from economic to environmental and social consequences. The most common impact respondents noted was the environmental effects (47%); respondents mentioned issues such as entanglement and ingestion (Figure 3.3).

Further, 15% of respondents felt the problem was that most plastic items are not biodegradable, and 11% felt the impacts on human health, such as microplastic ingestion, were the problem with plastic pollution. A notable 10% of respondents believed the issue with plastic pollution lay in its impact impeding natural river and water flow. In addition 8% felt leaching chemicals from plastic pollutants while in rivers was an issue.

The closing question asked respondents how the amount of plastic pollution in rivers and streams could be reduced. The most common solutions proposed by respondents were better waste management infrastructure (17%), and better education about the environment and the issues posed by pollution (16%). Significant fines for littering and illegal dumping (13%) were also a common solution, while only 4% suggested incentives for cleaning environmentally friendly products. Controversially, 8% of respondents felt the answer lay with a change of governance, citing a lack of political will and corruption:

'The government needs to stop corruption because when corruption is alive, everything else dies!' – (Respondent #1)

A further 5% of respondents felt the solution was to raise greater awareness of plastic pollution. Similarly, 5% felt a behavioural change toward acting pro-environmentally was the solution, while 6% felt the answer was wider-ranging and more intensive cleaning operations.

Riverine ecosystem

Across the Jukskei River within the water column, there was a significant variation in the number of plastic items moving through each site. Site J1 at the river's headwaters ranged from 3 457 items daily in the dry season (May and August) to 4 704 items daily in the wet season (November and February), with a peak in February of 6 072 items daily. Site J2 in Kyalami ranged from 3 012 items daily in the dry season to 5 431 items daily in the wet season, with a peak of 5 856 items daily in February. Site J3 produced the highest number and the most significant range in the number of items across sampling campaigns within a site in the Jukskei River. Site J3 ranged from 93 435 items daily in May to 517 679 items in August, with an average of 216 226 items across sampling campaigns (Figure 3.4).

Figure 3.4 *The number of macroplastic items moving through sites along the Jukskei River across the four sampling campaigns*

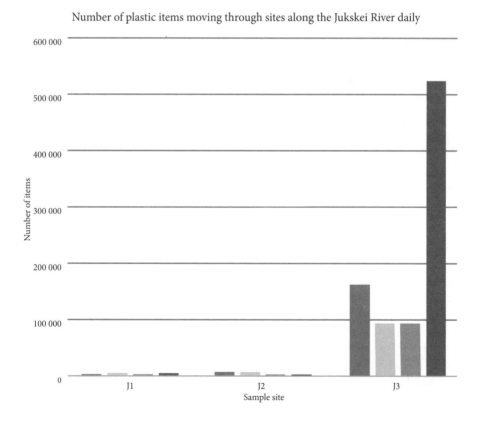

Site J1 ranged from a weight of 1 kg daily in August to 31 kg in May, with an average daily weight of 15 kg. Site J2 ranged from a daily weight of 4 kg in August to 13 kg in February, with an average of 8 kg daily. Site J3 ranged from 71 kg daily in August to 234 kg in November, with an average daily weight of 174 kg. A significant plastic pollution source is noted entering the Jukskei River after site J2 in Kyalami. This finding is fascinating as the region between sites J2 and J3 is characterised as a mix of urban development on the city's periphery, followed downstream by open land, private reserves, and nature estates.

Across all sampling campaigns and sites within the Jukskei River, Low-Density Polyethylene (LDPE), Polypropylene (PP) and Polystyrene (PS) comprised 91% of the plastic items found within the water column; LDPE 31%, PP 17%, and PS 43%. These types of plastics are commonly associated with single-use items. When investigating plastic pollution, one of the most critical analyses undertaken is the size of these items. Their size directly relates to these items' negative societal and environmental implications. Across sites and sampling campaigns along the Jukskei River within the water column, there was consistency in the most common size of plastic items found; 86% of items were smaller than five centimeters.

Along the riparian zone of the Jukskei River at site J1, items less than 5 cm accounted for 55% of the sample across sampling campaigns, while items 5–20 cm in size were 38%. At site J2, items less than 5 cm comprised 16%, while 5–20 cm formed 63%. At site J3, items less than 5 cm were 24% of the sample, 5–20 cm accounted for 48%, and 20–50 cm was 20%. A greater variety in the size of plastic items collected across sites and sampling campaigns is found along the riparian zone, as compared to items within the water column. A constant, ubiquitous presence of plastic pollution along the riparian zone, averaging 28 items/m^2, was found across all sites. The most common types of plastic pollution present across sites along the riparian zone were Low-Density Polyethylene and Polystyrene, commonly used in single-use plastics and commonly found within the water column of freshwater environments.

Conclusions

The Jukskei River is essential to our social, economic, recreational, cultural, and physiological thriving. It has, however, come under increasing pressure from macroplastic pollution. The amount, types and size of most plastic items within the Jukskei River are of concern for several reasons. The high load of plastic pollution, size, and types of items threaten the natural environment through ingestion, degradation, and deposition. Small plastic items are expensive and difficult to remove from aquatic ecosystems, and single-use plastics are designed to degrade quickly. Additionally, macroplastic pollution threatens society by transporting and retaining pathogens, increasing flood risk and placing an economic burden on local communities. A high pollution load entering the Jukskei River outside the city also raises further questions as to the sources of pollution in this river. Through more significant government and industry involvement, community activism and increased pro-environmental behaviour, there is an opportunity to reduce plastic pollution and restore the Jukskei River to benefit the local community and the environment.

Notes

1   Bonthuys, Jorisna. 'Death in a drop: study explores microplastic pollution-emerging pollutants.' *Water Wheel* 17, no. 1 (2018): 12-15.

2   Cook, Cayla R., and Rolf U. Halden. 'Ecological and health issues of plastic waste.' In *Plastic Waste and Recycling*, Academic Press, (2020): 513-527.

3   Windsor, Fredric M., Isabelle Durance, Alice A. Horton, Richard C. Thompson, Charles R. Tyler, and Steve J. Ormerod, 'A catchment-scale perspective of plastic pollution.' *Global Change Biology* 25, no. 4 (2019): 1207-1221.

4   Yan, Yuanyuan, Fengxiao Zhu, Changyin Zhu, Zhanghao Chen, Shaochong Liu, Chao Wang, and Cheng Gu, 'Dibutyl phthalate release from polyvinyl chloride microplastics: Influence of plastic properties and environmental factors' *Water Research* 204 (2021): 117597.

5   Jambeck, Jenna R., Roland Geyer, Chris Wilcox, Theodore R. Siegler, Miriam Perryman, Anthony Andrady, Ramani Narayan, and Kara Lavender Law, 'Plastic waste inputs from land into the ocean.' *Science* 347, no. 6223 (2015): 768-771. Liro, Maciej, Tim van Emmerik, Bartłomiej Wyżga, Justyna Liro, and Paweł Mikuś. 'Macroplastic storage and remobilization in rivers.' *Water* 12, no. 7 (2020): 2055.

6   Yan, Yuanyuan, Fengxiao Zhu, Changyin Zhu, Zhanghao Chen, Shaochong Liu, Chao Wang, and Cheng Gu, 'Dibutyl phthalate release from polyvinyl chloride microplastics: Influence of plastic properties and environmental factors.' *Water Research* 204 (2021): 117597.

7   Van Emmerik, Tim, and Anna Schwarz, 'Plastic debris in rivers.' *Wiley Interdisciplinary Reviews: Water* 7, no. 1 (2020): e1398.

8   Van Emmerik, Tim, and Anna Schwarz, 'Plastic debris in rivers.' *Wiley Interdisciplinary Reviews: Water* 7, no. 1 (2020): e1398.

9   Hurley, Rachel, Hans Fredrik Veiteberg Braaten, Luca Nizzetto, Eirik Hovland Steindal, Yan Lin, François Clayer, Tim van Emmerik et al., 'Measuring riverine macroplastic: Methods, harmonisation, and quality control.' *Water Research* (2023): 119902.

10 Jambeck, Jenna R., Roland Geyer, Chris Wilcox, Theodore R. Siegler, Miriam Perryman, Anthony Andrady, Ramani Narayan, and Kara Lavender Law, 'Plastic waste inputs from land into the ocean.' *Science* 347, no. 6223 (2015): 768-771; Khan, Farhan R., Bahati Sosthenes Mayoma, Fares John Biginagwa, and Kristian Syberg, 'Microplastics in inland African waters: Presence, sources, and fate.' *Freshwater Microplastics: Emerging Environmental Contaminants?* (2018): 101-124.

11 Gabbott, Sarah, Sarah Key, Catherine Russell, Yasmin Yonan, and Jan Zalasiewicz, 'The geography and geology of plastics: Their environmental distribution and fate.' In *Plastic Waste and Recycling*, Academic Press, (2020): 33-63.

12 Hurley, Rachel, Hans Fredrik Veiteberg Braaten, Luca Nizzetto, Eirik Hovland Steindal, Yan Lin, François Clayer, Tim van Emmerik et al., "Measuring riverine macroplastic: Methods, harmonisation, and quality control." *Water Research* (2023): 119902.

13 Gold, Mark, Katie Mika, Cara Horowitz, and Megan Herzog, 'Stemming the tide of plastic litter: A global action agenda.' *Tul. Envtl. LJ* 27 (2013): 165.

14 Khan, Farhan R., Bahati Sosthenes Mayoma, Fares John Biginagwa, and Kristian Syberg, 'Microplastics in inland African waters: Presence, sources, and fate.' *Freshwater microplastics: Emerging environmental contaminants?* (2018): 101-124.

15 Weideman, Eleanor A., Vonica Perold, and Peter G. Ryan, 'Limited long-distance transport of plastic pollution by the Orange-Vaal River system, South Africa.' *Science of the Total Environment* 727 (2020): 138653.

16 Mboweni, Tribute J., and Engela P. de Crom, 'A narrative interpretation of the cultural impressions on water of the communities along the Vaal River, Parys, Free State.' TD: *The Journal for Transdisciplinary Research in Southern Africa* 12, no. 1 (2016): 1-7.

17 Weideman, Eleanor A., Vonica Perold, and Peter G. Ryan. 'Limited long-distance transport of plastic pollution by the Orange-Vaal River system, South Africa.' *Science of the Total Environment* 727 (2020): 138653.

18 Matowanyika, Wadzanai, 'Impact of Alexandra Township on the water quality of the Jukskei River.' PhD diss., University of the Witwatersrand, 2010.

4 Bacterial contamination in the Jukskei River in Gauteng Province, South Africa

Kousar Banu Hoorzook and Atheesha Singh

The Jukskei River in Gauteng Province, South Africa, is crucial for domestic, agricultural, and recreational use but suffers from severe pollution, due to urbanisation and industrial activities. This chapter investigates the river's water quality, revealing high levels of harmful bacteria, antibiotic resistance, and toxic metals. These contaminants pose significant health risks, making the water unsafe for drinking, recreation, and irrigation. Our comprehensive analysis, including physio-chemical properties, microbiological content, and antibiotic resistance, underscores the urgent need for effective water quality management and public health interventions. Immediate actions are necessary to clean up the Jukskei River to ensure the safety and well-being of both the people and the environment. This study highlights the critical importance of addressing pollution to protect human health and ecological integrity.

Introduction

The Jukskei River is one of the major rivers in the Gauteng Province of South Africa. Originating in the northern parts of Johannesburg, it flows through urban and rural areas, before joining the Crocodile River. It has played a pivotal role in the historical and environmental landscapes of Johannesburg. The river provides water for domestic, agricultural, and recreational purposes for millions of people living along its course. Historically, the Jukskei River was a pristine watercourse, but with the growth of Johannesburg and associated urbanisation, it has faced numerous challenges. The river is also severely polluted by various sources of contamination, such as sewage effluent, industrial waste, stormwater runoff, and informal settlements. Among the pollutants, deteriorating water quality of the Jukskei is alarming, given its potential to harbour waterborne pathogens which are tiny disease-causing organisms, such as bacteria, viruses, and parasites, that live in water. Waterborne bacteria pose a significant threat to human and environmental health, as they can cause various diseases and disrupt the ecological balance of the river.

In this chapter, we summarise the findings on the extent of bacterial contamination in the Jukskei River, based on our study[1] that analysed the Jukskei River water samples for physio-chemical properties (physical and chemical water properties), microbiology (harmful bacteria), antibiotic resistance of bacterial isolates, genetic markers, and potentially toxic metals. This comprehensive analysis helps understand how safe the water is for human use and the environment. We also discuss the implications of these findings for water quality management[2,3,4] and public health interventions.

As a guide to non-specialist readers, Table 4.1 offers an alphabetical list of the scientific acronyms and abbreviations that are used in this chapter, along with short introductory definitions where needed.

Table 4.1 *Glossary of key terms and health implications related to water quality in the Jukskei River*

Acronym/ abbreviation	Long name	Definition	Consequence if ingested
aafA	Aggregative adherence fimbriae	Virulence factors of enteroaggregative *E. coli.*	N/A
AH	*Aeromonas hydrophilia*	Bacterium commonly found in fresh water and sewage.	Gastrointestinal infections, septicaemia
AL	Aluminium	Chemical element.	Neurotoxicity at high levels
AMP	Ampicillin	A type of penicillin antibiotic. Used to treat a wide range of bacterial infections.	Allergic reactions, gastrointestinal issues
AS	Arsenic	Poisonous element.	Acute poisoning, cancer risk
Ba	Barium	Chemical element.	Acute toxicity, gastrointestinal issues
bfpA	Bundle forming pilus	Associated with the aggregation of bacteria.	Identification for EPEC
Cd	Cadmium	Heavy metal.	Acute toxicity, kidney damage
CFU/100 mL	Colony forming units per hundred millilitres	Unit to quantify the number of viable bacterial colonies in 100 mL of water.	Measurement of bacterial cells
CHL	Chloramphenicol	Antibiotic. Used for serious infections like typhoid fever and meningitis, but has serious side effects.	Bone marrow suppression, anaemia
cdtB	Cytolethal distending	Lethal to cells.	Bacterial identification
CP	*Clostridium perfringens*	Anaerobic bacterium that produces gas and toxins.	Food poisoning, gas gangrene
Cr	Chromium	Chemical element.	Acute toxicity, skin irritation
EaeA	Enterohemolysin	Hemolysin produced by enteropathogenic strains.	Destruction of red blood cells
EAF	Enteropathogenic adherence factor	Factor causing disease in the intestinal tract.	Intestinal disease
EAEC	Enteroaggregative	*E. coli* strains causing acute or persistent diarrhoea.	Persistent diarrhoea, dehydration
EHEC	Enterohemorrhagic	*E. coli* strains causing bloody dysentery.	Bloody diarrhoea, kidney failure
EIEC	Enteroinvasive	*E. coli* strains causing syndrome identical to shigellosis.	High fever, profuse diarrhoea
ENT	Enterococci	Bacteria that indicate the presence of faecal material in water.	Urinary tract infections, endocarditis

Acronym/ abbreviation	Long name	Definition	Consequence if ingested
EPEC	Enteropathogenic	*E. coli* strains causing disease of the intestinal tract.	Diarrhoea, food malabsorption
ERY	Erythromycin	Macrolide antibiotic. Treats respiratory infections.	Gastrointestinal issues, onset of cardiac arrest
estA	Heat liable enterotoxin	Toxin causing diarrhoea in ETEC infection.	Watery diarrhoea
Fe	Iron	Chemical element.	Iron toxicity, gastrointestinal issues
FOX	Cefoxitin	Antibiotic used for bacterial infections. Often used before surgery to prevent infections.	Allergic reactions, gastrointestinal issues
GEN	Gentamicin	Aminoglycoside antibiotic. Used for severe infections caused by certain bacteria.	Kidney damage, hearing loss
ipaH	Invasion plasmid antigen H	Promotes actin cytoskeleton rearrangements at the site of bacterial contact.	EIEC identification
KAN	Kanamycin	Aminoglycoside antibiotic. Treats severe infections, especially when other antibiotics don't work.	Kidney damage, hearing loss
Li	Lithium	Chemical element.	Lithium toxicity, tremors
Mn	Manganese	Chemical element.	Neurotoxicity at high levels
NAL	Nalidixic acid	Antibiotic for urinary tract infections.	Gastrointestinal issues, photosensitivity
Ni	Nickel	Chemical element.	Allergic reactions, cancer risk
PA	*Pseudomonas aeruginosa*	Bacterium found in water and soil.	Skin infections, pneumonia
Pb	Lead	Heavy metal.	Neurotoxicity, brain developmental issues
PCR	Polymerase chain reaction	Tool used to quantify microorganisms in water.	Multiplication of DNA for identification
SA	*Staphylococcus aureus*	Bacterium that can cause skin infections.	Skin infections, food poisoning
Se	Selenium	Chemical element.	Selenium toxicity causes hair loss
stx	Shinga toxin	Toxin produced by certain strains of *E. coli*.	Haemolytic uremic syndrome
TET	Tetracycline	Antibiotic. Treats infections like acne, respiratory infections, and sexually transmitted diseases.	Tooth discoloration, gastrointestinal issues
VAN	Vancomycin	Glycopeptide antibiotic.	Nephrotoxicity, ototoxicity
VC	*Vibrio cholerae*	Bacterium that causes cholera.	Severe diarrhoea, dehydration
Zn	Zinc	Chemical element.	Zinc toxicity, gastrointestinal issues

Course of the Jukskei River

The Jukskei River, located in Metropolitan Johannesburg, stands as one of ten prominent river catchments in South Africa – areas of land where all the water that falls as rain or snow flows into a specific river. This river is linked to the Limpopo River's system, eventually discharging into the Indian Ocean.[4] Its origin is traced to the Bezuidenhout Valley, where it is often concealed by stormwater infrastructure. Navigating northward, the Jukskei traverses various urban zones, including densely populated residential sectors. Notable is Alexandra, an area characterised by high population density, presenting challenges of infrastructural strain. This occasionally results in sewer overflow incidents, contributing to river pollution.

Before its confluence (point where two or more rivers meet and merge into a single watercourse) with the Crocodile River – a feeder to the Hartbeespoort Dam – the Jukskei is joined by three subsidiary streams: the Braamfontein Spruit, Klein Jukskei Spruit, and Modderfontein Spruit.[1,4] A concerning aspect of the Jukskei water environment is the influx of pollutants. Nearby industries, unregulated waste dumps, and agricultural zones have been identified as significant contributors to this pollution. The river's catchment is heavily urbanised, an observation supported by spatial data (map) depicted in Figure 4.1.

Figure 4.1 *Visual location of the upper Jukskei catchment study area (with permission from Hoorzook et al., 2021)*

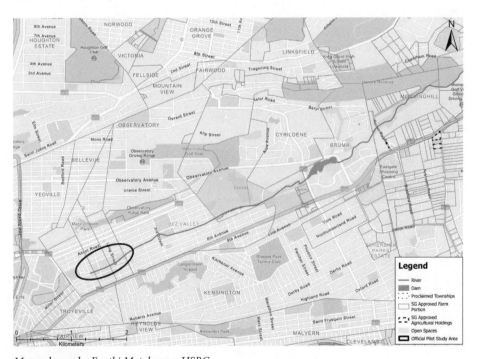

Map redrawn by Enathi Motolwana, HSRC

Sources of contamination in the Jukskei River

The Jukskei River in Gauteng Province faces contamination from multiple sources. Industrial discharges introduce chemicals and heavy metals, while agricultural activities contribute pesticides and bacterial runoff from livestock. Additionally, untreated sewage infusions bring a host of pathogens and pharmaceutical residues. The sources of contamination are:

- Industrial Discharges: Industrial zones adjacent to the Jukskei River may discharge untreated or insufficiently treated effluents (liquid waste or sewage discharged into the environment) into the water. These effluents can contain a plethora of contaminants, from heavy metals such as cadmium, lead, and mercury, to various hazardous chemicals, depending on the nature of the industry.
- Agricultural Runoff: Agricultural activities in proximity to the river contribute to contamination through the runoff that can introduce pesticides, herbicides, and fertilizers. Additionally, bacteria from animal wastes and organic fertilizers can seep into the river system.
- Untreated Sewage Discharge: The discharge of untreated or inadequately treated sewage introduces a wide range of pathogens, including bacteria, viruses, and protozoa. Alongside the pathogens, sewage can also carry pharmaceutical residues and personal care products, which can have an array of environmental and health implications.
- Urban Stormwater Runoff: As rainwater traverses urban areas, it collects various contaminants from streets, industries, and households, such as motor oil, heavy metals, and synthetic chemicals, eventually draining into the river.
- Illegal Dumping: Unauthorised disposal of waste, including hazardous waste, near the riverbanks or directly into the river, can introduce both chemical and bacterial contaminants. This activity remains a recurrent issue in many water bodies worldwide.
- Mining Activities: Where there are mining operations near a river, contaminants such as arsenic, cyanide, and other heavy metals can leach into the water system, either through direct discharge or via groundwater pathways.
- Natural Sources: Although human activity is a primary contributor to contamination, natural sources like soil erosion can introduce metals and minerals into the river.

Additionally, wildlife can be a source of bacterial contamination, especially in areas with significant animal populations.

Physio-chemical properties of the Jukskei River water

The physio-chemical properties of water reflect its quality and suitability for different uses. We[1] measured several parameters, such as electrical conductivity (EC), total dissolved solids (TDS), turbidity, pH, dissolved oxygen (DO), and temperature, at two sampling sites over a period of three months along the Jukskei River in 2018.

The key water quality parameters can be explained as follows:

a) Electrical Conductivity (EC): Measures water's ability to conduct electricity, indicating the presence of dissolved salts and minerals.

b) Total Dissolved Solids (TDS): Refers to the total concentration of dissolved substances in water, affecting its purity and taste.

c) Turbidity: Indicates the cloudiness or haziness of water caused by suspended particles, which can impact aquatic life and water quality.

d) pH: Measures the acidity or alkalinity of water on a scale from 0 to 14, with 7 being neutral. It affects chemical reactions and biological processes in water.

e) Dissolved Oxygen (DO): The amount of oxygen dissolved in water, essential for the survival of fish and other aquatic organisms.

f) Temperature: Influences water chemistry and the health of aquatic ecosystems, affecting dissolved oxygen levels and metabolic rates of organisms.

The results obtained in this study[1] were also compared with the previous data collected from 2010 and 2015, as well as with the South African water quality guidelines for domestic, recreational, and irrigation purposes.

The results showed that the EC, TDS, and turbidity of the river water increased significantly since 2010, indicating a high level of salinity and suspended solids in the water. The EC and TDS values exceeded the guidelines for domestic and irrigation water at all sites, while the turbidity values exceeded the guidelines for recreational water at most sites. The pH values ranged from 7.2 to 8.4, which were within the acceptable range for all uses. The DO values ranged from 3.9 to 7.6 milligrams per litre (mg/L), which were below the minimum requirement of 8 mg/L for aquatic life. The temperature values ranged from 16.5 to 23 °C, which were within the normal range for river water.

The high EC, TDS, and turbidity of the Jukskei River water suggest that the river is receiving a large amount of dissolved and particulate matter from various sources of pollution, such as sewage effluent, industrial waste, storm water runoff, and informal settlements. These pollutants can affect the water quality by reducing its clarity, increasing its salinity, altering its pH, decreasing its DO, and changing its temperature. These changes can have adverse effects on human health and aquatic life.

Microbiology of the Jukskei River water

The microbiology of water reflects its sanitary condition and potential risk of infection. We analysed the river water samples for various bacteria to assess contamination and potential health risks. The tested bacteria include indicators of faecal contamination (Total Coliforms (TC), *Escherichia coli* (EC), *Enterococci*

(ENT)), opportunistic pathogens which cause infections when the immune system is weak (*Pseudomonas aeruginosa* (PA), *Aeromonas hydrophilia* (AH)), and specific disease-causing bacteria (*Salmonella spp., Shigella spp., Vibrio cholerae* (VC), *Staphylococcus aureus* (SA), *Clostridium perfringens* (CP)). These analyses help determine the safety and quality of the water. We then compared these results with the South African water quality guidelines for domestic, recreational, and irrigation purposes.

The results[1] showed that all samples were positive for TC and EC at levels ranging from 12 000 to 18 million colony forming units (CFU – number of alive bacteria in a sample) per 100 millilitre (CFU/100 mL) and from 1 000 to 10 million CFU/100 mL, respectively. These levels exceeded the guidelines for domestic[4] (<10 CFU/100 mL for TC and <1 CFU/100 mL for EC), recreational[3] (<1 000 CFU/100 mL for TC and <130 CFU/100 mL for EC), and irrigation[2,3] (<1 000 CFU/100 mL for TC) water at all sites. The samples were also positive for ENT at levels ranging from 1000 to 1 million CFU/100 mL, which exceeded the guidelines for domestic (<1 CFU/100 mL) and recreational (<35 CFU/100 mL) water at all sites. The samples were positive for PA at levels ranging from 100 to 100 thousand CFU/100 mL, which exceeded the guideline for domestic water (<1 CFU/100 mL) at all sites. The samples were negative for *Salmonella* spp., *Shigella* spp., VC, and CP, but positive for AH at levels ranging from 100 to 100 thousand CFU/100 mL and for SA at levels ranging from 10 to 1 000 CFU/100 mL.[2,3,4] To translate these numbers for faecal contamination, they are millions of times more and thousands of times more pathogens present than is considered safe.

The high levels of TC, EC, ENT, PA, AH, and SA in the Jukskei River water indicate that the river is heavily contaminated by faecal material from human and animal sources.[2,3,4] These bacteria can cause various diseases in humans, such as gastroenteritis, urinary tract infections, wound infections, septicaemia, endocarditis, and skin infections. Some of these bacteria are also opportunistic pathogens that can infect immunocompromised individuals. Moreover, some of these bacteria can carry antibiotic resistance genes that can be transferred to other bacteria and pose a threat to public health.

Antibiotic resistance of bacterial isolates from the Jukskei River water

Antibiotic resistance happens when bacteria change in a way that makes antibiotics no longer effective against them. This means infections become harder to treat, can last longer, and may need stronger or different medications. The antibiotic resistance of bacteria reflects their ability to survive and grow in the presence of antimicrobial agents (the 'antibiotics' that are prescribed by doctors when people are sick). We isolated and identified 120 bacterial strains[1] from the Jukskei River water samples, including *E. coli* (n = 40), *E. faecalis* (n = 20), *E. faecium* (n = 20),

PA (n = 20), AH (n = 10), and SA (n = 10). We also evaluated[1] the susceptibility of these strains to nine antibiotics commonly used in human and veterinary medicine: ampicillin (AMP), cefoxitin (FOX), chloramphenicol (CHL), erythromycin (ERY), gentamicin (GEN), kanamycin (KAN), nalidixic acid (NAL), tetracycline (TET), and vancomycin (VAN). Additionally, we determined the presence of genetic markers for antibiotic resistance and virulence factors in *E. coli* and *E. faecalis/E. faecium* isolates by polymerase chain reaction (PCR). PCR is a method used to multiply millions to billions of copies of a specific section on the DNA, which can then be studied in greater detail.

The results showed that all *E. coli* isolates were resistant to AMP and NAL, while most of them were resistant to FOX (95%), TET (90%), CHL (85%), KAN (80%), and GEN (75%). Only one isolate was resistant to ERY, and none was resistant to VAN. The *E. coli* isolates also carried various genes encoding resistance to AMP (blaTEM), FOX (blaCMY-2), TET (tetA), CHL (catI), KAN (aphA1), GEN (aacC2), NAL (gyrA), and ERY (ermB). These antibiotics represent common treatments for various bacterial infections in both humans and animals. The *E. coli* bacteria in the river water showed high resistance to many of these antibiotics, indicating that infections caused by these bacteria would be difficult to treat with standard medications.

Moreover, the *E. coli* isolates carried genes encoding virulence factors such as intimin (*eaeA*), enterohemolysin (*ehxA*), Shiga toxin 1 and 2 (*stx1* and *stx2*), heat-stable enterotoxin a and b (*estA* and *estB*), heat-labile enterotoxin I and II (*eltI* and *eltII*), invasion plasmid antigen H (*ipaH*), aggregative adherence fimbriae I and II (*aafA* and *aafB*), plasmid-encoded toxin (*pet*), enteroaggregative heat-stable enterotoxin (*eagg*), cytolethal distending toxin (cdtB), bundle-forming pilus (bfpA), enteropathogenic adherence factor plasmid (EAF). These genes indicate that the *E. coli* isolates belonged to different pathotypes, such as enteropathogenic *E. coli* (EPEC), enterohemorrhagic *E. coli* (EHEC), enteroinvasive *E. coli* (EIEC) or enteroaggregative *E. coli* (EAEC). These findings highlight the potential health risks posed by the river water, as these resistant and virulent bacteria can cause serious infections that are difficult to treat with standard antibiotics. The spread of such bacteria could have significant public health implications, underscoring the need for improved water management and contamination prevention strategies.

All *E. faecalis* isolates were resistant to AMP, FOX, CHL, ERY, KAN, NAL, and TET. The high level of antibiotic resistance of bacterial isolates from the Jukskei River water indicates that the river is exposed to a variety of antimicrobial agents from human and animal sources. The presence of resistance genes in bacterial isolates also suggests that horizontal gene transfer (movement of genetic information between bacterial organisms) can occur among bacteria in the river water. This can facilitate the dissemination of resistance genes among different bacterial species and increase the risk of multidrug-resistant infections in humans and animals.

Potentially toxic metals in the Jukskei River water

Potential toxic metals are microscopic particles suspended in water and are not there on purpose. They are present due to contamination of the water supply by minerals or contamination by industrial or agricultural activities or leaching out of piping or cookware. Low levels are tolerated by the human body. High levels can be harmful to health of humans and animals. They may also be passed on into food or drink processed with this water. We measured the concentrations of 16 metals in the river water samples: aluminium (Al), arsenic (As), barium (Ba), boron (B), cadmium (Cd), chromium (Cr), copper (Cu), iron (Fe), lead (Pb), lithium (Li), manganese (Mn), nickel (Ni), selenium (Se), sodium (Na), vanadium (V), and zinc (Zn), and compared these results with the South African water quality guidelines for domestic, recreational, and irrigation purposes.[2,3,4] The results[1] showed that most metals were below the detection limit or within the acceptable range for all uses. However, these metals exceeded the guidelines at some sites: Na exceeded the guideline for domestic water (<200 mg/L) at all sites. Zn exceeded the guideline for domestic water (<3 mg/L) at four sites Ni exceeded the guideline for domestic water (<0.1 mg/L) and irrigation water (<0.2 mg/L) at three sites, Li exceeded the guideline for domestic water (<2.5 mg/L) and irrigation water (<5 mg/L) at two sites, and Pb exceeded the guideline for domestic water (<0.01 mg/L), recreational water (<0.015 mg/L), and irrigation water (<0.2 mg/L) at one site.

High levels of several metals in the Jukskei River water suggest that industrial or agricultural operations (i.e. dumped, spilt accidentally or carelessly, or by deteriorating infrastructure) have contaminated the river. These metals can have toxic effects on human health and aquatic life. For example: Na can increase blood pressure and cause hypertension; Zn can cause nausea and vomiting; Ni can cause allergic reactions and lung cancer; Li can cause kidney damage and neurological disorders; and Pb can cause neurological damage and developmental delays.

Public health implications of contaminants in the Jukskei River

Bacterial and chemical pollutants in the Jukskei River present multifaceted public health concerns. Consuming or contacting this compromised water can lead to gastrointestinal disorders, hepatic (liver) and renal (kidney) complications, and skin and eye infections due to bacterial agents. Additionally, chemical pollutants can disrupt endocrine (hormone) functions, while metal contaminants, such as lead and mercury, can cause neurologic (nervous system) and brain developmental issues. The river also potentially harbours antibiotic-resistant microbes, which compounds the problem of bacterial infection treatment and heightens global antimicrobial resistance alarms. Chronic (continuous) exposure to these contaminants may weaken the immune system, result in the building up of toxic chemicals and metals (because they can't be easily broken down or removed), and elicit long-term health challenges. Safeguarding water quality remains pivotal for the health of those reliant on the river.

Conclusion, implication and recommendation

The Jukskei River is a vital source of water for millions of people in Gauteng Province, South Africa. However, the river is also severely polluted by various sources of contamination, such as sewage effluent, industrial waste, stormwater runoff, and informal settlements. Our study revealed that the river water has poor physio-chemical quality, high bacterial contamination, high antibiotic resistance of bacterial isolates, and high concentrations of some potentially toxic metals. These findings indicate that the river water poses a serious threat to human and environmental health. Therefore, there is an urgent need for effective water quality management and public health interventions to protect the river and its users from further deterioration. This chapter serves as an educational bridge between complex scientific research and public understanding to empower individuals to make informed decisions regarding their health and the environment. It stands as a testament to the importance of disseminating scientific knowledge in an accessible format, thereby contributing to the broader goals of public health and environmental conservation.

The contaminated state of the Jukskei River highlights the need for comprehensive measures to address pollution and protect the health of communities that rely on it and live nearby. Initiatives such as the 'Water for the Future' project that have been launched to tackle river pollution through the convergence of art, science, and activism should be supported. More efforts should be made to raise awareness, create employment opportunities, and implement sustainable solutions to restore the health and cleanliness of the Jukskei River and its surrounding environment.

Notes

1   Hoorzook, Kousar Banu, Anton Pieterse, Lee Heine, Tobias George Barnard, and Nickey Janse van Rensburg, 'Soul of the Jukskei River: the extent of bacterial contamination in the Jukskei River in Gauteng province, South Africa.' *International Journal of Environmental Research and Public Health* 18, no. 16 (2021): 8537.

2   Department of Water Affairs (DWA), Water Quality Management Series: Operational Guideline for Disposal of Land-Derived Water Containing Waste to the Marine Environment of South Africa (Revision 1). Pretoria: DWA; 2010.

3   Department of Water Affairs (DWA), Water Quality Management Series: Operational Guideline for Aquatic Ecosystems: Instream Water Quality Guidelines (Revision 1). Pretoria: DWA; 2015.

4   Department of Water Affairs (DWA), South African Water Quality Guidelines Volume 1: Domestic Use (Second Edition). Pretoria: DWA; 1996; Department of Water Affairs (DWA). South African Water Quality Guidelines Volume 2: Recreational Use (Second Edition). Pretoria: DWA; 1996.

5 Upper Jukskei Catchment Management Plan

Stuart Dunsmore and Ernita van Wyk

The Upper Jukskei Catchment Management Plan (CMP) was commissioned by the City of Johannesburg with a vision for integrating improved stormwater use, land use planning and an opportunity to restore river health. The chapter describes the targets of the CMP and presents prospects for action.

The Jukskei crisis: Old and new

The Jukskei River is no exception to the long, and at times antagonistic, relations between human settlements and the rivers that both enable and imperil them. Arguably, the Jukskei River is disproportionately plagued by rapid urbanisation and issues of governance. It has for many decades been dubbed 'South Africa's dirtiest river.'[1] Even the hardiest of aquatic life struggles to maintain a presence and in long sections of the river there is no life at all. Although the Jukskei River has not historically been a major water provider for the City,[2] it can still potentially provide a wide range of benefits to urban residents, including improved water security. But its problems are serious: ageing sewerage and stormwater infrastructure, faecal and solid waste pollution, chronic seasonal flooding and drought and encroachment of formal and informal settlements onto the river. These realities, together with the risk of climate impacts (i.e. accentuated floods and droughts), shaped the priorities of the Catchment Management Plan.

At the same time, Johannesburg City has been in the grip of chronic disruptive party politics resulting in high turnover of political leadership. The result is instability in the execution of municipal functions. Power outages and failures in water and other infrastructure now extend into days and even weeks. Municipal processes that should unlock implementation plans and budget commitments and mobilise actions that could start to restore the Jukskei system, are paralysed.[3] The current situation is particularly unsettling given South Africa's constitutional right to a healthy environment[4] and the global recognition that a clean, healthy, and sustainable environment is a human right.[5] Under these conditions, society's resilience depends on the ability to secure access to natural resources and minimise risk amidst the ongoing failure of public service provision.

Figure 5.1 *Severe flooding in the upper Jukskei catchment, November 2016. Image posted on Twitter.*

An opportunity for creative transformation?

We suggest that the Jukskei River and catchment system, including ecological, social and governance elements, has entered into a phase of 'collapse,' hallmarked by a substantial loss of resilience, both human and natural,[6] driven by political dynamics that maintain an unstable state of governance.[7] Reorganisation following collapse offers opportunities. It is typically a phase of uncertainty, novelty and experimentation and this is a time of greatest potential for either destructive or creative change in the system. It is indeed a time when human actions and interventions can have the greatest impact.[8]

There is plenty of evidence for this as community action and contributions from the business sector illustrate capacity for adaptation. Individuals monitor ecology and water quality; community-based organisations undertake river cleanups; NGOs invest in green infrastructure, food security and water re-use projects; and developers protect wetlands and convert river corridors into open space natural assets. An underlying belief in these activities is that positive change begins by doing things differently.

Origins of the Upper Jukskei Catchment Management Plan

Despite political turmoil and related municipal challenges, the City of Johannesburg Environment and Infrastructure Services Department (EISD) commissioned the development of the CMP (2018–2022) to offer a scientific basis for feasible actions to restore the catchment water resource and its services to people. A major request by the City was to explore the potential for stormwater management to support the achievement of other catchment objectives, notably adjusted land use and development planning and the need to reintegrate the river into the landscape as an asset of the urban space.

Based on the CMP, this chapter proposes what may be realistic actions for the city governance, service delivery and technical systems and how communities can get involved to support emerging experiments and solutions. While this chapter presents a highly simplified overview, curious readers will come away with insights on the importance of targets to stimulate a whole-of-society approach[9] to restoring catchment health and access to river-based benefits.

An unsustainable water balance

Figure 5.2 *The study catchment location within the quaternary catchment system*

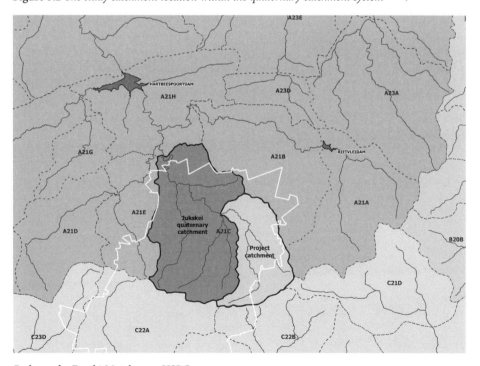

Redrawn by Enathi Motolwana, HSRC

The 760 km^2 Jukskei catchment is quaternary catchment[10] A21C. It is one of eight quaternaries that supply the Hartbeespoort Dam, a regional water resource asset. The Jukskei covers 19% of the dam's supply catchment area but it contributes almost 40% of its annual inflow. Almost two thirds of this inflow is wastewater from consumption in the Jukskei catchment. Some of it is outflow from treatment works; the rest is raw sewage that leaks from the city's sewer networks. Instead of drawing the supply water from Hartbeespoort Dam, it is drawn from the Vaal Dam in a separate water resource region. This highlights a severe imbalance where clean, potable water is imported from as far as Lesotho (via the Vaal Dam), then mixed with effluent in Johannesburg and exported to another part of the country. This situation is surely unsustainable and inherently unjust.

Upper Jukskei catchment characteristics

The baseline data are summarised in the table below. Although the CMP covers only the upper third of the quaternary catchment, it is still a large urban catchment. It has moderate slopes apart from the upper parts of the watershed. Averages of paved surfaces and population densities are moderate to low, however there are key areas where there are extremely high densities. These are mainly in the upper and middle sections of the catchment, and they have a dominant effect on stormwater response patterns that affect the lower areas of the catchment. The natural soils of the catchment have good soil water characteristics (e.g. good filtration and retention) for stormwater management. The current annual stormwater yield from the catchment is equivalent up to 90% of the annual residential water consumption.

Table 5.1 *Baseline parameters for the upper Jukskei catchment*

Total area	241 km^2	Population (est. 2020)	810 000
Average slope	8% (0.3% to 47%)	Population density	33/ha (8 to 475/ha)
Main soil types	Sandy loams and Sandy clays	Water consumption (est.)	73 x 10^6 m^3/ann
Length of main river	34.9 km	Portion to sewers (est.)	60 x 10^6 m^3/ann
Average channel gradient	0.8% (max 1.4%)	Mean ann runoff (natural catchment)	~3% MAP
Percent impervious	28.4% (2% to 93%)	Mean ann runoff (natural catchment)	3 x 10^6 m^3/ann (approx. 4% present day consumption)
Mean ann ppt (MAP)	680 mm	Mean ann runoff (present day)	~30% MAP
Mean ann (potential) evap (MAE)	1700 mm	Mean ann. runoff (present day)	39 x 10^6 m^3/ann (approx. 53% present day consumption)

Catchment management targets

The brief for the Upper Jukskei CMP was to develop targets that reflect the potential water resource for the upper Jukskei catchment, especially when stormwater is included as a useful component of the overall available water resource. In addition, the aim was to reveal implications for land use planning and for river health. The recommendations of the Upper Jukskei Catchment Management Plan were simplified to four main targets.

Table 5.2 *Recommended catchment management targets*

Target	Implication
Stormwater harvesting: 20% of catchment rainfall is to be made available for harvesting through sustainable stormwater management and not just rainwater harvesting.	Stormwater is a significant resource for the upper Jukskei. The 20% target would satisfy around 64% of the annual consumption requirement of the estimated 2020 population of the catchment area.
Prioritise reduced sewage loads to improve water quality: Instream water quality is to be managed to comply with the Department of Water and Sanitation's designated Resource Quality Objectives,[11] RQO's.[12]	The sewage loads in the streams and stormwater systems are extremely high. It will be difficult to achieve the RQO's unless the overload of the sewers is addressed. This will require work on the sewage networks, but it should be supported by reducing the magnitude of storm runoff that spills into the sewer networks. However, urban runoff is generally polluted by dust, chemicals, hydrocarbons, etc. that accumulate on roof and paved surfaces. Treatment of runoff before it enters the main drainage networks is now deemed good practice, and forms part of the CMP recommendations.
Reduce Effective Impermeability (EI) to less than 10%: Utilise areas for water to be absorbed and filter into the soils. The 'hardness' of the catchment, increased by hard paving and tarred surfaces such that water cannot filter into the soils damaging streams and rivers. To achieve the 10% target, storm runoff should be diverted to permeable ('spongy') areas before it enters the drainage network.	EI represents those hard surfaces that are directly connected to drainage lines and streams. In the high density areas, it is between 60% to 80%, but overall it is estimated to be at 22% of the catchment. This means that there is much potential to achieve the target by disconnecting impervious areas (i.e. 'hard surfaces'). This requires interventions that are designed to divert runoff to permeable surfaces.
Interventions to manage larger floods: 'Regional' (i.e. larger scale) flood detention solutions, such as flood detention basins, will be retrofitted in the catchment to address extreme flood events.	The measures above will go some way to reducing flood responses, but more will be required to mitigate against the larger events. The solutions are in line with conventional flood management (e.g. provision of detention basins). These will be strategically located and dependent on the success of EI reduction in the catchment. Creative use of space may be needed to achieve adequate protection in retrofit applications.

Recommended stormwater management approach

The traditional approach to stormwater management involves channelling it into pipes for efficient discharge into rivers. A more modern and sustainable practice advocates for the use of Sustainable Drainage Systems (SuDS). SuDS manage stormwater at its source – where it runs off roofs and pavements – encouraging infiltration back into the ground through techniques such as specially designed gardens, sand-filled soakaways, or permeable pavement systems.

However, the most straightforward and cost-effective approach utilises existing open spaces such as gardens, parks, road verges, and servitudes. These landscaped systems typically require minimal structural control (like inlets or weirs). The Catchment Management Plan (CMP) recognises the crucial role of these open spaces in restoring the broader Jukskei catchment. They will support three of the four targets of the CMP in Table 2.

To address Target 2 (i.e. 'reduce sewage loads'), it will be essential to continue managing stormwater separately from sewage and wastewater. While SuDS technologies significantly improve the quality of stormwater runoff, untreated wastewater can overwhelm these systems, especially in densely populated areas. Therefore, a key success factor lies in rehabilitating and upgrading the sewerage system within the catchment, alongside the CMP's implementation.

In a natural catchment (i.e. no development), some rainfall filters into groundwater and some filters back into streams, but urban development severely limits these functions. By implementing Sustainable Drainage Systems (SuDS) principles, we can mimic natural functions and even enhance them by retaining excess runoff for harvesting or to support ecological systems. SuDS technologies can be engineered to infiltrate stormwater at a much higher rate than natural ground, but the analysis showed that just utilising available open spaces, without engineered enhancement, could significantly progress towards these goals. This low-cost solution makes it a viable option for householders and communities to take action.

The Upper Jukskei CMP analysis considered the practicality of accessing all open space areas. Low-density areas offer greater potential than high-density areas, so realistic targets were set for achievable performance levels across different parts of the catchment. A target of 20% harvestability of annual rainfall was deemed ambitious yet feasible. Key success factors include:

- Ensuring stormwater runoff is detained for sufficient time for abstraction or to support river and wetland ecosystem function. This contrasts with rapid, short-lived stormwater responses.
- Recharging the natural storage in soils. This includes ensuring that the remaining soils are effectively used. Every hectare of paved surface in the Jukskei potentially results in substantial loss of natural water storage.
- Recharging subterranean storage, such as the 'vadose zone' (i.e. the shallow, unsaturated soil zone) and groundwater, which are crucial for water retention and storage, but are often disrupted by urbanisation. The vadose zone lies

between the topsoil and the groundwater zone. It feeds both groundwater and streamflow.

- Minimising evaporation and transpiration (evapotranspiration) losses by using SuDS to drain stormwater below active root depths and into the vadose and groundwater zones.
- Utilising open spaces creatively to maximise stormwater management effectiveness, supported by appropriate policies and regulations.

Achieving these targets would naturally lead to an advanced level of catchment restoration by moderating stormwater release, reducing flood risks, restoring ecological functions, and improving water resource yield.

However, the CMP highlights challenges, particularly in retrofitting SuDS technologies into conventional stormwater networks in older and informally densified areas. This is financially demanding for municipalities but can be addressed by leveraging available space and applying simple SuDS techniques, thereby decentralising stormwater management and alleviating budget pressures.

A significant outcome of the CMP is the decentralisation of significant areas of the stormwater network to householders and communities, overseen by municipal authorities. This shift necessitates critical policy review to support effective implementation and community participation. Incentivising household and community involvement will be pivotal to CMP success.

Controlling stormwater at source brings stormwater management responsibilities into each stand and household. An intervention at household level can be as simple as diverting a downpipe from a roof onto a lawn or flowerbed (or water tank), rather than into drains. The wider the implementation at source, the smaller the scale of intervention needed downstream. This will reduce the municipal burden but will also rely on active community participation. Hence a significant portion of the stormwater management network will be 'decentralised' from municipal management. But how will this take effect? Incentives for householders and communities may be a critical part of the success of the CMP.

What should we expect to see if the proposals are implemented?

Storm responses in urban rivers like the Jukskei are described as 'flashy'. Water levels rise rapidly soon after the start of a storm and pass quickly like a wave of water passing along the river channel. In the upper Jukskei this wave passes in around six hours after a typical summer storm, but it may rise to its peak in less than 30 minutes.

Not every storm results in a flood, but each one still presents violent conditions for aquatic habitat and will eat away at riverbanks. Figure 5.3 shows the frequency of storm responses in the Jukskei River in its present state (grey lines) and an assumed natural state (black lines). The black spikes are much fewer and smaller than the grey spikes. Threshold levels of water depth and velocity are used to measure the threat to aquatic systems.

Figure 5.3 *Frequency of storm responses in the Jukskei River natural catchment (black) vs urban catchment (grey)*

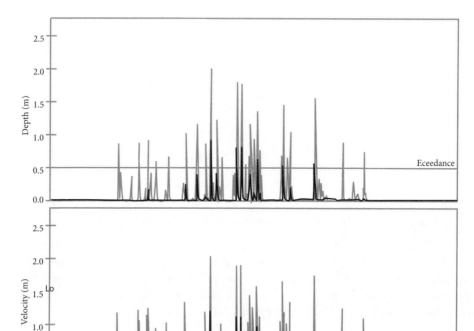

The SuDS proposals in the CMP will not prevent flooding, but they will reduce the magnitude of large storm flood responses. In a sample summer season, Figure 5.4 shows the benefits of diverting stormwater runoff to available open spaces (black line), compared to the conventional stormwater network (grey line). A range of thresholds in the insert show that the SuDS based system shows exceedance counts much closer to a natural catchment function. That means it acts as a natural buffer against the unnaturally high runoff quantities from urban surfaces.

These outcomes will be visible to communities along the Jukskei River and tributary streams. The rate of transition will depend on the programme of implementation. It could take a decade or more to achieve.

Figure 5.4 *The benefits of diverting stormwater runoff to available open spaces (black line) compared to the conventional stormwater network (grey line)*

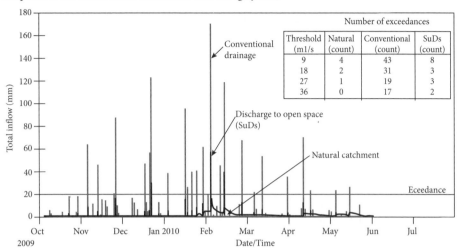

Is the retrofit equation practical?

The CMP has underscored the necessity of integrating SuDS into existing developed areas of the catchment to achieve significant improvements in river conditions. As part of this effort, the CMP explored the feasibility of retrofitting SuDS in older, densely developed regions.

The effectiveness of SuDS technologies is closely tied to the ratio of impervious ('hard'/non-porous) area draining to them relative to the SuDS surface area. This ratio indicates the stormwater loading, with higher ratios necessitating more

Figure 5.5 *Water's journey on different surfaces in the catchment area. Planning the stormwater 'load' diverted to an unpaved area of the catchment.*

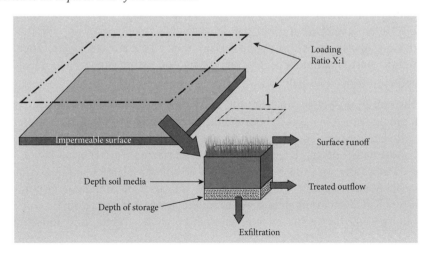

engineered SuDS units. Loading ratios typically range from 1:1 (low) to 15:1 (very high).

The CMP identified a practical ratio of 6:1 for spatial planning and retrofit applications. This suggests that approximately 17% of an impervious area should be allocated for stormwater runoff infiltration. This is realistic for new development or for land re-development, but is it practical for retrofitting SuDS in already developed areas?

The study revealed:

- 80% of the catchment has less than 40% impermeable area, implying over 60% of the catchment consists of permeable spaces. Allocating only a quarter of open spaces for SuDS results in a loading ratio of 2.6:1 or less, making rain gardens highly effective with a very high potential for successful implementation.
- Areas with 40–50% impermeability cover 10% of the catchment. Allocating a quarter of open spaces for SuDS results in a maximum loading ratio of 4:1. While higher performing SuDS (e.g. bioretention systems) may be needed in some areas, rain gardens remain widely applicable with a high potential for implementation success. SuDS would cover 90% of the cumulative catchment area.
- Areas with 50–60% impermeability cover 5% of the catchment, bringing SuDS coverage to 95%. Allocating a quarter of open spaces for SuDS results in a maximum loading ratio of 6:1. Here, greater use of higher performing SuDS is necessary, though rain gardens continue to play a role, presenting a reasonable potential for implementation success.

Therefore, the CMP study suggests that significantly reducing Effective Impervious areas (EI) across most of the catchment is indeed practical.

Decentralised stormwater management

Achieving the target reduction in Effective Impervious (EI) areas requires a focus on treating stormwater at its source, typically near where rainfall impacts occur. In many older developed areas of the city, available open spaces are often located on private property or within public service areas like road servitudes. Therefore, community participation becomes pivotal in addressing stormwater challenges within the Jukskei catchment.

Two cost-effective options are rainwater harvesting tanks and rain gardens, both of which provide direct benefits to households, and they reduce runoff volume entering the stormwater system. The next step involves retrofitting infiltration trenches, swales (i.e. shallow, wide, and vegetated channels), and bioretention systems in road reserves. These systems offer versatile combinations of detention, retention, and water quality treatment. Moreover, they can recharge the vadose zone and local groundwater systems, enhance environmental flows to watercourses, and create opportunities for community water harvesting, such as through boreholes. While some interventions may be situated in municipal spaces, their planning and management are most effective when carried out collaboratively with or led by local communities.

This approach decentralises a significant portion of the catchment's stormwater network, shifting planning, maintenance, and management responsibilities to local communities. The role of local government then evolves to include policy development, planning, investment in decentralised systems, oversight, facilitation of community support, and monitoring system performance. This model supports system sustainability, as communities invested in local infrastructure are more likely to maintain it, given ongoing benefits. Conversely, infrastructure perceived as solely municipal responsibility often deteriorates and may be neglected or misused by the community. Another rationale for community-led action is the municipality's current limitations in developing resilience plans or adequately maintaining existing infrastructure.

As local initiatives take root, the extent to which communities across the catchment collaborate in challenging environments may become clearer. Nevertheless, the CMP underscores how downstream communities are directly affected by upstream performance, highlighting their strong interest in the success of upstream efforts.

Emerging role players

Given the political and governance realities in Johannesburg, it appears unlikely that the CMP will receive coordinated support across various stakeholders operating at different spatial and temporal scales, alongside an enabling institutional environment and strong buy-in from municipal departments and politicians – though this would be ideal. Interestingly, the most significant support for the CMP's initiatives has emerged from community-level initiatives, driven by the need for practical, scientifically sound interventions.

In cases where the state fails to provide critical services, communities, civil society (both formal and informal), and the business sector often invest in actions to enhance their resilience. In Johannesburg, this trend is already evident, with some successes in the Jukskei catchment, such as Victoria Yards and Alexandra. Efforts by society to bolster resilience against water-related challenges should be further developed and expanded with state support. However, there is a risk that when communities enhance their own resilience, the state may view them as self-sufficient and thus less in need of state assistance. Ideally, the state's capacity and functions should be strengthened to fulfil its role as custodian, even as communities build their resilience autonomously.

Conclusion

The City of Johannesburg's concerns over the Jukskei River, focusing on flood hazards and water quality, prompted the development of the Catchment Management Plan

(CMP). The CMP aimed to assess the feasibility of achieving a healthy river while addressing flood and water quality issues, enhancing water security, and empowering communities.

The CMP presents a comprehensive strategy to address stormwater challenges in the Jukskei catchment through innovative SuDS solutions and community involvement. By decentralising stormwater management and leveraging existing infrastructure and open spaces, the plan not only aims to enhance water quality and reduce runoff, but also fosters community resilience and ownership. Moving forward, effective collaboration between stakeholders will be essential to achieve the plan's objectives and sustainably manage the catchment's water resources. This holistic approach not only benefits the environment, but also enhances the quality of life of residents, making the Jukskei catchment a model for integrated and sustainable urban water management.

Key outcomes include:

1. Managing Urban Stormflows: Urban pavement contributes to damaging stormflows but also provides a water source absent in natural catchments. The CMP demonstrates achievable stormflow management using Sustainable Drainage Systems (SuDS), allowing river recovery while utilising this additional water volume.

2. Mitigating Floods: SuDS effectively mitigate a significant portion of flood responses. Although conventional detention systems are still necessary in some areas, their size can be reduced through widespread implementation of SuDS measures across the catchment.

3. Reducing Pollution: Stormflows contribute to pollution through surface runoff and sewer overloading. SuDS solutions treat urban runoff in filter media, reducing both pollution load and sewer overflow frequency. Addressing sewage network faults alongside SuDS implementation is recommended.

4. Aligning with River Health Goals: The CMP aligns requirements for flood and pollution control with established Resource Quality Objectives for the Jukskei River, ensuring holistic river health improvements.

5. Long-term Vision: Beyond immediate goals, the CMP envisions using SuDS networks to harvest rainfall, enhancing groundwater recharge in strategic locations.

6. Effective SuDS deployment hinges on utilising available open spaces across the catchment. Localised SuDS interventions provide limited benefits; thus, municipal leadership is crucial for scaling up efforts and achieving cumulative hydrological effects. Community engagement is pivotal for long-term SuDS adoption and initial innovation.

The emergence of new stakeholders like communities, NGOs, and private sector funders is a potential catalyst for urban infrastructure investments. New funding opportunities, including blended climate and biodiversity finance, provide support for initiatives like the Jukskei transformation. Encouraging leadership within multi-actor networks is essential for incubating and funding innovative water management approaches.

The CMP highlights technical and governance trade-offs, such as of capacity SuDS to manage flood peaks alongside the need for scaled efforts and policy shifts. A hydrological model developed in the study will continually inform decision-making, enhancing water security and reducing flooding risks. Successfully implementing these strategies requires a paradigm shift in urban water cycle management and strengthening local government capacity as policymakers and joint custodians with affected communities.

The CMP positions the Jukskei system for positive transformation, advocating for integrated water management approaches, amidst evolving urban challenges. By embracing innovative solutions and fostering collaborative governance, Johannesburg can navigate complexities and sustainably manage its water resources for future generations.

Notes

1 Hoorzook, K. B.; Pieterse, A., Heine, L., Barnard, T. G.; van Rensburg, N. J., 'Soul of the Jukskei River: The Extent of Bacterial Contamination in the Jukskei River in Gauteng Province, South Africa,' *Int. J. Environ. Res. Public Health* 2021, 18, 8537. https://doi.org/10.3390/ ijerph18168537.

2 Rand Water, 'Where Does Our Water Come From?' https://waterwise.co.za/site/water/Where_Does_our_Water_Come_From/.

3 Paul Burkhardt, 'Power Crisis Triggers Water Cuts in South Africa's Economic Hub,' January 30, 2023. https://www.bloomberg.com/news/articles/2023-01-30/power-crisis-triggers-water-cuts-in-south-africa-s-economic-hub#xj4y7vzkg.

4 'South African Constitution,' 1997; Section 24.

5 'UN General Assembly declares access to clean and healthy environment a universal human right.' https://news.un.org/en/story/2022/07/1123482.

6 Cumming, G. S., Peterson, G. D., 'Unifying research on social–ecological resilience and collapse.' *Trends in Ecology & Evolution,* 32(9): 695–713 (2017). https://doi.org/10.1016/j.tree.2017.06.014.

7 Abel, N., Cumming, D. H. M., Anderies, J. M., 'Collapse and reorganisation in social-ecological systems: questions, some ideas, and policy implications,' *Ecology and Society* 11(1): 17 (2006). [online] URL: http://www.ecologyandsociety.org/vol11/iss1/art17/.

8 Walker, B., Salt, D., *Resilience Thinking: Sustaining Ecosystems and People in a Changing World.* Washington, DC, USA: Island Press, 2006.

9 Kjellen, Marianne, Catherine Wong, Barbara van Koppen, Labisha Uprety, et al. *The United Nations World Water Development Report 2023: Partnerships and Cooperation for Water,* Paris: UNESCO, 2023. 173-182. ISBN 978-92-3-100576-3. https://cris.unu.edu/governance-%E2%80%98whole-society%E2%80%99-approach.

10 Quaternary catchments are the principal hydrological and water management units in South Africa. They were demarcated in 1946. https://www.dws.gov.za/Groundwater/Groundwater_Dictionary/index.html?introduction_quaternary_catchment.htm.

11 Resource Quality Objectives are water resource objectives, gazetted by government and expressed as numerical and/or descriptive statements about the biological, chemical and physical attributes that characterise the water resource in line with its level of protection, defined as a 'class' (DWS, 2019).

12 DWS (2019). *Determination of Water Resource Classes and Resource Quality Objectives for the Mokolo, Matlabas, Crocodile (West) and Marico Catchments.* Department of Water and Sanitation. Notice 562 of 2019. Gazette No. 42775.

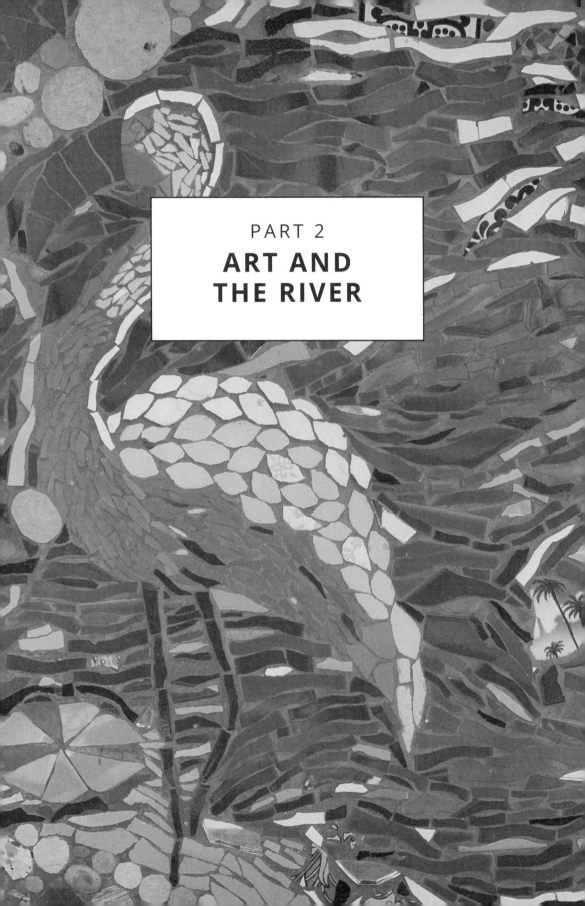

PART 2
ART AND THE RIVER

6 For the one that dances with jiggling brass: Compositions for the Jukskei

Dunja Herzog

The chapter offers a reflection on the importance of rivers in the art of Dunja Herzog. The artist relates how she made her first instruments with beeswax and the help of a river and how subsequently she travelled to Johannesburg with them, where she chose to work close to the Jukskei. The creative journey to the installation HUM is outlined and how finally the sound of the brass instruments is used to metaphorically heal the Jukskei.

Introduction

HUM (2022) is a sonic installation produced using brass instruments first realised in bees wax and then cast using recycled brass drawn from electronic waste in Benin City in southern Nigeria. These instruments and their soundings were conceived as a homage to the Yoruba river deity Ọṣun. A digital archive was realised using the recordings of the instruments and shared with musicians via a sound bank. The musicians commissioned to respond are geographically connected to my travels or the story of the global copper trade. The compositions were shared in a two-channel installation directed towards the Jukskei River in Johannesburg as part of the Riparian Urbanism Symposium. The sonic compositions were intended to be heard by the Jukskei River, and by extension all rivers, paying tribute to Ọṣun's presence and energy in all rivers.

Upon reflection, rivers have played an important role in my life as lifelong companions that I return to. These stretch from the small stream in Alsace, France, where I spent my childhood, to the Rhine, an arterial in the heart of my hometown Basel. For several years I've had a love affair with the Wouri River in Cameroon. I consider the shallow Doubs River in the Jura Mountains in Switzerland a pilgrimage. The Ọṣun River in Yorubaland in Nigeria fundamentally changed my relationship with rivers. Through it I understood that Ọṣun is not just a river, but a deity. The Birs River gave way to new work; while working alongside the Jukskei in Johannesburg deep resonances emerged and a sonic element entered my installations.

My practice and sensibility were informed by my stay in the Cameroonian grasslands as a child. Returning to Cameroon often, I spent time in the fishing village of Bonendale, on the banks of the Wouri River where ArtBakery, founded by Goddy Leye, is located. In 2006 I travelled to Fumban with Salifu Lindu, an artist and friend from Douala with connections to a bronze casting workshop.

Returning nine years later I experimented with casting, which lead to the project and the jewellery line, *Red Gold Import Export,* and later to casting brass instruments in tribute to the river deity Ọ̀ṣun. The sounds of these instruments were first shared publicly in the installation *HUM* realised in my studio located next to the Jukskei River in Johannesburg in June 2022.

In 2014, grappling with my identity and to better understand my position as a white artist working on the African continent, I became consumed by the Austrian avant-garde artist Susanne Wenger who travelled to Nigeria in 1952 and subsequently became a Yoruba priestess. At the request of the Yoruba community in Osogbo, she began renovating the Yoruba shrines in the sacred grove and subsequently created concrete sculptures depicting aspects of Yoruba cosmology. Compelled by these sculptures and her life, I travelled to Osogbo and stayed at her house with her adopted daughter, Doyin Fani Olosun, high priestess of Ọ̀ṣun. Doyin showed me the sacred grove and introduced me to Ọ̀ṣun, the river that flows through the grove. She explained to me that Ọ̀ṣun is the deity of fertility, beauty, and love, who has a weakness for honey and brass objects. Not only a nurturing being and a healer, the river also carries great floods when displeased.

Drawn to the mythology surrounding Ọ̀ṣun and the beauty of the sacred grove and Ọ̀ṣun in river form, what resonated most with me was how Doyin communicated with Ọ̀ṣun. She announced her arrival with a bell, praised her, and talked to her. This evoked something familiar in me, and there was a deep sense that I had arrived at a place where the river was understood as alive. When I was a child playing in the stream in Alsace, this play was more of a conversation with the stream. Being absorbed into the realm of the stream allowed me a greater understanding of its essence. I walked in the water and conversed with it and the plants and animals that lived in its realm. I had a sense I was home and felt deeply understood. When I had to leave, I missed that merging and that sense of belonging and of being one with something I felt so strongly connected to.

Intrigued by the brass bell Doyin used to announce our arrival at the Ọ̀ṣun river, the high-pitched tone made me realise that not only was I in the presence of a river but that the river was a deity that wanted to be honoured and addressed in a specific way. It allowed me to access a new mode of openness and deep listening. I also found the bell itself compelling, the fact that brass was used to communicate with Ọ̀ṣun. I had the intuition to continue working in brass and felt a strong desire to make Doyin a bell for Ọ̀ṣun to show her my appreciation for introducing me to Ọ̀ṣun's realm. At that time, I met brass casters in Oshogbo and undertook my first trip to Benin City, the historic centre of bronze casting in Nigeria.

Working with Phil Omodamwen, a seventh-generation bronze caster, in Benin City, I made a brass bell for Doyin, a shaker, and a singing bowl. When I heard the instruments for the first time, I was sure that they would play an important role in my future work. Before immersing myself in the realm of sound, I first had to engage with the fact that copper (the main ingredient of bronze and brass) plays an important role in global trade. In 2006 the presence of Chinese trade in Cameroon caused copper prices to skyrocket, threatening the livelihoods of traditional brass casters. In 2018, as part of the *Red Gold Import Export* project, I became particularly interested in the history of Benin City and the copper trade.[1] I looked at the trans-Saharan trade from the copper belt to Nigeria, as well as the history of copper mining in the 15th century in Europe. Manillas (bracelet-like objects) and other brass objects were exchanged by Europeans for slaves off the west coast of Africa and used by the King of Edo to cast the famous Benin bronzes.[2] The Benin Kingdom was destroyed in 1897 by the British who stole most of the bronzes in a punitive expedition. Today the Benin Bronzes are dispersed among European museums and are often at the centre of ongoing restitution endeavours.

A lot of electronic waste enters Nigeria today, and therefore much of what is made in Benin City is made from this recycled waste. It is important for me to work in Benin City, because I see the bronze casters' practices as alchemical and profoundly transformative. Slave money was transformed into sacred bronze heads of kings and queens through which the royalty could contact their ancestors, as well as into panels that visualised and made evident historical facts in the Edo Empire. Today, the casters turn electrical scrap into panels depicting the kingdom's shattered history and subsequent hardship. I also try to create objects that have the ability to transform the depleting spiral of extraction, land dispossession, accumulation, oppression, and contamination into something new. This should be something that resonates differently, that allows beauty to be experienced, that creates jobs, and that honours the work of people and the deep metallurgical knowledge passed down through many generations. These objects should create awareness of the past, be made from the waste of the present, to become conductors for the future.

The instruments I have realised are all in tribute to Ọṣun. I understand her as the transversal deity, speaking to the water aspect of all living beings and matter. As humans we are fluid and susceptible to various influences, being made of 65% water. Through water and DNA we are connected to and vibrate with our living environment as well as the context to which we are exposed.

Sound is waves, particles moving in matter, and energy created through vibration. I am drawn to cymatics (study of sound and vibration) and its experiments,[3] as it demonstrates how rhythm shapes matter. I fabricate instruments from brass, the main component of which is copper, which in itself is a transmitter of electrical force and is sometimes considered a kind of battery that can store (spiritual) energy. This is a way to work with physics on the one hand and to engage the spiritual world on the other. Copper is extracted from the depths of the earth, smelted from its ore in a complicated chemical process, and subsequently used in electronic devices to transmit electricity and information. At some point,

FOR THE ONE THAT DANCES WITH JIGGLING BRASS

it ends up as electronic waste and goes through a recycling process, only to be resold and begin a new cycle as a conductor. Taking some of the material from this cycle to make brass instruments evokes the memory of the experience of the material; this resounds on each occasion the instrument is played. But there is even more in the frequencies you hear or in the vibrations you feel, as the material is melted at 1000 degrees Celcius to be cast into new forms.

In 2020, at the invitation of the art institution Salts, I had the opportunity to collaborate with the Birs River in my hometown of Basel. At the time Ọṣun was not happy, or wanted to support my endeavour, as the river flooded and washed up a lot of driftwood. Aware of the beehive in the garden the project began to evolve with beeswax and natural materials used to make moulds for the brass casting using the lost-wax technique. Bees provided the wax and the Birs River the driftwood and I was finally able to fabricate the instruments that I had longed to create!

In early 2021, I travelled with the sculptures to Nigeria, where I cast them in bronze at Phil Omodamwen's foundry. Subsequently I travelled directly with them to Johannesburg, where I was undertaking a residency. During the residency, I wanted to work with the instruments and learn more about the context of Johannesburg. When I was pointed to a studio in Victoria Yards, I was immediately interested, given that the Jukskei River flowed behind the studio. The studio location offered the possibility of connecting with another stream. I was curious about the Jukskei as the river seemed out of balance and in poor health, and it struck me that it wasn't accessible, other than from Victoria Yards.

Playing the brass instruments, I soon realised I wanted to record their sounds in order to share these through the copper wires of the digital network to musicians who were connected to the project through their context or contact with me and were open to realising experimental compositions. Collaborating with percussionists Farai Matake and Yao Agbodohu we went to the famous DownTown Music Hub in Johannesburg to record the sounds and the label Subterranean Wavelength created a soundbank. I began making enquiries about a local beekeeper and on first meeting Thembalezwe Mntambo we immediately connected and discussed square beehives which are designed for maximum extraction, as opposed to the traditional hives made of clay, which are more in line with the bees' natural design. We discussed land ownership and its importance to beekeeping, and how small the black beekeeping community is, due to lack of access to land.

After undertaking research, I was interested in making amorphous organic ceramic hives out of Johannesburg soil that would meet the needs of the bees and not have an extractive agenda. The intention was to work towards an exhibition at the end of the residency where the hives would first be shown as sculptures along with the compositions, and subsequently transferred to nature as functional hives.

The exhibition took place in my studio at Victoria Yards, in close proximity to the Jukskei, a brick wall separating the studio from the river. The sonic compositions would be heard by the river, paying tribute to its presence and its embracing energy that first brought me to the studio at Lorentzville and enabled me to develop the idea of making hives for bees – building homes for the creatures that are crucial for the life cycle on our planet and themselves symbols of hope. Aware that Ọṣun desires honey and that honey is a salve, it seemed apt to have an exhibition that saw the creation of beehives along the Jukskei River – a gesture of metaphorically healing the Jukskei.

Together with Thembalezwe and the ceramist Cosmas Ndlovu, we worked to develop and fabricate the beehives in clay sourced from a deep industrial clay pit south of Soweto. It made sense to realise beehives in the post-industrial and extractive context of Johannesburg. I wanted to create something life-affirming, something that gives instead of takes; something that does not extract anything from this city that is itself formed by extraction. Homes for bees provide a counter-narrative, one which has been my experience of Johannesburg.

In the installation *HUM* seven hives were presented on pedestals, while the sound of various composers, as a metaphor for the buzzing of the bees, resonated from cone speakers in an 8-channel installation, surrounding the hives and directed towards the Jukskei River. This sound installation and the instruments that were made to realise it constitute *For the One that Dances with Jiggling Brass,* which was realised in two channels for the Jukskei River as part of the Riparian Urbanism Symposium in September 2022.

It was important to me to send the instrument soundings to musicians that had a connection to the development of the project. I invited Ade Omotade, Damola Owolade, Dion Monti, Gugulethu 'Dumama' Duma, Elsa M'bala, Grace Kalima N./ Aliby Mwehu, Jill Richards, Rikki Ililonga and Dani Kyengo O'Neill to respond to the material. The compilation of all the different tracks created a tapestry of sound that made the exhibition space vibrate with the sounds of *For the One that Dances with Jiggling Brass,* for the Jukskei, and for all rivers.

My perception of the world changed when I first heard Doyin Fani Olosun call and honour the river deity Ọṣun with her bell. This experience reshaped my practice and led me to consciously seek out rivers and explore the transformative possibilities of sound vibrations, as well as to recommit to a sensory, embodied and experiential art practice.

Figure 6.1 *HUM, 2022, Multimedia installation with seven ceramic beehives and an 8-channel sound installation. Work by Dunja Herzog in collaboration with Thembalezwe Mntambo and Cosmas Ndlovu, Victoria Yards, Johannesburg*

Notes

1 Eugenia W. Herbert, *Red Gold of Africa: Copper in Precolonial History and Culture* (Madison: University of Wisconsin Press, 1984).

2 Wu Mingren, 'The Benin Bronzes: A Tragic Story of Slavery and Imperialism Cast in Brass,' *Ancient Origins*, May 1, 2021, https://www.ancient-origins.net/artifacts-other-artifacts/benin-bronzes-008565.

3 Hans Jenny, *Cymatics: A Study of Wave Phenomena & Vibration* (Basel: Basilius,1967-1974), https://monoskop.org/images/7/78/Jenny_Hans_Cymatics_A_Study_of_Wave_Phenomena_and_Vibration.pdf.

7 Where water once stood, it shall stand again: Stances on fluvial art practice

Nina Barnett, Refiloe Namise and Abri de Swardt

This chapter results from a conversation between three artists, Nina Barnett (NB), Refiloe Namise (RN) and Abri de Swardt (AdS), who make work concerning bodies of water from the vantage of Johannesburg. Our dialogue flows from the city but is not bound to it, joining several rivers and dams with our own watery embodiments. We each grapple with the Jukskei River differentially, thinking *with* and *through* its presence to direct us to particular hydro-relations. Collectively, the Jukskei represents a watershed, a moving constant, a series of fragmented zones in excess of containment. In each of our practices, the Jukskei is an existing or potential medium. We generated the writing and editing process through several discussions prompted by our varied approaches to this river. We have structured our conversation through poetic invitations rather than 'scholastic' subsections, as expressions of converged writing. These invitations engage notions of riparian infringement, water ownership, site-responsive materiality, elemental adaption to toxicity, and modes of storytelling as self-preservation. We propose these notions as pressing to fluvial art practice.

Cold, soft, far, here, how: What is the Jukskei River to you?

NB: The Jukskei is an origin point, a high place that drains northwards to the Crocodile River, the Limpopo and the Indian Ocean. The Jukskei's particulate, what it carries as sedimentary, diluted and suspended flow, is embedded in and messaged to the larger rivers and oceans it feeds. This river is singular – its territory and materiality are particular to its fluvial pathway, its riparian, atmospheric and submerged environments. When arriving at this river, I acknowledge its agency and specificity beyond its use as a resource for humans. I want to know this river, and the other water bodies in my practice, as a collaborating force, an anchor and an adversary.

AdS: I access the Jukskei through a series of scattered vantages, in incongruous – even incompatible – places, seeing its waters used differentially, simultaneously and indelibly. The river is both resource and medium, exceeding any act of framing: beyond laundry, leisure, spirit or art. I approach the Jukskei as its flow leads me away from the immediacy of the city, while still holding it materially. The Jukskei signalled a moment in my practice where I returned more deliberately to a convergence of the digital and the elemental, enacting each through the other.

Though that work might not be about the Jukskei only, the river moved me to a process of listening to it.

RN: I consider the Jukskei River as a moving body. I engage different parts of the river running through Alexandra, north of Johannesburg, and think about its constant presence – how it geographically situates place. In Alex there are various riparian areas, called East Bank (which lies east of the riverbank), West Bank (west of the riverbank), and Far East Bank (far east of the riverbank). The river also separates old and new Alex (new Alex consists of subsidised housing). There are parts of the river where certain activations happen, such as baptisms. In this way I reflect on the river as a body in motion initiating constant practices.

Entering rivers as trespassing/violation/saturation

AdS: Nina, you anecdotally spoke of the Rupert Museum staff bleaching water from the Orange River which you, Dee Marco, Sinethemba Twalo, and Amy Watson in *The Orange River Project* had collected on your field trip for display in your collective installation at the Social Impact Arts Prize 2022. How do you negotiate this management of bringing river matter – the fluvial – into institutions that routinely impose containment upon the 'natural'?

NB: In *The Orange River Project*, Sinethemba Twalo, Dee Marco, Amy Watson and I followed the Orange River from the Gariep Dam to Alexander Bay in late 2022 as a way to begin to understand the many iterations and evolutions of this particular flow. We collected water from several key sites along the trajectory, which became part of our installation in the Rupert Museum in Stellenbosch.

Museums or gallery spaces are often places in which water – whether in the form of moisture or leaks – is a sign of destruction, decay and loss. The presentation of specific watery materiality as the subject of an artwork complicates this position. This complication highlights the fluid, unfixed nature of water – that though it may be attractive in its pristine form, water is also an evolving biome. The Rupert Museum's actions articulate their position: insisting on certain conditions of conservation, concerned about the possibility of sensory discomfort from that which might grow or evolve in the water. In his book *What is Water?*, academic Jamie Linton describes the notion of modern water – as a utility; as benign; considered in terms of its quantity rather than its specificity to place or make up.[1] The Rupert Museum's actions were not our intention, but they do illustrate the disruption caused by the fluid and the temporal in spaces historically committed to stasis and sterility.

AdS: Refiloe, in your exhibition *Segopotso sa Gomora – Open Studio* (2022) at The Point of Order in Braamfontein you approach the Jukskei River running through Alexandra as material and narrative collaborator. By exploring questions of self-sufficiency, community mobilisation, and the governance of economic realities, your work engages how histories of housing in the area are entangled with the riparian. Do you consider the river as an archive of housing, or in excess of what the archive can house?

RN: Segopotso, a research practice that I've developed over the past few years, is embodied in different sites in Alex, by different kinds of bodies. Treating the exhibition like an ongoing working space was a way for me to visualise and consolidate my work elsewhere. The open studio offered perspective, understanding Alex through a different lens. This type of mobilisation also echoes the ways in which communities of Alex gather: thinking about agency, trust and self-sustainability.

Breaking my time at The Point of Order into three episodes allowed for specific types of gatherings, ultimately drawing towards bigger concerns of how we historicise, and where (outside of formal history holders) material can exist, be held, engaged with, re-understood and re-imagined. Episode 1: *The Conversation with Joel Thamba that took place at no. 39 13th Avenue, Alexandra* (Figure 7.1) is a re-enactment of a conversation (held in August 2021) with Joel Thamba, a resident who lives on 13th Avenue in Alex. The re-enactment takes shape in the form of brick-making, using Jukskei River sand with 'gold nuggets,' and water from the river. The house where Joel lives and grew up in was built by his uncle, Themba Thamba, using Jukskei River sand. I was thinking about how the house can serve as a 'monument' of the river.

Episode 2: *Bus ya ko 7: The Inauguration* is a video screening of a bus that I painted red as a reminder of the bus boycotts that took place in January 1957. The bus is parked in MaNtombi's yard on 7th Avenue opposite what is now a heritage site where Nelson Mandela lived in 1942, across the street from the Alexandra Heritage Museum. Here I explored ways of thinking about heritage sites – how we memorise and memorialise. In Episode 3: *Ditshwantsho tsa Rona* (Figure 7.2), I photocopied the bricks that I made in Episode 1. The phrase *ditshwantsho tsa rona* means 'images of us' in Setswana.

Figure 7.1 *Refiloe Namise, images taken during Episode 1 of* Segopotso sa Gomora, *installation-based performance, 2022, The Point of Order, Johannesburg*

Figure 7.2 *Refiloe Namise, images taken during Episode 3 of* Segopotso sa Gomora, *installation-based performance, 2022, The Point of Order, Johannesburg*

NB: Abri, how do you see the river as translatable into the forms you work with – photography, film, sound, storytelling or poetry? I have always found your work to be generous to the gallery space, while still managing a sense of risk or exposure to material presence. Is this a conscious move on your part?

AdS: Author Olivia Laing, in '*To the River,*' ponders on the independent emergence of writing beside the Euphrates, Tigris, Nile and Yellow Rivers in Sumer, Babylonia, Ancient Egypt, and the Indus Valley respectively, stating it is no 'coincidence that the advent of the written word was nourished by river water.'[2] It is as if the babbling of fresh waters calls forth impression and narration. My engagement with the fluvial intensified after coming across graffiti beneath Coetzenburg bridge in Stellenbosch reading *Real EYES Realize Real Lies* – which I took as a herald of Fallism, and as a prompt towards my ongoing moving-image trilogy on the Eerste River. I explore how white supremacy is expressed through, and attenuated by, this river in *Ridder Thirst* (2015–18), and ask 'if the river's mouth could speak, what would it say?' in *Kammakamma* (2022–24). Differing parts of the river summon different approaches. In the latter work, I am collaborating with the Indian Ocean historian Saarah Jappie and the Kaaps poet Ronelda S. Kamfer on a screenplay that reflects divergent communities linked by the river. Storytelling becomes a way to approach the river as a hydro-social commons, rather than a regulating borderline; as a place for gathering and capaciousness. Though rivers are repositories for submerged stories which expand with every convergence and tributary, translating these can never fully epitomise the entirety of the river.

The fluvial offers material conditions of flow, confluence, saturation and spill that permit inter- and trans-disciplinary proliferation. In my work, dissimilar affects can accumulate as an expanded collage in being about, with and *of* the river. In *Ridder Thirst* (Figure 7.3), for instance, I use motion-tracked costuming, dense voice-over narration, anti-monumental paralinguistic gestures and a princely flautist to address photography.

Figure 7.3 *Abri de Swardt, stills from* Ridder Thirst, *2015-18, HD Projection with double seating structure, 13'38 min*

Fluvial materials, such as objects spewed from the river mouth in the condom-like *Eerste Waterval* (2018) sculpture, or sand mined from the estuary dunes in *Kammakamma* do offer olfactory, tactile residues of riparian-human violation in my exhibitions. Drawing from scenography, I have of late invoked the dim glow of photographic and queer darkrooms, the hierarchy of sports seating, and the stagecraft of flood prevention to reorientate the viewer and bring awareness to the body.

Strategies of sampling and seeping define your installations, Nina. Would you consider your work as primarily phenomenological, and if so, how can localised, watery sensoriums contribute to how we recognise the world?

Figure 7.4 *Nina Barnett,* On Breathing – Vapour *(installation view), 2022, Adler Museum of Medicine, Johannesburg*

NB: I feel that immersive installation work should make a viewer aware of their own presence and sensory knowledge, and encourage the possibility that all bodies, human or otherwise, are implicated in the exhibition. Towards this, I set up relationships in which there is a sense of fragility or risk: sometimes to the viewer's body, sometimes to the installation itself, which may encourage an emotional, immediate understanding of materiality. In the exhibition *On Breathing* (2022), in collaboration with Jeremy Bolen, we used humidifiers on pedestals and bricks to fill the Adler Museum of Medicine's glass cabinets with steam (Figure 7.4). The contained moisture clouds made the air a physical, quantifiable entity in a defined environment to be scrutinised by the visitor. Condensation dripped down the interior of the glass, creating a sense of concern for the integrity of the museum cabinets and the institution itself. The implied risk of electrical shorts heightened the sense of precarity.

Riparian slippage and rituals of return

NB: Refiloe, your description of Ntate Thamba's basement, the water emanating from the drain, makes me think of the Jukskei as a spectre, a haunting presence that continues to bleed or seep out of the earth. Do you think of your practice as a witness to the Jukskei and that which is performed for it, next to it or in it?

RN: I've grappled a lot with the feeling of witnessing, of being an insider or outsider. Can one be a community member and objectively engage Alex as a place? Central to Segopotso as a practice is developing ways of understanding past and present moments. Segopotso here re-enacts spoken narratives, beliefs or myths, in and around the river, as a way to understand how the river moves, and the mythical and social impact that it has on the surrounding communities. These re-enactments and interventions are ephemeral, fluid and uncontainable – posing questions as to what and how moments are historicised. Ntate Thamba's house

Figure 7.5 *Nina Barnett,* Incidental Rift, *2016 documentation of intervention at Origins Centre, Johannesburg*

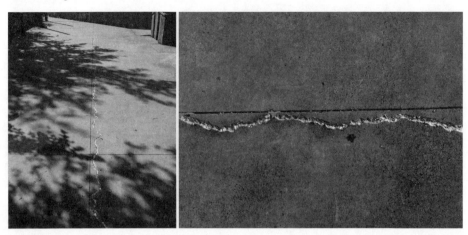

acts as a representative of the making and survival of a place and its people: a monument made from gold-nuggeted sand and water from its own river, to which it shall in the end return.

Nina, how does your intervention, *Incidental Rift,* make visible that which is not seen? Was it performative, or were you depositing the gold leaf over days, by hand, alone?

NB: *Incidental Rift* (Figure 7.5) was made in 2016, in the courtyard of the Origins Centre in Johannesburg. This museum is built on the crest of the Witwatersrand Ridge, that runs from east to west through the city. The ridge is known for its dense quartzite rock, inside of which runs a seam of gold ore. These deposits were central to the formation and growth of the city. The Witwatersrand Ridge is also significant in the greater landscape as a high point that divides two watersheds. When rain falls to the south of the ridge, it drains into streams that feed the Vaal and Orange Rivers, which flow into the Atlantic Ocean. When rain falls to the north, the water joins the Crocodile and Limpopo rivers, eventually leading to the Indian Ocean. The Jukskei is an anomaly in some ways. It surfaces on the south side of the watershed by Ellis Park, but eventually winds its way north (see the map on pp. xiv-xv).

At the museum I noticed a long crack in the concrete floor surface. It formed from the force of rainwater pulling in opposing directions to the north and south. The crack was a marker of an origin point for a number of major water bodies. I bonded gold leaf to the interior of this fault, from end to end, alone over the course of six days while eight and a half months pregnant. Like many of my intervention works, it was not intended as a performative act, and yet it became one in the moment. The gold leaf linked the geology of the city, established in relation to gold and its extraction, to the movement of its waters. Gold and water are intrinsically connected in this city in many environmental, industrial and political ways.

Abri, your text 'Riverwork' (2021) expresses such desire to have the river as a collaborator, and failures of attempting collaboration. The river is unkempt and uncaring and also very attractive, almost magnetic. Do you think that a collaboration with a river is doomed to fail, or be undone by its relentlessness?

AdS: I consider 'Riverwork' a speculative manifesto on fluvial art – its creation, display, viewership and cultural reception. It was commissioned by the online platform wherewithall for their library on independent curatorial and artistic practices in Johannesburg, and informed by working within rivers, including tributaries of the Jukskei. 'Riverworkers' are artists who resolve to only show their work within 'the river.' This mode of working is a fledgling practice for them. I grapple with how 'the river's conditions – its unrelenting instabilities of filtering, temperature, and pressure, of sweep and swell, forever browning and refracting, its steady dissolutions' is a 'congruence impartial to former functions.' These conditions effect a total renegotiation of artistic process, form and community wherein 'work mutated in concert with its bearer, past terrestrial recuperation.'[3] I position the river as a 'sensorium of estrangement, compelling new interpretations, other forms, experimental sociality.'[4] These include the development of several factions, disagreeing on how best to engage, embrace, or repudiate, riverwork: namely *Benders*, *Crossers*, *Rapids* (Dry or Amphibian), *Spewers*, *Koppies* and *Arids*.

These formations show how this river is subjected to its community at every turn:

> [t]he river was commuting through the city, a resident, hostage and exile alike, fashioned and twisted by intention's bucketing flow. The river was a class divide, a baptism, the air worms breathed....The river, though measured, zoned, charted, managed, forsaken and owned, was irreducible to its parts.[5]

As much as 'Riverwork' proposes riparian relations beyond hydraulic possession and re-engineering, these already are the river's material conditions through coloniality. Archaeologist Matt Edgeworth terms rivers both 'cultural' and 'wild artefacts': they are marked by human occupation yet cannot 'be entirely contained.'[6] He writes that the 'river is an artefact that can escape the bounds of its culturally applied form.'[7] My interest in fluvial art practice is in this potential of waters to exceed categorisation through wildness, alongside challenging evocations of 'naturalness.' I would not say rivers necessarily undo work – they are not inherently foreboding nor toxic – rather working fluvially generates a non-settling that alters intent. Riverwork means resurfacing.

We've spoken about what it means to collaborate with the fluvial, but not so much about how existing modes of collaboration might influence such approaches. Refiloe, I'm wondering about how your earlier collective work as anticlockwise

INGWEMBE with Siyanda Marrengane and Tsholofelo Seleke inform the *Segopotso* episodes with regards to costume and the division of labour?

RN: There are overlaps in my personal work and the work that we do as anticlockwise INGWEMBE. The collective existed during our studies at the Wits School of Arts, pooling together our concerns around storytelling, text-based work, object-based installations and performances where the body is central. The collective was indeed a good and safe space to bounce off ideas, both as a working space and friendship fed by our individual practices.

Anticlockwise INGWEMBE was established in 2014. *Ingwembe* means 'wooden spoon' in siSwati. We take on the notion of a wooden spoon as a tool and signifier of power that instils discipline, domestication, mixing and remixing. Much of our work is centred around the body in public space, exploring ways in which spaces can be re-read, complicating the understood behaviours between private and public practices. In thinking about costume, we generally wear black dresses. Though this unifies us, we think of the collective as one figure made up of three bodies, like in Morwalo wa Metla (which means 'constant luggage' in Setswana) a performative intervention we did in 2017, as part of *A Monument to Freedom,* at NIROX Winter Sculpture Fair, NIROX Sculpture Park. We walked slowly in unison throughout the site, each firmly striking a wooden spoon against the palm of our hand, our eyes covered in red strands undone from the China bag, wooden spoons sewn onto and hanging from our black dresses. The sounds of the spoons hitting against each other echoed the aggressive and violent contact between security forces and students, during Fees Must Fall.

During my own performances and interventions, the key aspect of what to wear is that the item must be red. This is central to the embodiment of Segopotso – which continues the use of the colour. The Alex Action Committee (AAC, implemented 1986) was successful in organising the communities of Alex. The committee had a red flag symbolising the workers struggle and wrote in red on their posters. I think of Segopotso as a writing body. In Episode 1, I was making bricks as a way to re-enact the conversation that I had with Joel Thamba. His uncle built the house himself, using river sand and river water from the Jukskei. In this way, I was embodying the act of making the bricks myself with the same fluvial material. In drawing on the conversation with Joel, and the collaborative acts of making, I reflected on the survival of a house – and at large, the survival of Alex, a place that was meant to be demolished and set up as a labour camp with hostels.

AdS: In a saturated solution, the overbearing presence of one substance can lead to a phase change. Water shifts colour, becomes soupy, or halts flow. Nina, how and with whom do you observe these fluctuating appearances at the Vaal Dam?

NB: I went to the Dam this week [March 2023] and sat on a pier at the bottom of a suburban garden watching the liquid surface. Cyanobacteria has saturated the top layer of the water, turning it acidic green and thick. The Dam's waves move slower, and the sun's reflection is held like a bright wobbling ball. I am working through ways of articulating this interaction between the water and the algae, which indicates and visualises the pollution present. By using strips of paper as a sort of litmus test, I record the fluctuations in level and density in a rudimentary way.

In these visits I am regularly conversing with those who encounter the dam daily. These residents, fishermen, cyclists and sailors are working and living in relation to a water body in flux. I check in with them regarding my observations: 'was the water like this last week?' 'how high were the levels after it rained?' Answers to the questions seem less important than the act of noticing together. This durational watching of the water can allow for a material or sensory 'reading' of the environment.

Astrida Neimanis asks: 'If our bodies are mostly water, where does this water come from? Where does it go, and what does it make possible? How does our wateriness condition how we live as bodies, and how we become implicated in the bodies of others?'[8] The subjective nature of my body (of water) witnessing the water that will ultimately flow through me (via pipes, treatment plants, reservoirs) is a kind of feedback loop, or a mirroring.

Drink irregularity

RN: Abri, at the end of 'Riverwork' you mention that '...If the river was to be a body of work, it could only be one in flux, a collection in overhaul, a museum of falling. But falling only signalled a longer contiguity and gestation, another repertoire of remembrance, ghosts in the valences of particles, slippery chronologies.' How do you explore some of these slippages? Are we haunted by these ghosts? How do we negotiate a kind of space that is flowing, liquid, not tangible, uncontainable, slippery?

AdS: In the closing paragraph, I'm making sense of the spatial-temporal effects of the fluvial practice I hypothesise. Though I am flirting with impossibility and abandon, I also think through the actual precariousness defining a lot of art production, of the struggle to persist, feel or effect touch. Conversely, I think of the decementising of art histories, of petrifying infrastructures, of missing, and messing, and amassing the transference between art and life. I think of the freedoms yearned for by ghosts, calling us beneath the waters, to join their journey of unsettling.

Refiloe, in your video *Noka ya Tsala*, you are shown sifting through the waters of the Jukskei as debris floats by. We see you seated on a river rock, with a red substance bleeding from your hands. Your gesture enacts histories of gold prospecting at the river, when the Jukskei's conditions were different. You therefore call forth this ghost version of the Jukskei, with its former flows of migration and economic opportunity. How do you perform ideas of redistribution and custodianship through this river?

RN: The poem *Jukskei Ghost* by Modikwe Dikobe made me think of a kind of end, a calm that would descend upon the communities living on the banks of the river. This would be an end to turmoil, and the unpredictable nature of living next to these waters. Dikobe was a novelist, poet, trade unionist, communist, soldier, and in the 1940s a secretary of the Alex Squatters' Resistance movements.

Jukskei Ghost

Be calm
Nobody dare unearth you
The searchlights you see
Are men's fears
On those who have passed death
Closeted in their apartment
Waiting for the day of resurrection.

Upon the Jukskei River bank
You've friends
Praying for your soul
That you may rest
In God's kingdom
Till eternity.

They've chosen you as neighbour
Rather than submit
To exploitation.

I ventured to pacify you
Be calm
Very soon it will be over.[9]

Noka ya Tsala (2017) is an intervention during which I wrote in/on the water using red food colouring. *Noka ya tsala* means 'the river gives birth' in Setswana. Being in the river was uncomfortable because it felt unpredictable, rocky, slippery and very cold. As I released it from my gold-painted fingertips, the food colouring spread in the water, slowly saturating the river, distributing and fading. One can also think of the act of casting a spell, enchanting the river to be calm, and to protect its friends, '[v]ery soon it will be over.'

NB: Refiloe, this reference to bleeding makes the movement of the Jukskei visible. I wonder whether the water is staining the red, or whether the red is staining the water. The water and the red feel like they might have suspicious qualities, they seem consequential to possible actions or events that have come before. The blood-like quality brings attention to what is at stake in the water: life and death.

RN: Something is washed away. In the same way that water takes, it also gives.

Ripple storying

RN: In *Ridder Thirst* there's a part where the narrator repeats the words 'at last', echoing the possible tranquillity of '…and now, a dry riverbed stone, last withered fingers clutching to the damp banks…gives no sounds of water, and cries out to the mountain, where they buried the river, where there is no water but only rock, mountains of rock without water…' While one is overcome with a sense of doom or ending, it can also feel like a beginning, a utopia, a calm before the storm, a calm after the storm. What are your feelings at this moment of the work?

AdS: This scene in the video marks a shift in narration towards tenderness. Preceding it, there are two emotive peaks: a verbal litany of brutality while four queer students' empty pitchers of milk into the Eerste River, and a melancholic wake at the river's artificial bank. The premise of the voiceover is that a force ('The Shadow Prince' and 'his Battalion of Shades') slips out of a camera and is tasked to 'roll up' this river and sift through what remains. Thereafter the river can be buried. As the visuals cut from the riverbank to the distant silhouette of the princely flautist on a boulder, the narrator imagines what a riverbed stone might say to the mountain it once broke apart from…Like much of the work, this is metaphoric, yet material!

In suggesting the mountain burial of the river, the water cycle becomes redrawn. I wanted to evoke a longing to breathe, to recuperate and assert that there is room for vulnerability, upheaval, collapse, for turning one's back, getting side-tracked, even for lagging behind. For marking the passing of place. The mountain and the riverbed stone are like a fable on the virtues of being anchored or being set in motion. *Ridder Thirst* holds so many instabilities and dispositions, premised on the river's run. Cinematographically, I use changes from black & white, solarised, and colour footage to register these. This scene is followed by a sunset overlooking Stellenbosch and the Cape Peninsula, with two dams noticeable in the foreground, reminders of the countless vessels the river is buried within.

What is the place of your own body in relation to the vastness of the Vaal Dam and Orange River in your work Nina? There is something about the flatness and variance of these waters which resist established understandings of containment, especially when visualised midday. How do you consider temporality when approaching these waters?

NB: I have been using this poem by Natalie Diaz[10] as a guide when thinking about my body's relationship to the vast expanse of the Orange River:

The Colorado River is the most endangered river in the United States –
also, it is a part of my body.

I carry a river. It is who I am: 'Aha Makav. This is not metaphor.

*When a Mojave says, Inyech 'Aha Makavch ithuum, we are saying our name.
We are telling a story of our existence. The river runs through the middle
of my body.*

*So far, I have said the word river in every stanza. I don't want to waste water.
I must preserve the river in my body.*

In future stanzas, I will try to be more conservative.

Water, and water systems like the Orange and the Vaal River, are unfixed entities. They are defined by flow, by the nature of their movement in relation to their environment. Rivers are only fixed in places that have been dammed, in colonial- or apartheid-fuelled efforts to contain the resource for human and industrial use. The Vaal Dam, and the Gariep and Vanderkloof Dams on the Orange River, insist that the river is its water, or the sum of its parts. It feels hopeful to think of my body in terms of a force, rather than a container.

A body of water, at least a big one like a river, a dam or a lake, is a marker of time. Seasonal shifts in flood and drought change the shape of the water, the moon plays a part also. In driving back to Johannesburg from Alexander Bay on our *Orange River Project* journey, Sinethemba, Dee, Amy and I experienced the river shifting into flood. The water rushed past, climbing quickly up the banks. The flood shifted the temporality of being next to the river, of observing – time quickened, it tumbled past us, taking branches and thoughts with it. We seemed in slow-motion, too slow to keep up with the pulsing torrent. And so too, when the Vaal Dam is still and glass-like, time pauses and I feel self-aware, like my presence might disrupt the suspended body.

AdS: Refiloe, one conversational prompt you sent is your photograph of a bridge in Alex featuring graffiti reading 'PSALMS 66:12/ YOU HAVE CAUSED MEN/ RIDE OVER OUR HEADS,' with the full verse being 'You have caused men to ride over our heads; We went through fire and through water; But You brought us out to rich *fulfilment.*' (AV). As mentioned, in my work I have taken words beneath bridges as prophetic texts, addressing power dynamics between above and below, between that which one moves away from, or towards. How does this verse resonate with Alex in your works?

RN: This phrase is written on a concrete structure, opposite from where I performed *Noka ya Tsala*. The placement of the phrase fosters a way of reading that is actively contextual – the bridge above and the river complete the phrase, the verse, the thought. I enjoy how you have interpreted the idea of such words being prophetic, narrating something that exists in the present moment and perhaps saying something about a future possibility. I have thought of this phrase as describing how Alex has survived. In 1955, the Department of Native Affairs and the Peri-Urban Areas Health Board assumed responsibility for governing Alex, deciding that the township would be converted into a hostel complex. The AAC

WHERE WATER ONCE STOOD, IT SHALL STAND AGAIN

contributed in mobilising resistance towards the implementation of the hostel policy, collecting signatures in its petition calling the government to reconsider. In 1974, property owners were informed by the West Rand Administration Board that they would have to vacate their properties, and failure to do so would result in an expropriation of their property rights. During this time, a rigorous formulation of committees emerged in protest. Rev. Sam Buti, leader of the Save Alexandra Party, worked closely with members of the community in driving the campaign to save Alex, and in 1979, it was officially announced in parliament that Alex would remain.[11] This ultimately draws on the biblical narrative, written about two demolished cities south of the Dead Sea: Sodom and Gomorrah. These were described as 'sin' cities, where rape, sodomy, sexual practices, pride, gluttony and laziness reigned.[12] Alex is colloquially known as Gomorrah/Gomora. The phrase was important as a starting point into thinking about the different parts of the Jukskei River and which parts of Alex they directly affect. This concrete structure is located across the river from an informal settlement called Stjwetla, along the riverbank where many families forcefully settled.

NB: Abri, in *Ridder Thirst* the photographs submerged in the river provoke questions about the future of the images, about disintegration and sediment. What is the relationship, for you, between image and liquidity? How are you thinking about the paper on which the images are printed?

AdS: That scene in *Ridder Thirst* uses inversion to comment on the effects of time: the digital photographic collage motion-tracked over the students before now manifest as actual cut-outs carried downstream, while the picturesque Eerste River pebble embankment undulates into a load of gabions. Here I linger on sinking, enmeshment, and substitution as states.

In my work, collage becomes a frenzied proxy of the photographic. I am drawn to image simultaneity and profusion. The operations of the lens lose their footing, become muddled, compounded and re-sequenced non-linearly into accumulations. In my ongoing series *Streams*, which I initially was photographing in a tributary of the Jukskei, I explore notions of emergence through metaphorically transposing the 'Stop Bath' in photographic film processing – a water tray where exposed images stop developing – to rivers. Differing river flows become a means of collaging without cutting, as bodies of photographs become wettened, sink and held from the waterfall's effervescence in *Streams (VI)* (Figure 7.6) to the estuary's lip.

Figure 7.6 *Abri de Swardt*, Streams (VI), *2021, Giclée Print on Hahnemühle Baryta, 500 × 750 mm*

Primarily my concern is this photographic gathering as the river's morphology. The stream *is* also the photograph/s. You see scenes of gestation. Implied is a transformative continuum, of photographs absorbing, and dissolving into, the river, only to be filtered and repurposed in the darkroom. The river becomes a queer, counter-sedentary way of archiving the photographic. However, the future of these images concerns not only their materiality, but also their instrumentalisation. I'm working through how photographs are unstable surfaces, linguistic substitutes and bodily extensions. This includes how they keep shifting their relation to memory, to constitutive acts. Photographic paper is one iteration in a discontinuous resurfacing: sometimes paper is the digital transfer to the physical, especially given the dematerialised nature of present photography. In other instances, paper is metonymic of the tug between containment and transportation, like in the laminations of albums and keepsakes, clutching and unleashing the past. It's no coincidence that photographs are stored in shoe boxes.

In preparing the compositions placed within the rivers in *Streams*, I initially printed on non-coated paper which creases, frays and pulps with handling, but recently I am working with resilient prints that require prolonged immersion and agitation to shift. I'm starting to combine these registers of ephemerality, as well as experimenting with prior hydration, to heighten palpable time.

WHERE WATER ONCE STOOD, IT SHALL STAND AGAIN

Figure 7.7 *Refiloe Namise, installation shots taken from Episode 3 of* Segopotso sa Gomora, *2022, installation-based performance, The Point of Order, Johannesburg*

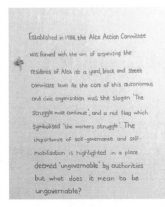

Refiloe, one key process in your work is remediation. By performing 'non-artistic' labour such as brick-making (*Episode 1*), painting a bus (*Episode 2*), and photocopying (*Episode 3*) you comment on the administration and acknowledgement of citizenship. Can you delve into how these processes find form in your work as a way of communing the everyday in the riparian zone?

RN: Photocopying the bricks and amplifying the sound was an act of rebellion against various forms of image-reproduction, and the conventional use of a photocopier. What does it mean for images to be from us, rather than *of* us? As each brick was placed on the photocopier in *Episode 3*, the continuous, mechanical sound of the machine filled the space. The photocopies generated were later handed out to members of the audience (Figure 7.7). The objectness of the machine, the microphone, the wheelbarrow, and the bricks, bring forth concerns around mass production, collective representation and sharing of imagery.

As Segopotso, I embody the middle-figure, taking on the labour of making, storing and sharing. Navigating the everyday becomes less personal in that Segopotso is a mediator that is not only me, but also the river and Joel Thamba's house, amongst other sites. These figures materialise Segopotso, in the labour that they perform during my encounter with them. They take on the role of holder, carrier, vessel and repository – storing, carrying and passing through information. Segopotso can therefore be understood as a practice that is largely informed by varying acts of mediation and translation.

Natural stagnancy is not neutral!

RN: Can you tell us about the water from the Vaal Dam you collected recently, Nina?

NB: I collected a sample of water in a jar from the Dam at Deneysville, at a site called Rate-Payers Bay, in early February. Nitrates in the water – from fertilisers, industrial

Figure 7.8 *Nina Barnett, Vaal water sample in the studio, March 2023 and Nina Barnett, Walking into the flooded dam 2023, documentation of experimentation*

effluent and untreated wastewater – have caused an abundant algae bloom. These particles of cyanobacteria are suspended in the silty Dam, concentrating near the water's edge like a green blanket on the surface.

Initially the water was murky – spots of brown silt and green algae teamed in the mid area, the top surface solidly covered in a green mass. After one month the algae had become browner, dying from lack of oxygen and flow. While the water was clear, it was also bright blue (Figure 7.8). As of now (May 2023), it has become paler, and the algae matter itself is a brown-green sludge hanging on the water's surface and settled on the bottom of the jar. It's a reminder on my desk of perpetual change and of variability in saturation. The term stagnancy is often used to describe a stillness, but this jar water articulates rapid state changes in the liquid medium.

Toxic archive on the edge of ownership

RN: 'Walking into the flooded Dam' is a kind of provocation into thinking about movement trajectories when 'walking': into, away from, alongside, with, on, in or through. How did you feel walking into a flooded dam? Can we think of walking into a space that is flooded as a way to unflood oneself? The act of letting go and taking on coincide. The gesture of you walking in water is reminiscent of the iconic spiritual gestures of people walking on water. What would it be like if the dam had no water?

NB: Many of my imaged gestures are prompted by a practical action or urgent experiment that becomes creative or symbolic in the making. I think about the river as a collaborating force and so the actions must be earnest and necessary.

'Can we think of walking into a space that is flooded as a way to unflood oneself?' – I love this provocation. Particularly because it acknowledges the watery nature of our bodies, that we may become flooded, and unflooding or releasing into water is an act of catharsis. This reminds me of the weightless pleasure of swimming, of being tuned into one's own watery-ness in submersion.

The image of walking into the Vaal Dam (Figure 7.8) does have the potential to seem like the body is hovering, rather than submerging or sinking. I link this to your prompt to think of the Dam without water. The Dam without water as a speculative projection might encourage visions of emptiness, of a vacuum, and may evoke a sense of anxiety about surviving without this resource. But I also consider the Dam before the water, when the area was Tswana grazing land through which a wide, seasonal brown river flowed. The Dam's emptying may expose a past terrain and history that has been erased or levelled by the water's surface.

RN: Abri, in *Ridder Thirst* I enjoy the flower-shaped cut-outs that briefly appear. They remind me of the times growing up when we would play with magazines and cut people out, and then go to the luxury home magazines and slice lines into the beds, kitchens, couches, etc., and slide those cut-out people in, pretending to be that person, living in that mansion. In many ways it's make-believe, fantastical, a desire. There's an active embodying, moving between being oneself and being this cut-out figure, simultaneously, the real and the very real. You become the figure that you cut out, and the cut-out becomes you. There's also a form of agency, in that you cut-out parts of an existing image that you want and make another – curated, imagined, controlled. How do you work through your process of collaging? Where do the images come from? How do you cut, paste, remove, re-member?

AdS: Your recollection Refiloe touches on questions collage raise: of surrogacy, fantasy and class. Collage is ghostly: along with what you see, there is what is no longer there – the occluded image. One becomes reminded that photography is a partial reality. In my work collage is inhabited as a form of haunting, where dismembered fragments become performed.

In *Ridder Thirst* there are numerous cut-outs, mostly motion-tracked over the four queer students performing in the work. Later cut-outs veil my face, and sprout upon the flautist's crown. Like camouflage, the cut-outs appear in the shape of oak and vine leaves, as well as grape clusters, forms of settler-colonial botany and agriculture along the Eerste River that conjure the cornucopia of land, and extractions from it. I position them heraldically, recalling university insignia at the time. As the video progresses, these overlays become increasingly tattered. In the artificial riverbank scene, they are rendered in – 'downloaded' into – the river as physical print-outs. Throughout, the cut-outs function to punctuate the narration, and derive from many sources relating to Stellenbosch: male student residence archives at Stellenbosch University, the *Die Matie* student newspaper, the advertising of the student clothing brand Stellies from the photobooks of German-Namibian ethnographic photographer Alice Mertens – who was the first tertiary tutor of the lens in South Africa, in relation to whom this work emerges – and finally, artworks by Namibian-South African queer artist Hentie van der Merwe, who taught me in my undergraduate degree at Stellenbosch. Ultimately, the cut-outs perform glitches

Figure 7.9 *The confluence of the Vaal and the Orange Rivers at Douglas, Northern Cape in 1997 (sourced from National Geomatics Management Services, Department of Agriculture, Land Reform and Rural Development)*

and leaks, baring the violent desires – and toxic embodiments – underpinning these representations of place in their accumulation.

AdS: Nina, how does the confluence of the Orange and Vaal Rivers affect your treatment of each? What do you anticipate this meeting holds for your future work?

NB: On visiting the confluence of the Vaal River and the Orange River outside of Douglas, in the Northern Cape, I imagined each trajectory prior to meeting. There are myriads of dams – Mohale, Katse, Woodstock, Grootdraai, Sterkfontein, Vaal, Bloemhof, Gariep, Vanderkloof – that hold each flow at different moments. Many cities drink from each dam's reserve and flush their treated or raw sewerage and industrial pollution into the depths that are carried downstream to the point of connection. The Vaal River is unnervingly blue and clear at the confluence, and the Orange is murky brown, visibly carrying particulate matter. In their coagulating, I wondered which colour and clarity might be infecting which?

The question of colour also brings attention to the name Orange – which alludes to a descriptive understanding while actually referring to the Dutch Royal House of Orange – a colonial reference, rather than a visual one. The nature of the river called 'Orange' is materially different before the confluence, and after it. The moment of mixing – where each water is saturated with the other – is something that I want to think about and develop. The author Joanna Zylinska calls for the 'reterritorialisation' of water:[13] that in considering water in terms of its location, its origin and mouth, we might move beyond the understanding of this medium as a resource, a commodity, and a means of waste-removal and flushing.

Bubble, spit, soak, sift, flood, float: Ask?

NB: I ask water to always be elusive. To only be known collectively by those who live with and from it, who are drawn to it, human and non-human.

AdS: I ask water to be our unit of measure, our clock-theatre-skin-sky.

RN: I ask water to be cold, warmed only by our mouths, our hands, our bodies.

Notes

1   Jamie Linton, *What is Water?: A History of Modern Abstraction* (Vancouver & Toronto: UBC Press, 2010), 8.

2   Olivia Laing, *To the River: A Journey Beneath the Surface* (Edinburgh: Canongate Books, 2017), 6-7.

3   Abri de Swardt, 'Riverwork,' wherewithall, 9 December, 2021, https://wherewithall.co.za/?library.head.167880239318.

4   Abri de Swardt, 'Riverwork.'

5   Abri de Swardt, 'Riverwork.'

6   Matt Edgeworth, *Fluid Pasts: Archaeology of Flow* (London: Bloomsbury, 2011), 21.

7   Edgeworth, *Fluid Pasts*, 21.

8   Astrida Neimanis, *Bodies of Water: Posthuman Feminist Phenomenology* (London: Bloomsbury Publishing, 2017), 41.

9   Modikwe Dikobe, *Dispossessed* (Johannesburg: Ravan Press, 1983), 38.

10   Natalie Diaz, *Postcolonial Love Poem* (Minnesota: Greywolf Press, 2020), 74.

11   Phillip Bonner & Noor Nieftagodien, *Alexandra: A History* (Johannesburg: Wits University Press, 2008), 286-293.

12   'The New King James Version, Psalm 66: 12,' Biblia, January 30, 2022, https://biblia.com/bible/nkjv/psalm/66/12.

13   Joanna Zylinska, 'Hydromedia: From Water Literacy to the Ethics of ' in Melodie Jue and Rafico Ruiz (eds), *Saturation: An Elemental Politics* (Durham & London: Duke University Press 2021), 45.

8 Radiation and rapture: Images of healing and pollution in the Jukskei River

Landi Raubenheimer

In this chapter I consider recent photographs of the Jukskei River by Gulshan Khan and Hannelie Coetzee. Working during the onset of the COVID-19 pandemic in 2020, they capture the contradictory qualities of the river by focusing on its material qualities which highlight urban decay and pollution, and simultaneously evoke its healing qualities in spell-binding images. Their work also reveals other qualities of this river which allude to layers of invisibility; while for some the river is a holy site, it is frequently thought to be an eyesore to be put out of sight of the developed 'world class' city of Johannesburg. While research foregrounds how townships and informal settlements contribute to pollution, more insidious sources of pollution are found below ground in the heart of the developed city, where the eye of the river is piped into stormwater and sewage systems.

Introduction

Setting out to discover more about the elusive Jukskei River at the outset of writing this chapter, I encountered the unsurprising fact that it is not only the river's origin that is murky and difficult to pinpoint, but images of this river are equally scarce. I have been interested in the landscapes and waterscapes of Johannesburg for some time, along with the mining industry that left such indelible scars in these places. Photographs of bodies of water polluted by acid mine drainage are more common than images of the Jukskei River; there are photographs by Mark Lewis, Jason Larkin, Eva-Lotta Jansson, and even Edward Burtynsky, who have all explored the aesthetic qualities of these toxic landscapes around the greater Johannesburg area. The Klip river has also received more attention that the Jukskei. Photographers like Santu Mofokeng have captured that river, which is polluted by mine waste, and it appears in countless photographs of religious healing ceremonies by documentary photographers.

The general dearth of representations of the Jukskei River is probably partly why the myth persists that Johannesburg is one of the few large cities in the world that was not built on or alongside a river.[1] In fact there are several rivers that flow through the city: the Jukskei, which flows north and joins the Crocodile River, and the Klip River which flows south and joins the Vaal River.[2]

In this chapter I consider recent photographs of the Jukskei River by two female practitioners: Gulshan Khan and Hannelie Coetzee. Khan's work as award winning documentary photographer appears in publications such as *National Geographic* and Coetzee's work entitled *Finding the eye of Jukskei River beneath Joburg* was exhibited online in the CURE exhibition hosted by the University of Johannesburg Gallery with guest curator Johan Myburgh. Both portray the contradictory qualities of the river by focusing on its material qualities which point to urban decay and pollution, and by simultaneously evoking its healing qualities. What is more, these photographs may prompt us to consider the role of race and class in how particular environmental problems are foregrounded or disregarded by citizens and authorities alike. Pollution linked to informal settlements and poorer income communities along the river appear in more representations than the pollution which originates from the city's sewerage systems, implicating middle-class citizens. The developed city's role in this pollution is harder to see.

While questions of environment are top of mind in the Anthropocene moment we are in (an era where humans have shaped the natural world for the worse), it seems urgent to remember that geopolitics (and hydropolitics, the social relations shaped by bodies of water) should be included in environmentalist debates. Decolonial scholarship (seeking to undo some of the influence of colonisation in countries where colonialism has ended) and even intersectional approaches (where scholars consider the inequalities that linger in society, based on people's race, class or gender) can bring geographically located concerns to bear in such research. Below I do not engage with these fields in depth, but take inspiration from them in considering how race and class, in particular, shape the visibility of the river and its perceived problems. There are layers of invisibility to the Jukskei. Parts of it are out of sight geographically, running alongside informal urban spaces, and continue to be thought of as unsightly, while its relationship to the developed city is literally buried below concrete and often remains unacknowledged. My approach in examining the visibility and invisibility of the river is also indebted to recent research making use of hydrocolonial views of the city, as explored by various scholars in Isabel Hofmeyr, Sarah Nutall and Charne Lavery's recent special issue in *Interventions* entitled 'Reading for Water'[3] Such views consider the relationships between colonialism and bodies of water, and demonstrate that control over water as resource can be linked to unequal power relations in South Africa's history.

Spiritual waters: A new nature

Khan photographed the Jukskei River over several years. One of the most evocative is her photograph of a man she refers to only by his first name: Listen.[4] He kneels as if struck down, on the nearest bank of the river, close to Alexandra, the large township nestled between the affluent area of Sandton and industrial areas to the north, west and east. Listen is depicted in the early morning, with rays of the sun peeking out above foliage and greenery on the far riverbank. To the left of him there is a large sewage duct. He kneels on top of construction waste and behind him there are islands of rubble, with drenched pieces of fabric and plastic draped over broken tree trunks and branches. Under the sewage duct the water gushes out energetically. Listen wears a makeshift garment out of fabric that looks like it was once white and covers his eyes with his left hand. The photograph, which Khan posted on her

Instagram account on 10 April 2020, is accompanied by a short narrative, where she explains that Listen belongs to the Holy Ghost Zion Church, and that during early lockdown, enforced when the pandemic broke out, gatherings of such churches were illegal. Listen therefore prays for a cure for the virus on his own. One presumes from the heart-breaking narrative that he has family members who depend on him to provide for them. Listen has no work, however, as the informal labour sector could not sustain employment opportunities during this time.

What is striking about the image and the narrative beyond the human suffering depicted, is the proximity of nature. Listen told Khan that he likes to pray alone by the river, because it allows him to connect to nature. Looking at the image, the aspects of nature present in the scene appear adulterated, however, indicating that there is more at stake here than Listen's personal story. This is not a pristine image, and it recalls comparable images of religious dedication in Gauteng's urban outskirts. In 2008, Mikhael Subotzky and Patrick Waterhouse photographed men praying on a hillock overlooking Ponte City, the infamous skyscraper that has degenerated into an urban slum several times in its post-apartheid lifetime.[5] The three men they depict are also making the most of the green spaces they can find in the inner city, but their idyllic scene, like Khan's, is punctuated by bits of rubbish. Despite this, their eyes are closed in prayer, like Listen's, and they are kneeling on the grass. One pair of white loafers is neatly placed off to the left, while behind them a pile of rubble echoes the foreboding tone of the grey skies. This image resembles many other images of praying churchgoers which local documentary photographers have often been fascinated by. It also captures the Johannesburg skyline, complete with both its landmark sky piercers: Ponte and the Hillbrow Tower. As in Khan's photograph, there is a close relationship between religious devotion and nature, although this too is urbanised, adulterated and polluted nature.

The so-called Zionists (a term which encapsulates more than 6 000 denominations derived from John Alexander Dowie's Protestant church in Zion, Illinois) have been photographed for a long time in greater Johannesburg.[6] Anthropologist Martin West amassed a substantial archive of photographs of their practices around Soweto in the 1970s, now housed in an archive at the University of Cape Town. Ruth Motau captured images of baptisms in the Klip river close to Soweto in the 1990s, and Santu Mofokeng also captured spiritual cleansing in the Klip river in the 2000s. Unlike West's and Motau's photographs, which focus on subjects emerging ecstatically from dazzling waters, Mofokeng's colour photographs foreground pollution, like Khan's photograph of Listen on the banks of the Jukskei. In Mofokeng's image the pollution has turned the water and banks unnatural shades of ochre and bright orange. The title of one photograph describes the water as 'radiant' – implying that they are perhaps more radioactive than salvation-bearing or holy.

Delwyn Verasamy's recent photographs of the Klipspruit also portray a disquieting scene; a devotee looks out over murky waters topped with strangely white foam, accompanying an article on the polluted tributary of the Klip river's dubious capacity as holy site.[7] The Pentecostal branches of Zion practice immersion healings in the rivers around South Africa, and many such ceremonies take place in the Klip river,[8] but they also take place along the Braamfontein Spruit, a tributary of the Jukskei, and no doubt other parts of that river. The abundance of photography of such immersions in South African documentary photography indicates how water itself is understood in the Southern African context. As Hofmeyr, Nuttall and Lavery suggest, in the post-colonial context of South Africa, water can be interpreted in relation to the local spiritualities associated with bodies of water. They refer to this as 'Multi-Spirited Water.'[9] It is more than just a resource, but may be seen as an 'inspirited and spiritual substance,' which is also associated with healing.[10]

Khan's photograph of Listen captures the 'inspirited' qualities of the Jukskei in this way too. As in Subotzky and Waterhouse's image, there is a pastoral quality to her photograph (reminding one of pastures where animals are herded). The atmospheric light of early morning lends a glow to everything in the image, and if one did not look closely, this might look like a scene of harmony and devotion. The truth is more muddled, as these images of religious devotion are set in 'spoiled' idyllic landscapes. These post-industrial landscapes have borne the brunt of urbanisation and industry. As such these photographs are uncomfortably contradictory. They are beautiful and aesthetically, even spiritually, charged, yet they evoke the grief and anxiety associated with the Anthropocene era and environmental crises brought on by pollution of all kinds. They also bring to mind the unequal geopolitics of the city which mark these sites as neglected by government attention, however. Zion and its practices is predominantly observed by black South Africans.[11] These portrayals are associated with spaces characterised by informality; the resort of citizens that were historically forced to live outside the city in townships and informal settlements.[12] In Khan's photograph the banks of the Jukskei next to Alexandra, and in Subotzky and Waterhouse's image the hillock next to Hillbrow (an area known for its highjacked buildings), communicate a sense of informal use of space, as worshippers claim pockets of nature for their practices. Informality persists in Johannesburg as a form of urbanity that evokes colonial and apartheid urban planning. Views of nature as unspoilt align with colonial views of urban planning, and informality fundamentally contradicts such interpretations in its associations with poverty, disorder and waste, which are clearly articulated in these photographs.

The Jukskei River has not always appeared as it does now. Like many other parts of the country, it was also once part of the 'unspoilt nature' that colonial representations constructed.[13] J.H. Pierneef, one of the most well-known of South Africa's landscape painters, painted it in his characteristic style.[14] While his landscape does have the browns and dusty teals so characteristic of Johannesburg winters, the scene nevertheless looks so far from Khan's Jukskei that it seems unbelievable it is the same body of water. Pierneef's river is portrayed snaking its way through an unblemished landscape. There are no signs of human activity, and no signs of humans either. Pierneef is known for his pristine paintings of South Africa's landscapes and his omission of human influence on the land has been interpreted as presenting a colonial view of the interior as idle land; ripe for development and enterprise. The absence of humans is seen as a colonial fantasy, painting the land as *terra nullius*; an unclaimed and empty paradise offered to colonial settlers.[15] Tom Scanlan, exploring colonial views on land and the history of how waste was regarded, refers to 17th-century English thinker John Locke, who expresses colonial and imperialist ideas of land and property rights.[16] Like the colonial notion of the 'white man's burden,' Locke sees it as a God-given duty for humans to work on and develop the land to make it productive and conducive to more life. There is a moralising tone to such thinking, which sees idleness as impious and even sinful.[17] When such a colonial reading of the landscape is extended to its bodies of water, it is clear that water too was seen as a resource without a pre-colonial history and was understood to be available to work for imperial and apartheid enterprise. In Pierneef's painting the Jukskei appears as empty as the landscape, and as ripe for human enterprise.[18]

In stark contrast to the empty body of water in Pierneef's painting, another of Khan's photographs, taken earlier in 2018, documents plastic pollution in the Jukskei River, and is glittering and brimming with waste (see figure 8.1). Khan portrays the river in a visually sumptuous way, despite the fact that plastic pollution is so toxic. The focal point of the image is two 2-litre bottles floating side by side, with sticky brown bubbles floating next to them in viscous dark water. In the foreground there is polystyrene packaging used in fast food restaurants. The image has extremely

Figure 8.1 *Gulshan Khan, Plastic and other waste litter the banks of the Jukskei River which runs through the Alexandra Township in Johannesburg on June 3, 2018. Image courtesy of the artist*

shallow depth of field (the background is out of focus), with shimmering bokeh (blurring effects of the camera lens being out of focus) in the fore-and background, where the pollution fades into the river.

This image is unique in that it does not portray the river as a water body in a landscape as Pierneef does, but as a still life in the tradition of *nature morte* or vanitas. Renaissance-era paintings of still lifes such as flowers and insects, or platters of food, served to remind viewers that life is finite, and that they should therefore live a pious life to deserve an afterlife in heaven. In Khan's photograph, aside from the water, however, there is little that was ever alive, and the image is a stark reminder of mass plastic production in post-capitalist society. In vanitas paintings one would predominantly see nature's abundance, with some morbid reminders of the cycle of life and death included, such as flowers with insects like flies, or platters of raw meat and dairy, with flies, maggots and some gruesome elements included such as blood, intestines or organ meats. Sometimes a human skull or a candle would indicate the swift arrow of time.[19] Here there is no time though, and Khan's still life reminds one more of the photorealistic still lifes by feminist painters in the 1970s, such as Audrey Flack. What does this image say, beyond the obvious, however? Photographs like these remind one that Johannesburg is haunted by more than its dark political past, but also by the industry that founded it in the first place. In Johannesburg, remembering industry always seem to be second on the agenda, as human suffering in the wake of apartheid grows more acute. Khan's images are reminders of the cycle and life and death that humans are impacting in how they live alongside the Jukskei but are also reminders that Johannesburg needs to reconcile its industrial past as much as its political past.

Khan's photographs gesture to the environmental questions that are arising in post-industrial cities, and in her photographs of the Jukskei one might go so far as to say that 'nature' seems to be completely inseparable from human influence. As the city is evolving beyond its colonial and apartheid past, it is also leaving behind colonial notions of unspoilt nature. Scholars writing about post-industrial landscapes marked by pollution and decay in the global context have considered the Anthropocene as the 'new nature,' arguing that human contact with nature is taking on new configurations.[20] In other words, we may begin to see rivers as sites of both pollution and of healing; a contradictory state of affairs which characterises Khan's striking photographs. Khan accordingly reconfigures western art conventions for depicting nature in these two images. She presents a post-industrial pastoral landscape where a devotee prays for healing amidst pollution and purity alike, as well as an already-dead still life glittering with plastic.

Out of sight, out of mind

Khan's photographs raise questions about the meaning of waste in African cities. Along with religious practices, informal waste removal has fascinated documentary photographers in Johannesburg. Mark Lewis' photographs of waste recyclers, in a 2015 publication and subsequently in a book written with Tanya Zack, and Khan's portrayals of the Jukskei River share many of the same qualities.[21] Both photographers' work have a dark, saturated palette, with high contrast in their images. This gives the images an aesthetic quality; they are beautiful to look at and satisfyingly dramatic. Both make use of natural light elements to highlight human actors in dystopian settings. Although both critique Johannesburg's socio-economic inequality, one might also bear in mind that both photographers' work could glamourise aspects of the lives of Johannesburg's poor to some extent. But these photographs share another quality: they connect the dots between waste and informality, an association often based on how informality is regarded in Johannesburg in both popular and urban planning discourse. Along with drawing attention to the post-industrial character of Johannesburg, Khan's photographs highlight a hidden quality of the Jukskei River; while it is polluted through and through, a lot of this pollution is attributed to its proximity to the township of Alexandra. Its portrayal here reminds one that townships (or informal spaces) are still associated with dysfunction in western urban planning agendas. From a hydro-colonial point of view, images of a polluted Jukskei reinforce colonial associations between waste and townships.[22]

The Jukskei River has been widely studied in relation to its pollution. Much of this is associated with townships and informal settlements that are situated along its banks, such as Alexandra. In 2001 the Alexandra Renewal Project was undertaken to upgrade infrastructure in the township. Despite the project making progress, in 2011, Candice Landie's[23] article warned that water infrastructure in the area was in danger of collapse due a backlog in maintenance, and that in the upgraded parts of the township there were still blocked stormwater drains, with leaking pipes causing overflow into the streets. At the time the upgrades that were planned included addressing the river in general, along with stormwater systems and ablution facilities. However, from current research, it seems that not much has been achieved in these areas.

In their recent study, Nzalalemba Serge Kubanza, Ruwadzano Mtshika and Charles Gimba Magha argue that waste pollution in the Jukskei River remains, in part, due to an acute problem in solid waste management in the township. They found that many residents deposit waste in the river among other makeshift solutions, because waste removal in the area is erratic and insufficient.[24] The outsourcing of services to the company Pikitup also seems to result in waste removal being focused on the formal residential areas of the city such as the suburbs, and the Alexandra community and the local authorities cannot cope with the resulting scale of the problem, which Kubanza Mtshika and Magha describe as 'huge'.[25] In 2017, a study found flame retardants used in electronics and furnishings in exceptionally high levels near an informal settlement on the river's banks in Eastgate.[26] The study is disparaging of townships' and informal settlements' effects on the river and speculates that high consumption of cheap electronics in informal settlements could be the cause of this pollution. Earlier, in a 2007 report to the Water Research Commission,[27] Nemai Consulting found that the major source of pollution in the Jukskei River was fecal pollution, mostly from Alexandra township. They do acknowledge that this is worsened by the superimposition of the sewage system with the stormwater system in the CBD, a point I return to later.

Informal spaces are often associated with the term 'waste,' which is in western urban planning contexts understood in a broad sense as 'something that is to be separated, removed or which has become devalued.'[28] Waste in this sense relates to supposed wasted space, spaces that are seen as 'wastelands,' as idle spaces or as dangerous spaces. This is because they do not function as (middle class, and in South Africa, predominantly white) society would have them.[29] Objects such as rubbish, garbage or waste are seen as things that have been detached from their social context and function.[30] Maree Pardy argues that within the 'moral economy or urban renewal' there are various kinds of waste: idle bodies, time that is wasted, and the improper use of space (or wasted space).[31] Urban waste and wastelands are seen as akin to wildness in this sense, and the people who live in these spaces are likewise construed as lacking the right to occupy them.

Interpretations like this also pertain to water and water infrastructure. Charne Lavery, writing on Antjie Krog's portrayal of the Vals river in Kroonstad in her memoir *A Change of Tongue*, suggests that wastewater in contemporary South Africa points to the legacy set up by colonial and apartheid urban planning.[32] Plumbing was not developed equally across cities, and townships were disenfranchised when it came to waste removal infrastructure. Louise Bethlehem, in writing about the fictional Johannesburg in Lauren Beukes' *Zoo City*, describes plumbing as a form of 'domesticated water' that is an 'affordance of class privilege.'[33] Images of a polluted Jukskei remind one that there may be a cyclical quality to how townships were historically developed and how they continue to appear in popular discourse, and in urban planning in practice.[34]

As above, so below: The eye of the storm

The Jukskei River does not only run alongside townships, however, but its tributaries (such as the Braamfontein Spruit) also run from the very core of the city, and through some of its most affluent suburbs, such as Craighall Park and Hurlingham. Such residential areas may actually be more culpable in contributing to the river's pollution than Alexandra is, for example. Nemai Consulting's report suggests that formal residential land use is more substantial than informal land use along the river, and contributes substantially to its pollution. They also point out that since the river flows through diverse areas of vastly different socio-economic communities, the waste each of these communities contributes is inherently difficult to quantify. The upper Jukskei suffers mostly from litter (this is the area where Alexandra is situated); very visible in Khan's photographs.[35] It is important to note, however, that other forms of pollution are far less visible than the pollution from informal residential areas such as Alexandra, making its way into the system through stormwater drains that deposit 'organic matter, oils, fuels and detergents' in the CBD, for example.[36]

In a 2021 study, surface water collected from the Victoria Yards, close to Ellis Park and one of the river's eyes, found evidence of high levels of *E. coli*, as well as Lithium, Nickel, Zinc, Lead and Sodium. It concluded that the river is a threat to human health when used for drinking, irrigation or recreation.[37] The study speculates that the superimposition of the sewage system with the stormwater drains in the city could contribute to this pollution, which is exacerbated further downstream in Alexandra. Some of the river's tributaries are more polluted by industrial waste, in turn. River pollution can come from 'point' sources and 'non-point' sources.[38] The latter are more insidious, where the sources are diffuse and difficult to pinpoint. In 2005 a study which surveyed the Jukskei River water quality from the 1980s to 2002 found that in the 1980s inorganic chemical pollution from the mining industry (such as sodium chloride, sulphate, fluoride, nitrate, and orthophosphate) was high, leading to acid mine drainage evident in low water pH.[39] The study found that this pollution was decreasing over time and that the water pH was increasing, pointing to the river recovering from mining pollution. The research could not account for how mining waste got into the Jukskei River system in the first place, however, as the mines should more readily affect the Klip river system to the south of the city. The abandoned mines around Johannesburg may therefore still be contributing pollution to tributaries of the Jukskei River as non-point sources of pollution.

While visible pollution is associated with informal settlements and the existing image these areas have as spaces of poor waste management, formal residential waste and the mining industry's remnants deceptively appear as if they contribute in less visible ways to the Jukskei River's demise, and this is perhaps because the river is below ground where these sources of pollution affect it. Though lack of infrastructure and service delivery in townships and informal settlements are often blamed for pollution, it is interesting that the developed sewage system in the city itself seems to be problematic in terms of its relationship to the river, not least because it coincides with the very source of the river.

The eye of the Jukskei has been the subject of some investigation over the last few years in popular media, and even appears in artistic explorations of the city. Along with author Sean Christie and some employees of the Johannesburg Roads Agency, eco-feminist artist Hannelie Coetzee was interested in the location of one of the river's eyes in 2020, hunting for it as the COVID pandemic broke out in the city.[40] Her visual documentation of this quest portrays something unexpected: not a natural spring bubbling up from an underground source, but a 'piped eye.'[41] On her website she describes the sight as shocking, and the artwork entitled *Finding the eye of the Jukskei River beneath Joburg* conveys just this.

Figure 8.2 *Hannelie Coetzee, still from* Finding the eye of the Jukskei River beneath Joburg[42]

While the water flowing in the still image from the video artwork in Figure 8.2 looks clear, the context is entirely dystopian. A concrete pipe juts out from a decayed and besmirched wall and the clear flows into a polluted culvert (tunnel) below. As in Khan's photographs of the river, there is very little evidence of 'nature.' Despite this, Coetzee refers to Michelangelo Pisteletto's notion of the 'third paradise,' an artificial paradise humans should build to get close to nature.[43] In the image one can see an infinity sign with a third loop, an image she takes from Pisteletto, and which refers to this third paradise. The river as it exists here is no paradise, however. The Jukskei can be understood as an urban river. Parts of it are submerged beneath impenetrable urban surfaces, parts are canalised, affecting its sinuosity (where it has bends) and changing its geomorphology (its shape and form in the landscape). In such rivers water quantity may then also be affected by the urban demands made on rivers, exacerbated by abstractions (taking water from a river, such as to irrigate land), as well as by degrading pipes, illegal water connections and improper use of the water.[44]

What Khan's photographs portray happening above ground is echoed by the sinister picture below the city where the river is thoroughly urbanised. In another one of Coetzee's photographs a curtain of plastic waste hangs from bits of pipe that jut out of the concrete ceiling of the duct. In the margins of the image Coetzee has scrawled some notes connoting the ominous tone of this place: 'onderwêreld,' 'onderstebo,' 'wie se sak hang so onderstebo?'[45] These scribbles evoke an underworld, an 'upside down' place, and she asks whose bags are hanging here, along with a short narrative describing her safety helmet falling into the effluent, which she says she 'thinks' is the Jukskei. The fact that there is sewage here is another indicator that all along the river's course, pollution is being deposited into it, including in the developed parts of the city, though these deposits made below ground are far less conspicuous than the pollution ascribed to informal settlements and townships along the Jukskei's banks.

Coetzee says of the artwork, which consists of a video and four still images, that her hope is that it will bring images of the eye to people who have not seen it. Her initial involvement in the NGO Water for the Future was also an effort towards remedying the current state of the river. This was to bring the clear water of the eye to the surface, and to 'flip the river into a usable stream, to regenerate toxic run off, to relieve the culverts, and prevent flash floods....'[46] Her implication that many have not seen the river's eye indicates its lost presence in the city, and the pollution it suffers is thus also out of sight, transferred to a problem elsewhere – in the townships.

The intersectional Jukskei

Despite the photographs discussed in this chapter appearing quite dystopian, they are all concerned with human relationships with the river. In some ways Listen finding a connection with nature on the river's banks echoes what environmental artists are doing across many different geographical locations. Scholars working in the field of environmental aesthetics are often concerned with how artistic interventions can help rehabilitate post-industrial sites such as abandoned mines.[47] Many argue that one of the most powerful ways in which representation can contribute to current environmental debates is to imagine new ways of understanding places and landscapes, or to be more expansive: nature itself.

Amanda Boetzkes writes along these lines about post-industrial landscapes within the field of environmental aesthetics. She uses the term 'ecotechnological,' which she borrows from Jean Luc Nancy, to describe post-industrial landscapes as entirely shaped by human influence.[48] Such landscapes may be impacted by global warming and other climate crises, by resource management or its lack, but also by efforts of conservation or towards sustainability. In other words, these ecotechnological landscapes are completely shot through with the effects of humanity on them. Perhaps in some ways they are the counterpoint to the colonial fantasy of *terra nullius* (nobody's land), and in other ways the outcome of the imperial drive towards industrialisation. The Jukskei River as an 'urban' river may be thought of along these lines as a post-industrial river or 'waterscape.' These landscapes (or waterscapes, to extend the discussion to bodies of water in post-industrial landscapes) are indicative of a change in the relationship between humans and nature, which is nowhere free from the traces of human impact. In fact, Boetzkes argues that contact between nature and humans will be completely reconfigured in time to come.

Both Khan and Coetzee attempt to make sense of such post-industrial waterscapes. They may be accordingly understood as working from an embodied perspective (they work from the position of their own identities), that shares many traits with environmental art practices in that they cast a light on unacknowledged or invisible spaces, and the problems that require urgent attention. Although these photographs of the river are clearly concerned with the river's health and as such engage with environmental debates in contemporary art, they also highlight one of the most important aspects of environmental approaches to understanding representations of land and water: decolonial perspectives. One cannot consider the environment in a city like Johannesburg, which is so drenched in colonial and apartheid inequalities without considering the geopolitical aspects of the city. Hofmeyr, Nuttall and Lavery refer to Lesley Green's call for scholarship which engages both these areas of study, and in the case of the Jukskei it is paramount.[49] One might go so far as to say that we require not only a decolonial view, but even an intersectional one. The Jukskei is not the same river to everyone living in Johannesburg. It is socially shaped by the race and class (and gender) of those who live alongside or on top of it.[50] These factors impact the visibility of certain versions and parts of the river, ones that are purposely ignored, scapegoated or even completely obscured from view and as such may be thought not to exist.

Notes

1   It even appears in reputable academic sources that I consult in this article, and which I believe are otherwise sound. See Louise Bethlehem's excellent article discussing imagery of water in Lauren Beukes' novel *Zoo City*: 'Hydrocolonial Johannesburg,' *Interventions* 24, no. 3 (2022): 340. See also Anthony Turton, Craig Schultz, Hannes Buckle, Mapule Kgomongoe et al., 'Gold, Scorched Earth and Water: The Hydropolitics of Johannesburg,' *Water Resources Development* 22 no. 2 (2022): 313-335, DOI: 10.1080/07900620600649827.

2   Jasper Knight, 'Transforming the Physical Geography of a City: An Example of Johannesburg, South Africa.' in *Urban Geomorphology*, ed. Casey D. Allen Mary J. Thornbush. Amsterdam: Elsevier, 2018. 129-147; Innocent Makwela, 'Assessing the role of wetlands in improving the aquatic health of the Braamfontein Spruit Catchment in Johannesburg, Gauteng.' University of Johannesburg, Master's dissertation (2022): 25.

3   Isabel Hofmeyr, Sarah Nuttall, and Charne Lavery, 'Reading for Water,' *Interventions* 24, no. 3 (2022): 303-322, DOI: 10.1080/1369801X.2021.2015711. They (pg. 309) describe the term as including critical approaches to colonisation as it was carried out by water (often by seafaring nations), and it could also include the colonisation of water itself as a resource along with land. Water could furthermore be seen along the lines of colonial territory to be defended: colonies could exist on water, or islands could be colonised, and the notion of water could carry colonial associations of being a resource for colonial enterprise. See also Isabel Hofmeyr, 'Imperialism Above and Below the Water Line: Making Space Up (and Down) in a Colonial Port City.' *Interventions* 22, no. 8 (2020): 1032–1044. doi: 10.1080/1369801X.2019.1659172, and Isabel Hofmeyr, *Dockside Reading: Hydrocolonialism and the Custom House* (Durham: Duke University Press, 2022).

4   This photograph may be viewed on Khan's Instagram profile at
    https://www.instagram.com/p/B-zvq9aJPY1/.

5   This immediately places the photograph somewhere in Berea, a part of the inner city now
    synonymous with crime, poverty and urban decay. Refer to Svea Josephy, 'Acropolis now:
    "Ponte City" as "portrait of a city."' *Thesis Eleven* 141, no. 1 (2019): 67-85.

6   Refer to Joel Cabrita's book *The People's Zion: Southern Africa, the United States, and a
    Transatlantic Faith-Healing Movement* (Harvard University Press, Belknap Press, 2018) as
    well as Greg Marinovich's 'Shembe: A Zulu Church,' *Transition*, No. 125, Religion (2018),
    pp. 34-41, and Paul Weinberg's 'Reflections on the making of the AmaBandla Ama-Afrika
    Exhibition 2011-2012: Martin West's Soweto photographs,' *Kronos* 38 (2012): 82-105 on the
    practices associated with Zion, and its photography.

7   Sheree Bega, 'Klip River's "holy water" a danger,' *Mail & Guardian*, August 15, 2021,
    https://mg.co.za/environment/2021-08-15-klip-rivers-holy-water-a-danger/.

8   Joel Cabrita, *The People's Zion*, 1-24.

9   Hofmeyr, Nuttall, and Lavery, 'Reading for Water,' 313.

10 Lazarus Lebeloane and Mokhele Madise, 'The use of different types of water in the Zion
    Christian Church,' *Studia Historiae Ecclesiasticae* XXXII no. 2 (2006): 143-152.

11 Joel Cabrita, *The People's Zion*, 20.

12 Townships and informal settlements are not the same thing, as the former typically indicates
    a development underpinned by urban planning, while informal settlements are not planned
    or built by authorities, but by citizens themselves. In many cases, however, they are associated
    with each other. Townships historically often did not provide sufficient housing in areas
    where populations were underestimated, such as in early Orlando (now Soweto), leading
    to informal occupation of land. Refer to Noor Nieftagodien and Sally Gaule, *Orlando West,
    Soweto: An Illustrated History*. (Johannesburg: Wits University Press, 2012), 1-9.

13 Jeremy Foster 'Land of contrasts' or 'home we have always known'?: The SAR&H and the
    imaginary geography of white South African nationhood, 1910-1930,' *Journal of Southern
    African Studies* 29 no. 3 (2003): 657-680.

14 The painting, which does not appear to be dated, appears on Aspire Art's website:
    https://www.aspireart.net/auction/lot/8-jacobus-hendrik-pierneef-south-africa-1886-
    1957/?lot=12&sd=1.

15 Foster, 'Land,' 657-680; Lize van Robbroeck, 'Afrikaner nationalism and other settler
    imaginaries at the 1936 Empire exhibition,' in *Troubling Images: Visual Culture and the
    Politics of Afrikaner Nationalism*, ed. Federico Freschi, Brenda Schmahmann, and Lize van
    Robbroeck (Johannesburg: Wits University Press, 2019), 43-65.

16 Tom Scanlan, *On Garbage* (London: Reaktion Books, 2005), 13-55.

17 Scanlan, *On Garbage*, 22-26.

18 Foster, 'Land,' 657-680.

19 See Harry Berger Jr.'s book *Caterpillage: Reflections on Seventeenth-Century Dutch Still
    Life Painting* (New York: Fordham University Press, 2011), 1-3, for a brief discussion of
    conventional iconographic interpretations of the genre, and for an alternative reading of the
    complexity of symbolism associated with such paintings.

20 Amanda Boetzkes, 'Waste and the sublime landscape,' *Canadian Art Review*: Landscape, Cultural Spaces, Ecology 35, no. 1 (2010): 22-31; Megan L. E. Kirkwood, 'Land as natural resource: representations of mining in contemporary South African landscape photography,' *Photography and Culture* 12, no. 4 (2019): 429-452.

21 Mark Lewis has been interested in the informal waste recyclers working in the city; see Lewis, and Tanya Zack, *Good Riddance* (Johannesburg: Fourthwall Books, 2015); Tanya Zack and Mark Lewis, *Wake up, this is Joburg* (Durham: Duke University Press, 2023). The recyclers also appear in the music video for pop musician Skrillex's *Raga Bomb*, and in a series Khan made in 2018 entitled *Life in Plastic*.

22 One of the first townships in the country, Langa in Cape Town, was, for example, in part created to separate the slave population from residents after an outbreak of the plague. Regarding separating out unhygienic spaces from those that had to remain hygienic and healthy, see Richard de Satgé and Vanessa Watson, *Urban Planning in the Global South. Conflicting Rationalities in Contested Urban Space* (Cham: Palgrave Macmillan, 2018): 71-72.

23 Candice Landie, 'Ageing infrastructure, population growth. The effect on South Africa's water systems.' *IMIESA* (July 2011): 60-62.

24 Nzalalemba, Serge Kubanza, Ruwadzano Matsika, and Charles Gimba Magha, 'Exploring the role of local authorities and community participation in solid waste management in sub-Saharan Africa: a study of Alexandra, Johannesburg, South Africa.' *Local Environment* 27, no. 2 (2022): 207-208. DOI: 10.1080/13549839.2021.2010186.

25 Kubanza, Matsika, and Magha, 'Exploring the role,' 201.

26 Adegbenro Peter Daso and Okechukwu Jonathan Okonkwo, 'Evidence of gross contamination of surface water from Jukskei River, South Africa with hexabromocyclododecane (HBCDD) and tetrabromobisphenol A (TBBPA) flame retardants.' Conference paper May 2017. https://www.researchgate.net/publication/319968229.

27 Nemai Consulting, 'Guideline to develop a sustainable urban river management plan.' Report to the Water Research Commission, December 2007, 16-18.

28 Scanlan, *On Garbage*, 10.

29 Scanlan, *On Garbage*, 10.

30 Tim Edensor, *Industrial Ruins. Space, Aesthetics, Materiality* (Oxford: Berg, 2005); Walter Moser, The acculturation of waste, in *Waste-site Stories: the Recycling of Memory*, ed. Brian Neville and Johanne Villeneuve (Albany: State University of New York Press, 2002): 85-105.

31 Pardy, 'A Waste of Space: Bodies, Time and Urban Renewal,' *M/C Journal* 13, no. 4 (2010): sp, https://doi.org/10.5204/mcj.275.

32 Lavery, 'Postcolonial Plumbing,' *Interventions* 24, no. 3 (2022): 357, DOI:10.1080/136980 1X.2021.2015707.

33 Bethlehem, 'Hydrocolonial,' 346.

34 Rob Shields, writing about marginalised spaces in *Places on the Margin. Alternative Geographies of Modernity* (London: Routledge, 1991), argues that over time a 'place-image' can evolve, shaped in part by popular discourse and planning discourse, by how space is used by inhabitants, its social reputation and also through planning discourse and practice. For more on township planning and its history in the country see Richard de Satgé and

Vanessa Watson, *Urban Planning in the Global South: Conflicting Rationalities in Contested Urban Space* (Cham: Palgrave Macmillan, 2018).

35 Nemai Consulting, 'Guideline', 113.

36 Nemai Consulting, 'Guideline', 27.

37 Kousar Banu Hoorzook, Anton Pieterse, Lee Heine, Tobias George Barnard, and Nickey Janse van Rensburg, 'Soul of the Jukskei River: The Extent of Bacterial Contamination in the Jukskei River in Gauteng Province, South Africa', *International Journal of Environmental Research and Public Health* 18 (2021) 8537. https://doi.org/10.3390ijerph18168537.

38 Nemai Consulting, 105.

39 Jan, M Huizenga, and J. T. Harmse, 'Geological and anthropogenic influences on the inorganic water chemistry of the Jukskei River, Gauteng, South Africa', *South African Journal of Geology* 108 (2005): 439-447.

40 Christie, 'Searching for the soul of the Jukskei', *Mail & Guardian*, January 2, 2014, https://mg.co.za/article/2014-01-02-searching-for-the-soul-of-the-jukskei/.

41 Hannelie Coetzee, '2020 Finding the eye of Jukskei River beneath Joburg', accessed June 9, 2023, https://www.hanneliecoetzee.com/portfolios/2020-finding-the-eye-of-jukskei-river-beneath-joburg/.

42 See https://www.hanneliecoetzee.com/portfolios/2020-finding-the-eye-of-jukskei-river-beneath-joburg/. Image courtesy of the artist.

43 Coetzee, '2020 Finding'.

44 Nemai Consulting, 2007, 6-9.

45 Coetzee, '2020 Finding'.

46 Coetzee, '2020 Finding'.

47 Jonathan Maskitt, ' "Line of wreckage": towards a postindustrial environmental aesthetic', *Ethics, Place and Environment* 10, no. 3 (2007): 323-337. DOI: 10.1080/13668790701586309; Jennifer Peeples, 'Toxic sublime: imaging contaminated landscapes', *Environmental Communication* 5, no. 4 (2011): 373-392.

48 Boetzkes, 2010, 29.

49 Hofmeyr et al., 2022, 304.

50 Though I have focused more on race and class in the configuration of informal settlements and developed parts of the city as counterpoints of visibility and invisibility in the Jukskei's image and its pollution, using an intersectional approach one could also consider gender in relation to the river's portrayal. Both of the practitioners I discussed here are women, and as such their work may also be investigated through the lens of eco-feminist discourse in the arts.

9 Community engagement at the Jukskei source: A photo essay

Lungile Hlatshwayo

Introduction

The Jukskei River, a vital waterway in Johannesburg, South Africa, has been the focus of community engagement efforts aimed at revitalising its surrounding environment and fostering local participation. This photo essay by Lungile Hlatshwayo encapsulates the dynamic and multifaceted approach to community engagement at the Jukskei River. Through walking tours, cultural ceremonies, youth involvement, scientific data collection, and collaborative cleanup efforts, the local community has been getting involved in the rejuvenation of their natural surroundings.

Figure 9.1 *A walking tour led by Grant Ngcobo from Dlala Nje in August, 2021 shows local community members from Bertrams at the river at the Victoria Yards culvert. The walking tour was co-created by Water for the Future and Dlala Nje*

Figure 9.2 *A group of women from the local Bertrams community look at the Jukskei headwaters in the culvert near Lang Street, Lorentzville*

Figure 9.3 *On World Water Monitoring Day in September, 2021, visitors to Victoria Yards were invited to come and see the ongoing rejuvenation work at the culvert*

Figure 9.4 *A full moon healing ceremony by the group Exotically Divine, convened for meditation and discussion near artist Io Makandal's land artwork* Extant Rewilding, *2019-ongoing as part of her MAFA (Wits) practical research*

Figure 9.5 *Children from the community were invited to take part in a collaborative art project about water sustainability in August, 2019. Here they are setting off on a 'droplet treasure hunt'*

Figure 9.6 *One of the children searches for a clue in the droplet treasure hunt, near the Jukskei daylight point near Snake Road*

Figure 9.7 *Community children help Victoria Yards urban farmer Siyabonga Nlangamandla to plant a tree in the EcoSeat designed by Hannelie Coetzee in dialogue with the community. The EcoSeat is an example of a sustainable urban drainage system*

Figure 9.8 *After alien invasive trees are removed from the culvert, one of the ways the wood is repurposed is into aesthetic woven fencing*

Figure 9.9 *The weather station, funded by Campbell Scientific, is located at the Victoria Yards culvert. Along with a Isco sampler sponsored by aquatic ecologist Dr Liz Day in the water at the same location, scientific data is collected*

Figure 9.10 *Local community members from Bertrams assisting with a citizen science data collection activity regarding different types of waste in the area, in Thames Street*

Figure 9.11 *A teenage reclaimer transports her recyclable goods past the Jukskei daylight point. Local businesses have supported recycling and reclaimer self-employment in Bertrams*

COMMUNITY ENGAGEMENT AT THE JUKSKEI SOURCE

Figure 9.12 *An activation took place at the daylight point to invite the community to share ideas about how to clean up the formerly heavily polluted site*

Figure 9.13 *A collaborative effort involving community members who are part of the President Stimulus Fund, Industrial Development Corporation, Johannesburg Inner City Partnership project and local business cleaned up the daylight point on Thames Street. It now features a beautiful mosaic created by artists from the nearby Spaza Gallery*

PART 3
RIVER POLITICS

10 Joburg and the sea: A squalid romance

Sean Christie

The City of Johannesburg is both landlocked and water-scarce, yet the presence of the ocean can be strongly felt. To the south of the city centre, the gold mining industry's slime dams resemble coastal dunes. The city also boasts the largest dry port in the world, and the built environment rests on geological formations that were laid down when the area was covered by a prehistoric ocean. In the suburbs to the north of the city, hoteliers and property developers have spent a fortune developing amenities that supposedly resemble paradisal lagoons. Palm trees proliferate in the parking lots of malls and casinos, and flyers for 'beach' parties regularly appear under vehicle windscreen wipers. In this chapter, the author has attempted to catalogue and account for the city's marine ties and references, setting up a contrast between the oceanic fantasies of its residents and the shockingly polluted state of the city's best known river, the Jukskei.

Introduction

Very little about veld-bitten Woodmead Drive suggests water. It is true that the road crosses the Jukskei River, but overgrown banks and creeping business park perimeter fences all but obscure the water on approach. Water has been privatised, occluded. Motorists and pedestrians face estate walls, dealership flags and large billboards: Classic Monday Burger; Granite Warehouse; Fragrance Sale. Most messages fail to catch even the corner of the eye but one, promising the impossible, compels a double take: EXCLUSIVE BEACH LIVING, the words printed above a poor artist impression of a large, sand-fringed pool, topped with red kayaks. The housing estate is named Munyaka (meaning crystal in Venda). A memory stirred, of a press release I was sent in early 2020, announcing the 'launch' of the development. I pulled over next to an advertising trailer and found it in my Gmail: '*We've been absolutely inundated by interested buyers over the past four days…sales totalling R850 million since opening, with a record 555 apartments sold to date,' commented Steve Brookes, founder and CEO of Balwin Properties.*[1]

The selling point?

The largest crystalline lagoon in the southern hemisphere with Crystal Lagoons technology at approx. 7 rugby fields.*[2]

That an island-style amenity of unprecedented proportions will soon shimmer in a flinty crease of the Witwatersrand is truly incredible, yet I was not surprised. Why was I not surprised? For some time now, I have been walking Johannesburg's filthy rivers to better understand the city's relationship with water. My curiosity was piqued in 2010, when a city engineer claimed that the sources of the city's main streams, the Jukskei and the Klip, had been lost under the buildings and tarmacadam of Doornfontein and Newtown respectively. These streams are the beginnings of the region's most important water sources, the Limpopo and the Orange rivers. To have lost the sources of both looked to me (to paraphrase Oscar Wilde) like carelessness and seemed to raise serious questions about the state of river catchment management on the highveld. Over the course of several years, I was able to locate, with the help of engineers working for the Johannesburg Roads Agency, the eyes of both rivers, which decant from small pipes into large subterranean storm water drains. Not long afterwards I spoke to hydrologist Simon Lorenz, who made me wonder if the rediscovery of the river sources was in any way meaningful. Lorenz had recently subjected water samples taken from the Jukskei's daylight point (the point at which the water emerges above ground for the first time) to isotope analysis. He found that the isotopic signature of that water was identical to that of water from the Vaal Dam, more than 100 kilometres to the south of city. In other words, the water flowing in Johannesburg's river channels is not identifying as water from subterranean Johannesburg.

Where, then, does Johannesburg's river water come from?

The mystery was a simple one to unravel. Johannesburg – a mining camp that rapidly grew into a city – was founded on a watershed, and the flow from local water sources was soon insufficient to meet the population's demand.[3] Exactly a century ago, in 1923, the city's water utility (Rand Water) dammed the Vaal River to create the Vaal barrage, 56 kilometres to the south of the city. By the 1930s, demand had again outstripped supply and so the Vaal Dam was built some distance upstream. Today, most of Johannesburg's potable water is pumped from the Vaal Dam, which in turn is fed by three inter-basin water transfer schemes. The largest of these – the Lesotho Highlands Water Project (LHWP) – originates in another country altogether: the Kingdom of Lesotho! The ability to transfer hundreds of millions of cubic metres of water to where it is most needed is the result of immense feats of engineering, both physical and social, yet nearly half of the water supplied to Johannesburg ultimately leaks out of the city's ageing and poorly maintained reticulation and sewerage systems.[4] It leaks out in such volumes that in the dry season, the greater volume of water flowing in certain of Johannesburg's rivers is treated water that has been pumped from afar – this is what Lorenz clocked when he tested the headwaters of the Jukskei.

In 2022, I set out to locate the sources of the potable water that mingles with and subsumes the city's naturally occurring water, a journey that led into the Lesotho highlands, to the source of the Malibamat'so River, which feeds the largest of the LHWP's reservoirs: Katse Dam. Along the way I met engineers who shed light on the little-known histories of the country's inter-basin transfer schemes, and I spent time with communities that have been impacted both by these schemes and by the neglect of river catchments on the South African highveld. I wanted to document these experiences in a book and felt nearly ready to sit down to the task.

Yet, all this time, I had been missing something: the ocean. What can one say about Johannesburg's relationship with the sea? Why does the development of a Seychellois lagoon alongside a river that is little more than an open sewer seem an unsurprising, perhaps even characteristic, Johannesburg juxtaposition? I decided to drive the city in search of answers. First, I wanted to know more about Crystal Lagoons*, a US-based business founded by Chilean biochemist and real estate developer, Fernando Fischmann. In the late 1990s – according to an official company history,[5] Fischmann needed a selling point for a residential development on the inhospitable shoreline of Chile's Central Coast. He had a vast pool dug at the foot of the development, large enough to accommodate a variety of water activities. When the water turned green, Fishman searched the world for a management solution, and finding none developed the proprietary technologies that have made Crystal Lagoons* into a billion-dollar company.

Munyaka was then some months away from completion, but after buying an exclusive Crystal Lagoons* license in 2018, Balwin chose The Blyde housing development outside Tshwane as the location for the first of five planned lagoons. The estate's website carries an uppercase warning: NO DAY VISITORS, and in fact the property's managers recently caught flak (homeowners protested at the gates of their own complex) for imposing a R250 access fee per guest of any resident.

At the Blyde's entrance boom I asked for 'lagoon manager' Ian Nel. I liked him immediately, with his soft manners and former-player-turned-coach looks. 'We opened on the first of March 2018 after a one-year build,' he said, walking directly to the pool, a thing less impressive in reality than it looks in the pictures. Nel had an explanation – 'the recent rains have thrown the chemistry out.' The pool was off-blue, a little milky. 'First time this has happened since we opened,' he said, stopping beside a young man in lifeguard attire, who had in his hands an oversized control device. 'Our pool drone, formally called a bottom cleaner, or suction cart,' said Nel, his eyes on a large dark shape beneath the surface.

Dosing is done from a centre based in Chile, using telemetry, with tweaks done in this physical space by Nel and his team. Chlorine, turbidity, manganese and iron levels are all controlled in this way.

'We use ten times less chlorine than the average home pool. At home you throw in tablets and pray. We have a bit more insight,' said Nel.

Keeping the lagoon in pristine condition is a full-time job.

'If you're not thinking about your wife, you're thinking about the pool. The guys call her Thandi,' Nel said, eliciting a laugh from the pool drone operator, who shouted back,

'Thandi's not happy today.'

By Crystal Lagoons standards this pool is a tiddler – 1.5 ha or about the area of two rugby fields. The biggest is in Egypt, the 12.5 ha Sharm El Sheik development. Still, for a water stressed part of the world, 1.5 ha at an average depth of 2.5 metres equals 35 million litres of water.

'I probably shouldn't have told you that,' said Nel, switching back to safer facts: '21 metres visibility…28 degrees on average in summer…gravity-fed filtration… lifeguards on duty all the time.'

He had exhausted the spiel before the end of our slow walk around the perimeter. Apartment balconies leant over us, and Nel confirmed that poolside residences cost much more than the properties in the tenements marching down the gently sloping terrain, each service road bearing a nautical name. Through a gap between the buildings a large security fence enclosed an area of orange excavated soil, stark against a bright blue sky.

'Crystal Lagoons seems made for the highveld,' I mused. Nel lifted his eyes and squinted. 'High evaporation rate, but *ja, almal wil 'n huisie by die see hê* [Afr. yeah, everyone wants a house by the seaside],' he said, referencing the plaintive Koos Kombuis song about South African middle-class fantasies of a better future, symbolised by ownership of a cottage by the sea, and a 4x4 in the drive.

The anthropologist David McDermott Hughes suggested that in Rhodesia (now Zimbabwe), white settlers, being 'children of the glaciers…appreciated a well-watered, Wordsworthian topography [and] lusted for seas and breaking waves.'[6] Their need for water, Hughes suggests, was satisfied by the development of a hydroelectric dam across the Zambezi river – Lake Kariba. 'Concrete…did the job of ice sheets and gave Rhodesians an inland sea.'[7]

Does the same facet of Euro-African psychology underpin Munyaka, and The Blyde? For guidance, I called on South Africa's greatest living (and alongside Gertrude Jekyll perhaps greatest ever) designer of gardens, Patrick Watson, the man responsible for landscaping of the Sun City complex two hours north of Johannesburg. Sun City's Roaring Lagoon – a wave pool that sends down 2 metre swells every 90 seconds – lies at the heart of a compound of hotels and casinos that are clad in temples and animal statuary. It is a proudly south African hyperreality, supposedly inspired by Sir Henry Rider Haggard's 1885 imperial romance novel, King Solomon's Mines. Watson's home in Greenside is surrounded by a dense forest of its own, although he insists 'there's no plan here, no ideology. I have just planted surplus trees from the jobs I've done.' His clients – some of the richest people on the continent – insist on narrower tastes.

'There's a shift towards wild planting and the indigenous but historically it has been the exotic that people want. The Victorians liked roses. Sol (Kerzner, the developer of The Lost City at Sun City) liked palms. I used to hate palms, but I came to like them,' Watson mumbled, punctuating the sentence with a characteristic 'Why not?' as we set out on a tour of some of his notable Johannesburg gardens.

In 'Indigenous Palms of Southern Africa' (1969), Hein Wicht writes that palms reminded white citizens of 'temperate zones…tall stems, crowned with feathery leaves, automatically suggest[ing] blue skies and freedom…'[8]

Watson reckons they remind wealthy Johannesburg residents of Mozambique, Mauritius and the Seychelles, 'places that are practically owned by South African developers, these days.' The most notable use of palms in Johannesburg is at Montecasino in Fourways, a Tuscany-inspired casino/mall, described by American expatriate blogger Heather Mason as 'a poor man's version of The Venetian Las Vegas, without the canal.'[9]

Watson was phlegmatic as we passed the edifice on Witkoppen Road.

'You build a casino; you plant palm avenues. It's practically a reflex,' he said, although it was the other way around with Sun City.

'Not many people know that the landscape was conceived before the architecture. Sol was a landscaper first and foremost, he knew he wanted forests defined by palms, and everything else followed from that.'

In recent years, Watson and his teams have planted a million indigenous trees and over 20 million indigenous plants ('I mean, why not?') on Steyn City estate, the brainchild of businessman Douw Steyn. The development is the largest and richest of the now virtually contiguous run of security estates that have sprung up along the banks of the Jukskei in Johannesburg north. The Waterfall City complex (of which Munyaka forms a part) is the first, then comes the Dainfern complex, followed by Steyn City virtually at the city limits.

'Douw [Steyn] is another visionary who loves landscape. He hates colour – he wanted the entire estate to look classical, so I gave him stinkwood trees because the leaves are small and pointed, like olive trees. The whole place is indigenous, not just to the highveld but to the Fourways area. I mean, why not?'

As we drove the estate Watson was by turns proud of what has been achieved ('in 20 years this will be a 2 000-acre forest') and appalled by certain aesthetic decisions he believes have been made by 'the accountants.' The greatest aberration, in his view, is the gigantic Crystal Lagoons-esque pool that has been developed at the highest point of the sprawling property. We stopped on Progress Lane and clambered through a line of stinkwood saplings to get a look at it. The estate website describes THE STEYN CITY LAGOON as a '300 metre seaside-style facility that brings you the best of a day at the coast.' In the site's drone shot the lagoon looks like a giant turquoise band aid, upslope from the dark, snaking Jukskei.

'The lagoon is filled with treated effluent from sewage works across the valley,' Watson said drily, an offhand comment of significant gravity because Johannesburg is water scarce, and Steyn City does not have a right to extract water from the Jukskei. To meet the estate's vast water needs the property managers struck a deal with Johannesburg Water, which operates Northern Wastewater Treatment Works, the country's largest sewage plant. When Steyn City bathers enter their little sea, they dip in journeyed water – water which rises on the Maloti-Drakensberg watershed, snakes into the vast Katse and Mohale reservoirs in Lesotho, is pumped through 26 kilometres of subterranean tunnels into South Africa's Ash River and making its way to the Vaal dam via the Liebingsvlei and Wilge rivers, is abstracted and treated in one of two gigantic purification plants, is pumped as much as 540 metres uphill via booster stations into reservoirs in and around Johannesburg, is released under gravity to homes and factories, is swilled down toilets and drains, is transferred in pipes of varying diameter leading to Northern Works and finally crosses the Jukskei River (the original source of the city's water, now deadly to life) to the tertiary sewage treatment works on Steyn City estate, which sends the stuff out to irrigate Watson's Stinkwoods, and replenish Steyn City lagoon.

By contrast, the lagoon on Munyaka Estate is filled from the Jukskei River, which as we know also carries large quantities of treated (and then lost) water from Lesotho. The abstraction is done using the original agricultural water right that belonged to Waterval farm, on which Waterfall City was developed.[10] The quality of the water drawn by Munyaka and the great Waterfall City complex is no better than the semi-treated effluent used by Steyn City, and is likely far worse. A Jukskei water study done by University of Johannesburg researcher Dr Kousar Banu Hoorzook et al. found that samples drawn from the upper reaches of the river were teeming with life, just not the sort of life you want to find in a river. She identified 35 different types of bacteria capable of causing gastro-intestinal, and a wide range of other diseases, five of which are extensively resistant to antibiotics.[11] Additionally, the levels of sodium, zinc, nickel, lithium, and lead exceeded the accepted levels even of irrigation water, leading Hoorzook to conclude 'that the river water is a potential health threat to downstream users.'[12] Thus, Jukskei water has to be treated on site before it can be used by the Waterfall City estate managers to irrigate lawns and top-up the vast Munyaka lagoon. It is unlikely that many users of the lagoon make the connection between the river they can undoubtedly smell (the stinking Jukskei is just a few olfactory footsteps away) and the limpid water in which their bodies immerse, because the filthy abstracted water is treated in an on-site ozone water treatment plant.

Munyaka is being billed as 'Joburg's first beach,'[13] but this isn't true – the idea that ocean-inspired amenities can boost business profits is a timeworn strategy on the South African highveld. Growing up in Johannesburg in the 80s, the only large-ish body of water I knew was Wemmer Pan, a former quarry five kilometres south of the city centre, flooded by City Deep Mine in the early 1900s in order to meet the water needs of its mining operations. Like Zimbabwe's Kariba, Wemmer Pan was 'coded white'[14] – a site of leisure for white residents, in the main. My father was a member of Wemmer Pan-based Viking Rowing Club, and on long regatta days some stimulation for the children of oarsmen could be found at Santarama Miniland on the north shore, with its full-scale replica of Jan van Riebeeck's ship, the Dromedarus. On the other side of Wemmer was the South African Institute for Maritime Research, which, it later emerged, was a front for a paramilitary organisation headed by 'commodore' Keith Maxwell, who used to appear at special occasions dressed as an 18th century admiral and claimed to have had a hand in the 1961 plane crash that killed UN secretary general Dag Hammarskjöld.[15]

I returned for the first time in 30 years on Good Friday. Several JMPD policemen stood guard at the entrance to Pioneers' Park, to prevent social gatherings in this time of COVID-19. We connected over memories of school visits to the theme park across the water. 'The ship is now gone. It has sailed,' quipped one. In an email, Luyanada Mzangwe – the IT and Assets Manager for SANTA, the tuberculosis organisation that developed the theme park in the 70s – explained that the Dromedarus 'perished in 2013, due to a fire started by vagrants that live in the veld.'

I walked around to the theme park's entrance, which is still guarded by a 30-foot van Riebeeck, and, on the inside by a snarling King Kong gorilla. The remaining scale models of notable buildings and locations from around South Africa, including a port in which 1:25 container ships float, were in various states of decaying. Gulls swarmed around the harbour waters, and waves of sacred ibis took flight, with one simply flopping around hideously in the water, regurgitating an orange substance.

In the grounds of the Wemmer Pan the rowing club boatsheds were locked and silent, and kayaks, skiffs and sculls lay mouldering behind chicken wire. The lock on the door of TURG DIVING CLUB ☎ 435-0403 was completely rusted over, reminding me of writer Ivan Vladislavić's observation, in *Portrait with Keys*, that Johannesburg has a 'reef, of course, but no diving.'[16]

If Wemmer's oceanic allusions are fading, almost nothing remains of nearby Shareworld, a theme park built to resemble a Mediterranean fishing village. In their meditation on the meanings of Johannesburg, *Not No Place*, Bettina Malcomess and Dorothee Kreutzfeldt describe Shareworld as having an artificial sea as a centrepiece, 'with concrete islands, a 2 000-foot sand beach and wave-making machines powerful enough to accommodate Africa's first-ever inland surfing competition.'[17] Opened in 1988, Shareworld was 60 percent owned by a total of 880 black investors. A *Los Angeles Times* article by David Crary quotes Reuel Khosa, then Shareworld's executive director, as saying, 'There's no question that Soweto is something of a recreational desert. This place came in as an oasis.'[18] The theme park was heralded as a milestone of both the de-segregation of leisure activities, and black economic empowerment – 'a victory for all those South Africans who still believe that there is hope in South Africa'[19] – but two years later the Shareworld was liquidated by its lender, and today the only visible remnant, swaying against the backdrop of the FNB stadium in which the 2010 World Cup final was played, is a single palm tree.

In seeking to bring a divided people together, the developers created an ocean amidst the mine dumps. Did they address the right collective yearning? The calabash-shaped FNB stadium is dwarfed by three vast, dune-like slag piles to the west, and

I am reminded that German photographer Jürgen Schadeberg's iconic 1953 photo shoot with jazz singer Dolly Rathebe took place nearby. Wanting a beach scene on a beachless highveld (and with many of the beaches along South Africa's coastline segregated by law), Schadeberg photographed a bikini-clad Rathebe atop a gold-mine dump overlooking Soweto. The two were spotted and duly arrested under the Immorality Act.[20]

In Johannesburg, the connection between 'white' residents and the sea is overt and can be neatly ascribed to European sensibilities, but a romance between 'black' Johannesburg and the sea is undeniable, and perhaps the strongest evidence for this is the Soweto Beach Party, which took place annually between 2006–2016 alongside Power Park Dam in Orlando. Pulling off Chris Hani Road, I opened a copy of *Third World Child: Born White, Zulu Bred*, the memoir of Soweto Beach Party founder, GG Alcock.

'It started with a chance remark from a client,' writes Alcock. 'We want to launch [Captain Morgan Spiced Gold] into Soweto...we need something monumental, something to capture people's imagination.'[21] In 2006, Alcock, with business partner Billy Chaka, delivered an ocean.

'Four hundred tons of beach sand were laid down, 20 6-foot yachts were launched and a host of Caribbean style bars were built along the "seashore" The Soweto surf report was broadcast on local radio stations and the best babes in Soweto, in their Captain Morgan branded mini bikinis wowed the crowds in taverns and shebeens.'[22]

Sowetans were disbelieving at first, and the first running of the party was marred by the discovery of a body in the dam in the middle of a media boating junket. By year four the venue was filled to capacity by 7pm, and not long afterwards, according to Alcock, 10 000 surplus revellers broke down the fences and surged in past security guards, who used plastic chairs as riot shields.

'At midnight when the customary fireworks went off, the explosions mixed with the sound of shotgun blasts from the riot police outside, while the smell of fireworks accompanied the faint smell of teargas. Never before had a party attracted so much passion among the people of Soweto.'[23]

In an email, Alcock explained that the Beach Party died from 'the opposite of too little interest.'

'It got too big for the venue and we could not find a space where we could run it. It did spawn a large number of copycat events everywhere from the Vaal to Polokwane, with varying degrees of success.'

The beach sand is long gone, but approaching the dam on foot I saw a couple of jet skis and a powerboat on the muddy shoreline, alongside an inflatable donut and water snake. A laminated page cable-tied to a fence of sticks carried the words Miami in Soweto. A man called Elias walked over to meet me, explaining that the business is new, and all of them – himself and the two men lounging among life jackets under a gazebo – had recently arrived in Soweto, having been poached from Sun City where they had worked at the water sports dam, not far from The Roaring Lagoon.

'People just stopped coming,' he said.

'You remember how it was, parasailing on the dam all day long. Now it is quiet. Even the crocodile park has closed.'

Miami in Soweto is faring no better.

'We have been trying on social media, but nothing so far,' said Elias. Who are they targeting? 'Everyone, but mainly tourists.' I walk over to the water, which smelled strongly of sewage. Elias recommended a jet ski ride but, fearful of the water quality, I paid for a rip in the power boat, which failed to start after we pushed off from the shoreline. The most thematically cool member of the team – white Oakleys, tattoos, long braids – came around with the jet ski, and towed us out of the bulrushes. The motor eventually fired, and we were off, the G's sending me to the bottom of the boat and my medical mask out floating over the water. We went around 3.5 times, and suddenly there was the sensation of stopping and sinking back in the water. Out of fuel. Elias waved the distress flag. Sitting there, hypertrophic gunk below the water's surface, iconic painted cooling towers above (one a gigantic advert for Vodacom), I had one thought – that it is here in this high, dry place, that we have beached. And for better or worse, this is how we beach.

Notes

1   'Balwin Sells 555 Apartments in Four Days for R850 Million,' *Property Wheel*, March 2020. https://propertywheel.co.za/2020/03/balwin-sells-555-apartments-in-four-days-for-r850-million/.

2   'Balwin Sells 555 Apartments in Four Days for R850 Million,' *Property Wheel*, March 2020.

3   Johann W.N. Tempelhoff, 'On Laburn's 'mystery' query – A prehistory of the Vaal River as water source of the Witwatersrand (1887-99),' *Historia*, 45, no. 1 (May 2000): 91.

4   'City of Joburg loses nearly half its water, costing billions,' *Moneyweb*, April 2023, https://www.moneyweb.co.za/news/south-africa/city-of-joburg-loses-nearly-half-its-water-costing-billions/.

5   'The Innovator's Dream,' Crystal Lagoons, accessed 23 October, 2023, https://www.crystal-lagoons.com/the-innovators-dream/.

6   David McDermott Hughes, *Whiteness in Zimbabwe – Race, Landscape, and the Problem of Belonging* (New York: Palgrave Macmillan, 2010), 14.

7   Hughes, Whiteness, 45.

8   Hein Wicht, *The Indigenous Palms of Southern Africa* (Great Brak: Howard Timmins, 1969), 63.

9   Heather Mason, 'A Little Piece of Fake Tuscany in Fourways,' 2Summers, March 2012, https://2summers.net/2012/03/02/a-little-piece-of-fake-tuscany-in-fourways/.

10   'Waterfall's HO strategy,' Waterfall City, May 2022, https://waterfallcity.co.za/news/waterfalls-h%E2%82%82o-strategy/.

11   Hoorzook, K. Banu; Pieterse, Anton; Heine, Lee; Barnard, T. George; van Rensburg, N. Janse, 'Soul of the Jukskei River: The Extent of Bacterial Contamination in the Jukskei River in Gauteng Province, South Africa.' *International Journal of Environmental Research and Public Health* 18, no. 16: 8537 (August 2021): https://doi.org/10.3390/ijerph18168537.

12   Hoorzook, 'Soul of the Jukskei,' 8537.

13   'Johannesburg's "first beach": Five things to know,' *The South African*, accessed 23 October 2023: https://ilovesouthafrica.com/news/johannesburg-first-beach-details-4-november-2022/.

14   Hughes, *Whiteness*, 69.

15   Emma Graham-Harrison, Andreas Rocksen and Mads Brügger, 'Coups and murder: the sinister world of apartheid's secret mercenaries,' *The Guardian*, 20 January 2019.

16   Ivan Vladislavic, *Portrait with Keys: The City of Johannesburg Unlocked* (London and New York: W.W. Norton & Company, 2009), 18.

17   Bettina Malcomess and Dorothee Kreutzfeldt, *Not No Place: Johannesburg. Fragments of Spaces and Times* (Johannesburg: Jacana Media, 2016) 44.

18   David Crary, 'New Theme Park Near Soweto Seeking to Bridge South Africa's Racial Gap,' *Los Angeles Times*, April 24, 1988.

19   Crary, 'New Theme Park.'

20   Tymon Smith, 'Making History,' *Arthrob*, 22 September, 2020.

21   G. G. Alcock, *Third World Child: Born White, Zulu Bred* (Bryanston: Tracey McDonald Publishers, 2014), 287.

22   Alcock, *Third World*, 2014, 290.

23   Alcock, *Third World*, 2014, 295.

11 Dirty river: Whiteness, pollution and the Jukskei

Nicky Falkof

In February 2011, Afrikaans musician Steve Hofmeyr made national headlines after tossing R5 000 worth of U2 concert tickets into the Jukskei. Hofmeyr was protesting statements made by the U2 frontman Bono, who had failed to condemn the controversial struggle song 'Kill the Boer', which was then being publicly sung by certain politicians. This chapter discusses the social and discursive meanings of Hofmeyr's act of political performance. It considers issues of whiteness, pastoral idealism and Afrikaans relation to the trope of 'the land' in order to consider what it might mean for a white Afrikaner to dramatically throw trash into a river. It asks what Hofmeyr's political littering can tell us about how the Jukskei is understood within a white South African imaginary, and about how notions of race and hygiene may impact on ideas about the purity of nature.

Introduction

On 14 February 2011, South African musician Steve Hofmeyr's Twitter feed made headlines across the country. Hofmeyr, an Afrikaans rock singer and self-styled minority rights activist, gleefully informed his Twitter followers that he had just 'dumped R5 000 worth of U2 tickets in the Jukskei', to a mix of applause and disgust.

Hofmeyr's protest was in response to a statement by the U2 frontman Bono, whose band was performing in South Africa that week. In an interview for a South African newspaper, Bono had been asked about the contentious struggle-era song 'Kill the Boer'.[1] He had told the journalist that 'there was nothing wrong with political songs, but not at public gatherings', and had said that it reminded him of the Irish Republican anthems he grew up singing.[2]

'Kill the Boer' has a long history in South Africa, first as an anti-apartheid call to arms and later as a cultural touchstone, sung in public by provocative politicians like former President Jacob Zuma and Economic Freedom Fighters leader Julius Malema. While Malema, then still heading the ANC Youth League, was found guilty of hate speech for singing the song in 2011, a 2022 ruling insisted that it could not legally be considered hate speech and that it is not meant to be taken literally.[3]

In the incident under discussion here, Hofmeyr appears to have decided that Afrikaans ethnic solidarity outweighed the international brotherhood of rock'n'roll, and that Bono's refusal to condemn the song was an unforgiveable insult to Afrikaners, best served by performatively tossing his expensive concert tickets into the Jukskei.

Hofmeyr's angry littering is a trivial moment in the cultural life of this abused river. In the grand scheme of things – sewage, *E. coli*, uncollected rubbish and all the other detritus of a neglected inner-city waterway – what did R5 000 worth of concert tickets really mean? Probably paper anyway, they would swiftly be consumed by the rest of the Jukskei's cannibalistic effluent. The protest was about the money rather than the physical tickets, about Hofmeyr giving up the chance to watch a legitimate 'god' of rock in action, a noble sacrifice nobly made in support of his put-upon people.

But as with most acts of political theatre in South Africa, Hofmeyr's overwrought gesture carries a host of probably unintentional meanings. In order to see it more clearly, and to understand what 'dumping in the Jukskei' actually suggests, we need to start by thinking about Steve Hofmeyr, about Afrikaner culture, about whiteness and about land.

Hofmeyr began his public career in the early 1980s, as an actor in the popular Afrikaans TV show *Agter Elke Man*. His persona soon morphed into singer and heartthrob and he produced a steady supply of singles and albums throughout the 1980s and 1990s, some of which were notable hits within the small but enthusiastic Afrikaans market. As his fame became entrenched, however, Hofmeyr's public pronouncements began to shift from bland and generic celebrity platitudes to something more overtly political and more explicitly troubling. During this period Hofmeyr aligned himself with an increasingly hysterical right wing consciousness which insisted that whites were the victims of reverse racism at the hands of the ANC, that whites were an endangered minority, and that whites were under threat of genocide and in need of exceptional support, protection and validation.

The Jukskei/U2 affair was the start of a series of controversial public statements, often made on Twitter, in which Hofmeyr clarified a paranoid worldview which insisted that white people were extraordinary victims, and that black people – at least the 'bad' ones, the ones allied to political parties – were directly responsible for the Afrikaans nation's apparently overwhelming series of crises. In 2011, soon after the event in question, he tweeted out lyrics to a song that contained the word 'kaffir,' probably the most offensive racial slur in South Africa, apparently in revenge for the continued public appearance of 'Kill the Boer.' In 2014 he informed his followers that 'in my books Blacks were the architects of Apartheid', again to much general outrage. Most significantly, in 2013 he fronted a campaign called Red October, which aimed to raise awareness of an alleged 'white genocide'.[4] Campaigners in South Africa, as well as in expat heartlands like London and Perth, Australia, released red balloons into the sky and sent lists of demands to government. During the campaign's main event at the Union Buildings in Pretoria, Hofmeyr read earnest poetry and entreated the crowd to remember how Afrikaners had voluntarily and altruistically given up power. (This one-sided reading of the 1992 referendum was remarkably free of any awareness of the anti-apartheid struggle, never mind the political and economic pressures that were making apartheid untenable.)

In Hofmeyr we see a familiar story: a professional entertainer who becomes radicalised, who immerses himself – and it is most often himself – in a particular kind of identity politics, while loudly eschewing the whole idea of identity politics as woke madness. From Stephen Baldwin and Dennis Quaid in the US to John Cleese and Laurence Fox in the UK, this figure is typically male and often white (although the public dissolution of Kanye West makes clear that being white is not necessarily a precursor to aligning oneself with white supremacist politics). He presents himself as speaking the hard truths that no one else will say aloud, and which inevitably suggest that people like him – people who are men, who are white, who are heterosexual and cisgendered (their gender identity is the same as their birth gender) – are the *real* victims of our cancel-prone culture, the real martyrs of the internet age.

As with so many global cultural phenomena, this trope appears in South Africa in recognisable form, but with a few local particularities. In Hofmeyr's case, his swing to the far right was framed in explicitly ethnic terms. He has reinvented himself as a campaigner for white rights, with Afrikaners, once central to and protected by apartheid, now represented as an abused and desperate minority, notwithstanding white South Africans' ongoing statistical monopoly on wealth.[5]

The issue of dumping in the Jukskei becomes particularly interesting when we consider that one of the major tropes of Afrikaner identity is its attachment to nature, to landscape and to the mythic idea of the land.[6] In the post-apartheid era, white and Afrikaans critiques of majority rule have often assumed that black South Africans are incapable of properly managing the country's vast landscape and natural resources.

The normative notion that white people are the only appropriate stewards for the natural world is hardly unique to South Africa. Indeed, it underpins the colonial enterprise from Kenya to Nepal, from hunting ground to national park, with white settlers imagined to be the only people with the wisdom, knowledge, skills and depth of feeling required to properly manage the environment.[7] Within traditional Afrikaans culture, this manifests as a deep and potent attachment to the idea of the land. The land is posited as a crucial element of the identity of the 'volk', the people/nation. The land can suggest both farmland and wild spaces, both the huge agricultural holdings that support Afrikaner wealth and the mountains, beaches, bush and national parks which are central to white leisure.

These associations of Afrikanerdom with land go back to the early days of white South African settlement, to Dutch farmers laying claim to swathes of the Cape, and later trekking north to take over the supposedly available spaces in the country's interior. Of course, the persistent myth of the empty land was continually disproven by the skirmishes, arguments, treaties, negotiations, purchases, lies and outright warfare that erupted whenever white migrants ran up against the people who were already living in those parts of the country.[8] During the periods of white migration into and expansion through South Africa it would have been abundantly clear that, far from being empty, the country was thoroughly populated, with complex social and economic systems and patterns of movement and migration. Nonetheless, Afrikaner political mythology held fast to the notion of emptiness, insisting that

Bantu tribes and white Europeans had moved into the interior of South Africa at the same time, the former from the north, the latter from the south. During apartheid this discredited fiction was transmitted to generations of South African schoolchildren.[9]

As in other colonised places, part of the moralising justification for white monopoly over land was that other inhabitants did not use it *properly*. Proper use, in the case of agricultural land, means to own it, parcel it out, tame it and make it profitable. In the case of 'natural' land, proper use involves managing, experiencing and appreciating it correctly, that is to say, in the way in which white people would. Landscapes appropriated by colonial endeavour 'would be rendered meaningful only because of capitalist intervention, and the spatial metaphors of both colonialism and adventure literature were based on the enunciation of capitalist values'.[10]

The Afrikaner preoccupation with land and nature retains a powerful role in post-apartheid mythology. Much far right organising in the past decade has, as I suggested above, focused on the idea of white genocide, which manifests in the crisis of farm murders. Farm murders are a classification of crime that is almost always applied to white people, and that discursively implies that whites are exceptional victims, disproportionately targeted because of their race.[11] While there are many instances of brutal murders on farms, and many of the victims are white, there is no evidence that these kinds of people suffer more or worse violence than other South Africans. Indeed, data suggests that people who are black and poor take the worst brunt of our endemic and shocking rates of violence. This is not to suggest that murders on farms are not terrible, or that they do not deserve our attention. Rather, 'while white farmers are the major victims of farm murder, a conceptualisation of such as "white genocide" does not adequately characterise the reality'.[12] Farm attacks are instances of the pervasiveness of criminal violence in contemporary South Africa, rather than proof of a targeted racial genocide.

The farm murder narrative is powerful in part because of the association of white Afrikaners with nature, the farm and the land. It suggests that isolated and vulnerable people are being brutally murdered because of their commitment to the land, because they are too attached to the natural environment to abandon it for the comparatively safer cities or for life overseas. The farm murder narrative implies that Afrikaners are being killed because of their deep relationship with nature, that their blood is seeping into the red dirt because they are too intertwined with it to leave. As well as inspiring much collective anxiety and entrenching South Africa as a sort of ground zero for global far right fantasy, farm murder stories reiterate Afrikaner love of and commitment to the land.[13]

While he is primarily concerned with the diminishing status of the Afrikaans language and with changes to place names, public holidays and monuments, Hofmeyr also makes clear that the association of Afrikaner culture with stewardship of the land remains a significant element of its political mythology. In his dramatic, code-switching speech at the 2013 opening event of the Red October campaign, at the Union Buildings in Pretoria, Hofmeyr read a lengthy poem to the enthusiastic crowd, which reproduced many common tropes of white South African victimhood: 'I am the Afrikaner. I am the one you should have kept close. The son of Africa you should have held to your bosom'. The poem is full of self-aggrandising hyperbole, in one instance explicitly stating that Afrikaners gave up their 'legitimate sovereignty' in the name of peace. It also makes a point of contrasting the violence of contemporary South Africa with the altruism and agrarian know-how of whites: 'I am the Afrikaner without whose employ this land would have once been the gem of Africa…I am the Afrikaner you tie to the sofa to watch the six-hour rape of his wife and daughters who wants to be nowhere else but on the land producing food for *your* family'.[14] In an interview with members of the press on the same day, Hofmeyr repeated the idea that Afrikaners are a simple people who just want to work the land and feed the nation, a description that blithely ignores the well-documented history of Afrikaner elites' power-hungry political manoeuvrings which led to the system of apartheid.[15]

Let us return now to the Jukskei. What might it mean when a cultural figure who claims to speak for a people that is intimately connected to nature is so casual about tossing a load of rubbish into a river? How does Hofmeyr get away with treating the Jukskei so cavalierly, when part of the myth that sustains him is that Afrikaners are naturally closer to and better carers of the natural world? The answer to this question lies in the difference between Afrikaans conceptions of nature and common understandings of the Jukskei as a dirty river, 'strewn with trash and laden with coliform bacteria'.[16]

White Afrikaner mythologies of land, from the farms of the Free State to the bush of the Kruger National Park, depend on specific relationships between humans and nature. As I suggested above, when the land must be heavily managed, as is the case with farming, this is best achieved by white men, who have the necessary emotional ties, instinctive skills, work ethic and modern knowledge. In the case of the bush – also heavily managed, although this is generally not acknowledged – it is again white men who best know how to read and move through these apparently wild spaces. In all cases, the land remains to some extent subservient to human endeavour. It is also separate in some way from the mass of humanity: the land is the thing that exists outside the cities where the Afrikaner nation was imperilled, and where its powerful culture industries emerged.[17] It is a shared heritage that exists outside of time and is thus, imaginatively, irrelevant or prior to race. This emotive conception places Afrikaner relations to the land outside the material and historic conditions of South Africa, free from the post-apartheid politics of guilt, shame and reparation.

The idea of the land is, then, imbued with a kind of ideological purity, an aspirational distance from the messiness of politics and the blurred racial/social boundaries that characterise urban life. When we think about the Afrikaner valorisation of nature we are also thinking about an idealised rural lifestyle, free from the density, compromise and racial mixing of the city. When culture warriors like Steve Hofmeyr gesture towards the centrality of nature in Afrikaner thought, and suggest the unique capacity of white people to appropriately steward nature, they are talking about an ideal that is both geographically and conceptually removed from the Union Buildings, from Pretoria.

The Jukskei is a natural body of water, it is true. But – at least in its first sections – it is also undeniably urban, intertwined with people and their city, their daily lives and their rubbish. Journalists call it 'Johannesburg's dirty little river', 'filled with excrement-filled water, trash and a putrid smell', a 'cesspool of decay and filth' that is as 'polluted as it is iconic'.[18] Public discussion of the Jukskei centres on what Mehita Iqani and Jessica Webster term 'faecal discourse': the 'implicit and explicit entanglement between politics, plumbing and the market' that reveals 'how the visible and affective traces of faecal matter in the river speak to a broader sense of post-colonial collapse of both infrastructure and trust in those responsible for it'.[19] As much of this book makes clear – in particular the chapters by Kyle van Heyde and by Kousar Hoorzook and Atheesha Singh – popular impressions of the Jukskei's muckiness and mismanagement are neither misplaced nor exaggerated. The river is indeed exceptionally dirty, to the point of being dangerous for those who wash in it, bathe in it and even drink from it. The Jukskei is an urban river, not only because it flows through the city, but also because it is polluted by its overly close contact with human life. From its emergence close to Ellis Park, through its journey past Alexandra township, its most noticeable characteristics are dirt, smells and trash, which grossly affect the poor black communities who live along its inner city banks.

Yes, the Jukskei is natural. However, it is not 'nature' in the sense demanded by Afrikaner political myth, with its warring conceptions of the rural as a white idyll and the cities as a source of pollution. 'In the folk-lore of Afrikanerdom, towns – particularly Johannesburg – were evil places' to which destitute whites were forced to migrate in the early 20th century.[20] Within this folklore, natural features within the urban landscape are not experienced as nature, if we consider nature as the glorified site of ethno-national wholeness and belonging.

The difference between Afrikaans conceptions of nature and popular understandings of the Jukskei explain why a figure like Steve Hofmeyr, whose shared cultural identity invokes the glorification of the natural world, could publicly sully and pollute this particular waterway. Because it is an urban river and a poor river, the Jukskei is excluded from sublime white relations to the land and so is not subject to the same injunctions as more pristine areas of South Africa. It is available for Hofmeyr to throw his concert tickets in, to dirty in protest against a perceived slight at Afrikaners, because it is not part of the mythology that underlines Afrikaner life. At least in Johannesburg, this is a river gone wrong, cut off from the devotion to the natural world that is a central tenet of South African whiteness.

I suggested at the start of this chapter that Hofmeyr's litter protest was just a minor incident in the larger cultural life of the Jukskei. It probably had minimal impact on the river's condition, and was quickly forgotten in the ensuing flurry of Hofmeyrist drama. It is interesting, however, for what it reveals about the river's debased or even non-existent place in certain white imaginations, which define it – and Johannesburg more broadly – as simply a place of dirt, danger and decay. But as the rest of this book has shown, rivers, and the cities they run through, are seldom as simple as they seem.

Notes

1 'Boer', Afrikaans for farmer, is often used as a pejorative term for Afrikaners.

2 'Hofmeyr Dumps U2 Tickets over Bono's Comments', *Mail & Guardian*, 14 February 2011, https://mg.co.za/article/2011-02-14-hofmeyr-dumps-u2-tickets-over-bono-comments/.

3 Tania Broughton, 'Judge Rules That 'Kill the Boer – Kill the Farmer' Is Not Hate Speech', *GroundUp News*, 25 August 2022, https://www.groundup.org.za/article/judge-rules-kill-boer---kill-farmer-not-hate-speech/.

4 Nicky Falkof, *Worrier State: Risk, Anxiety and Moral Panic in South Africa* (Manchester: Manchester University Press, 2022), 48–73.

5 It is true that many white people in contemporary South Africa are insecure in a way that was unimaginable under apartheid. Nonetheless, research makes clear that whites *in general* experience less poverty than other population groups, that insecurity experienced by whites is often less acute than for other groups and that whites retain a disproportionate hold over both economic and land wealth. To put it another way, Hofmeyr's 'minority rights' crusade ignores that the fact that millions of South Africans experience risk and poverty, often in more pressing ways than white people. See, for example, Statistics South Africa, 'Inequality Trends in South Africa: A Multidimensional Diagnostic of Inequality', 14 November 2019, http://www.statssa.gov.za/?p=12744; Carlos Gradín, 'Race, Poverty and Deprivation in South Africa', *Journal of African Economies* 22, no. 2 (1 March 2013): 187–238, https://doi.org/10.1093/jae/ejs019; Christi Kruger, '(Dis)-Empowered Whiteness: An Ethnography of the King Edward Park' (PhD thesis, Johannesburg, University of the Witwatersrand, 2017), http://wiredspace.wits.ac.za/handle/10539/24136.

6 Jennifer Beningfield, 'Native Lands: Language, Nation and Landscape in the Taal Monument, Paarl, South Africa', *Social Identities* 10, no. 4 (1 July 2004): 509–525; Scott Burnett, *White Belongings: Race, Land, and Property in Post-Apartheid South Africa* (Washington: Lexington Books, 2022); Herman Giliomee, *The Afrikaners, Biography of a People* (London: Hurst and Company, 2003).

7 See for example Grace Musila, *A Death Retold in Truth and Rumour: Kenya, Britain and the Julie Ward Murder* (Suffolk: James Currey, 2015); Rob Nixon, *Slow Violence and the Environmentalism of the Poor* (Cambridge, Mass.: Harvard University Press, 2011).

8 Anne McClintock, 'Family Feuds: Gender, Nationalism and the Family', *Feminist Review* 44, no. 1 (1993): 61–80.

9 Leonard Thompson, *The Political Mythology of Apartheid* (New Haven and London: Yale University Press, 1985), 58.

10 Jeanne van Eeden, 'The Colonial Gaze: Imperialism, Myths, and South African Popular Culture', *Design Issues* 20, no. 2 (2004): 25.

11   Nicky Falkof, 'White Victimhood: Weaponising Identity and Resistance to Social Change,' in *The Routledge Handbook of Social Change*, ed. Richard Ballard and Clive Barnett (London: Routledge, 2022), 67–76.

12   Adeoye O Akinola, 'Farm Attacks or 'White Genocide'? Interrogating the Unresolved Land Question in South Africa,' *African Journal on Conflict Resolution* 20, no. 2 (2020): 65.

13   Lloyd Gedye, 'White Genocide: How the Big Lie Spread to the US and Beyond,' *Mail & Guardian*, 23 March 2018, https://mg.co.za/article/2018-03-23-00-radical-right-plugs-swart-gevaar/; James Pogue, 'The Myth of White Genocide,' Pulitzer Center, 15 February 2019, https://pulitzercenter.org/reporting/myth-white-genocide.

14   Focus 2 Frame, 'Red October, a Peaceful March to the Union Buildings Pretoria,' YouTube, 13 October 2013, https://www.youtube.com/watch?v=Tz9lK9V80tQ.

15   Praag.org, 'Steve Hofmeyr Interview during Red October March, Pretoria,' 15 October 2013, https://www.youtube.com/watch?v=fgRdTdj76ew; GH Pirie, CM Rogerson, and KSO Beavon, 'Covert Power in South Africa: The Geography of the Afrikaner Broederbond,' *Area* 12, no. 2 (1980): 97–104.

16   Joe Walsh, 'How Johannesburg's Dirty Little River Could Help Ease Water Woes,' *Bloomberg. Com*, 20 August 2021, https://www.bloomberg.com/news/features/2021-08-20/a-dirty-river-may-be-key-to-south-africa-water-security.

17   David Welsh, 'Urbanisation and the Solidarity of Afrikaner Nationalism,' *Journal of Southern African Studies* 7, no. 2 (1969): 265–276.

18   Walsh, 'How Johannesburg's Dirty Little River Could Help Ease Water Woes'; Pongrass Import, 'Jukskei River in Alexandra is a Shadow of its Former Self,' *Alex News*, 14 April 2023, https://alexnews.co.za/215740/residents-pollute-juskei-river/; Leonie Wagner, 'The Jukskei River Used to Give Us Fish and Frogs, but Now There's Nothing,' *TimesLive,* 9 October 2022, https://www.timeslive.co.za/sunday-times/opinion-and-analysis/insight/2022-10-09-the-jukskei-river-used-to-give-us-fish-and-frogs-but-now-theres-nothing/.

19   Jessica Webster and Mehita Iqani, 'Johannesburg's Shitty Little River: Faecal Discourse and Discontent Regarding the Jukskei,' *Social Dynamics* 50, no. 1 (2 January 2024): 109.

20   Welsh, 'Urbanisation and the Solidarity of Afrikaner Nationalism,' 265.

12 Reporting on the Jukskei: Behind three headlines

Jamaine Krige

This chapter provides a narrative exploration of how the Jukskei River reflects and perpetuates South Africa's deep societal divides. Through personal stories from the author's career as a journalist in Johannesburg, it examines the river as both a geographic barrier and a powerful symbol separating affluence from poverty, offering a multi-perspective view into how environmental and social systems are inextricably linked. Vignettes cover topics like tracking a hippo's journey through wealthy suburbs, the tragic death of a child swept away in township floods, and a devastating fire that laid bare the daily injustices faced by residents of informal settlements on the river bank. The unifying thread is how the river demarcates vastly different lived realities and ecosystems of privilege and deprivation. The author grapples with the limitations of journalism to enact change, arguing that until systemic barriers are dismantled, the river will continue to divide rather than bind South Africa's people.

Introduction

As a news reporter in Johannesburg, I have witnessed first-hand the societal divides that plague South Africa. These divides are evident in every aspect of life, from the sprawling townships to the affluent suburbs. But perhaps nowhere is the divide more apparent than along the Jukskei River.

Rivers are the cords that bind our society, but in South Africa, widely considered the most unequal society on earth, rivers also divide us. Johannesburg is the country's economic hub. Here the Jukskei River serves as a powerful geographic, social and economic partition that reflects both our past and our present and influences those on either side of this divide in vastly different ways.

My career in journalism is underpinned by a deep love for stories. I am a story-hearer first, a storyteller second, and after that, perhaps, a news reporter and media practitioner.

With its source almost at the centre of the city I call home, it should not come as a surprise that so many of the stories and experiences that have touched my life and shaped my career flow from the Jukskei.

While I was never explicitly forced to examine my relationship to or my interactions with the city and its stories through this watery lens, I'm now acutely aware of how my experiences have been shaped by the river's role as a divider, and how its surface ripples reflect a much deeper, complex interplay between geography, politics and

Hunting hippos for headlines

I have, on more than one occasion, spent days tracking a wayward hippo on its journey through Johannesburg's affluent suburbs and up-market gated communities of Chartwell and Dainfern; the Jukskei River a convenient waterway for wild animals and their suburban excursions from the Hartebeespoort Dam.

I knew it was going to be one of those days when my phone rang 30 minutes before my shift started. It was my assignment editor. I needed to drop the story I had planned to work on because the news diary had been updated: a hippo had been spotted in Chartwell, and my top priority was to track it down.

Chartwell is one of the affluent Northern suburbs, consisting of sprawling luxury estates that market themselves as semi-urban farms, despite being only minutes from suburbs like Fourways and rarely producing anything farm-worthy.

I decided to head to the office and reach out to animal wrangler and wildlife expert Vicky Brooker to find out what to expect before I launched my search party; after all, I'd never tracked a hippo before. She would be available for a formal interview within the next hour, she told me, adding that she believed the animal, dubbed in some media reports as 'Chippo the Chartwell Hippo', was actually Hartebeespoort Dam's resident hippo affectionately known as Harpo. I scrolled through social media, paraphrased a statement from local authorities and jotted down what she had told me, quickly recording a voicer to be played on the next bulletin, before heading through to the office.

As I got into the car, the hourly news bulletin began. 'Residents of Chartwell and Olivenhoutbosch in the North West of Johannesburg have been warned to be on the lookout for a hippo wandering in the area. The Gauteng Department of Agriculture and Rural Development says they're investigating the situation after a number of people posted sightings of the hippo on social media platforms.'

Next, my own voice, sounding like someone who had been summoned to work half an hour early, who definitely felt that there were more pressing news issues on the agenda and did not feel like tracking an animal through the suburbs as the world prepared for New Years celebrations: 'Hippos have been known to migrate between bodies of water, but few people are prepared when one of these animals wanders across their property. Photos posted to social media show the large animal walking across a grassy lawn alongside the banks of the Klein Jukskei River in Chartwell, Johannesburg. Social media is now abuzz about where this unlikely visitor came from, with some people speculating that this may be Harpo, a well-known hippo from Hartbeespoort Dam, who travelled upriver. Authorities are investigating and people have been urged to stay away from the animal. Though the hippo has not shown any signs of aggression, it remains a wild animal and could be dangerous if approached. Jamaine Krige, SABC News, Johannesburg.'

When I arrived in the newsroom, almost deserted and operating on a skeleton staff as most of the public broadcaster's employees spent time at home with their families, I quickly typed and recorded an update while waiting for Vicky to make herself available. By the time she was ready for our recording, the next bulletin was already on the air: 'Wildlife authorities say they are exploring all options in an attempt to capture a hippo that's been spotted in Chartwell, north of Johannesburg. The Gauteng Department of Agriculture and Rural Development says it is working with local communities, conservation practitioners and the police to raise awareness and ensure the safety of both people and the hippo.'

'In a statement, the Department of Agriculture and Rural Development has warned people not to approach or feed the animal while they investigate ways to capture and relocate the hippo. The department says that if the hippo is not fed it will likely return to its home, which is suspected to be the Crocodile River. Should these options fail, however, the department says there will be no other option than to engage the Provincial Hunters Association to put down the animal. Conservationists, however, say this hippo has been visiting the area for many years and will not pose a threat to people if simply left to find its way back home.'

Vicky did not like that bulletin. That sentiment was echoed by many of our listeners. The hippo could not be shot! Even darting the animal could prove fatal, she explained: 'It is just not an option unless you involve the top experts, for the simple reason that in an open river like that, if you dart her she will go into the water. Once the immobilising drugs take effect, she will drown. Even if you do manage to keep her out of the water, it will stress her out completely!'

Also stressed out were the city's residents downriver from where she had been spotted, who unlike their 'neighbours' in Chartwell, lived in informal housing just metres from the river and did not have the sprawling lawns between their homes and the area's new visitor. But, said Vicky, Harpo would not harm anyone if they just left her alone.

Later that afternoon, after driving up and down the tree-lined suburbs alongside the river at the behest of my eager editors in search of an animal that was largely nocturnal by nature, I took a break at a local pub. The TV was on and a news anchor was introducing Vicky, who after our interview that morning had been inundated with media enquiries. As I wolfed down a sandwich and a beer, the news anchor introduced Vicky and the story with the words I had written for the radio bulletins earlier that day. He started his interview with a big smile and a jovial tone. 'So let's talk about Harpo,' he laughed.

She reciprocates and the tone of the interview is set from the start. 'We're dealing with a very clever hippo here because despite her regular outings she's managed to stay under the radar for quite a few years now.'

Vicky goes on to explain that the summer brings heavy rains, with rising water levels facilitating her travels up what is largely considered the most polluted river in South Africa: 'The water is cleaner and the river is more accessible for her. There is plenty of grazing for her on the river banks so she's not hungry or looking for anything specific – she's just exploring.'

Despite the obvious anthropomorphising of this 'clever, curious Harpo,' Vicky does emphasise that it is important to remember that the wild animal is just that – a wild animal, and a dangerous one. 'They can honestly move, they can gijima and baleka like you cannot believe, and running is not an option.' The presenter smiles at the blonde conservationist's use of Zulu ('to run' and 'to flee') to get her point across. She continues that it is best to leave the hippo alone, adding that Harpo will likely be going back to the dam when the water levels start to drop. 'But it's a nice thing to have her here and it's a nice story, as long as people know how dangerous she is and that they leave her alone.'

The presenter nods and asks whether it is true that hippos are responsible for more deaths than any other animal, both in South Africa and elsewhere on the continent. She laughs, adding that to date they've even killed more people than the COVID virus! This was said jokingly in December 2020, and I remember that that comment made me uncomfortable. Reflecting on it today still gives me an uneasy feeling in the pit of my stomach, especially considering so many of the other stories I've told on those river banks.

'The problems come when there is conflict between the villagers, the water and the hippos,' she explains, or when the villagers get between the hippos and the water. 'And they are dangerous; they don't mock charge or first pretend to come at you once or twice to scare you off like an elephant or a lion would. They just come one stap finish-and-klaar [charge and it's done with], and they're fast. They baleka like you cannot believe, and they are big and powerful and always angry. They don't have a sense of humour.'

The news anchor laughs. 'Well, this one seems to have a sense of humour, because Harpo has been spotted in that area for many years, and maybe because people do leave her alone and they don't bother her, she feels it is good to come back because she is welcome!'

Vicky laughs and her voice is warm and less stern: 'I hope so. And you know I really admire the people along the river who live with her, because they have respected her. Conservation services in North West are aware that she is travelling up and down and they are aware of her being in Hartebeespoortdam.'

She reiterates that darting the animal is not an option because she risks drowning. 'And anyway, where do you take her? She's very happy where she is. It's her habitat, and she's behaved herself. She respects people and their space and doesn't seem too worried about dogs. So it's a lovely story, in a way…if people can just stay out of the equation and allow her to be.' As the interview wraps up, the presenter then goes on to give the conservationist an on-air Zulu lesson, equipping her with a new word to add to her vocabulary – *imvubu*, meaning hippo.

I never did find Harpo, despite days of tracking her, both on social media and through the streets of Johannesburg. As the news cycle turned and the fervour died down, I continued to follow the story.

I read with mild amusement that controversial celebrity private investigator Mike Bolhuis, an ardent animal lover, had appointed himself Harpo's personal bodyguard after it was rumoured that wildlife authorities had issued a permit for her to be shot at the start of December, weeks before she embarked on her journey to the city. Not only was he following every lead to track the animal, but he was also raising funds for her protection and possible relocation: 'We take these things very seriously. When I was contacted by community members from Hartbeespoort who are concerned about the hippo's safety, I immediately agreed to get involved. I gave our task team orders to look after the hippo. We were appointed by the community of Hartbeespoort, the tree-huggers, the carers in South Africa, to protect Harpo and we will do it free of charge. Anyone who has a problem with the hippo must please phone us. Do not attack each other, do not get emotional. Just call us and we will take the responsibility,' Bolhuis told the Harties community newspaper. He said his company would be conducting a risk analysis, because 'it is not just about the safety of people, but also about the safety of the hippo. The dam might be dangerous for the hippo to be in.'

He also told local reporters that any person claiming to have a permit to shoot her would have to go through him and his team. 'We will verify the legitimacy of the permit and take it from there. We will act strongly against anyone who makes moves and takes the law into their own hands. We want to make sure that everyone, including the hippo, chill for now. It is December, nothing is going to happen now. If we find that the hippo is a danger to the community, we will organise a professional relocation,' he said.

Late January, after flying under the radar and amid rumours that she had been killed in one of the communities she was passing through, conservation authorities confirmed that Harpo had returned home. I thought that would be that, but in July 2021, on one of my off days, the newsroom called again, looking for contacts who could speak to the story. It seemed that Harpo had made her way up the Jukskei again, but this time had made herself a bit too comfortable on a golf estate. After her first sighting, the Steyn City Management Association (SCMA) tracked her movements along the river and the estate's dams with cameras and infrared drones, and when she moved into what was considered 'close proximity to the residents' homes,' a permit for her relocation was sought, 'with the safety of both the animal and residents in mind.'

According to a statement from SCMA, the hippo was darted and captured under the supervision of trained veterinarians and representatives from nature conservation authorities: 'However, the veterinarians responsible for the relocation of the hippo later advised that the hippo sadly died while in transit as a result of breathing complications. It was a devastating blow to our team on the ground, as well as the specialised task team who had done everything possible to protect this hippo. After a long and strenuous day, we had hoped for a good outcome and a happy ending.'

I never did find out if Bolhuis had more success in tracking her than I did that December. And we never did receive feedback on whether the breathing complications were a result of drowning.

Angel Sibanda

In 2016, not far from those luxury estates and rolling golf courses that would eventually host Harpo the Clever Curious Hippo's demise years later, I stood ankle-deep in a small stream that cut through Diepsloot township. A helicopter circled overhead. It was my third day covering a search and rescue mission for a six-year-old girl swept away during flash floods.

Angel Sibanda was crossing the small stream, one of the many tributaries that feed into the Jukskei River. It was a route that Angel Sibanda travelled – down the road, across the veld and through the trickling water – between school and the shack she shared with her parents and three elder siblings. On this Thursday afternoon, however, a downpour upstream caused the waters to swell into raging rapids.

Within moments, the waters rose by half a metre…and then another…and another. By the time a security guard saw the children in distress, the waters were 2 m deep. Angel's four older travel companions managed to cling to safety until they could be rescued, but the Grade 1 learner was not strong enough to hold on.

The South African Police Service was on scene with their water wing and their dog unit, police rescue vehicles had driven down the slope and parked in the mud at the water's edge. The river had subsided substantially, but the previously ankle-deep trickle was still raging at waist-depth in some places. Above the river, the City of Johannesburg's Aquatic and Urban Rescue Unit had set up base with several red fire trucks.

Dozens of community members gathered in restless groups – they had been forbidden from joining the search due to safety concerns and fear of further incidents. Despite strict instructions not to wade into the waters to assist authorities, some mobilised to search the riverbanks and reedbeds. Others contributed in the only way they were allowed to – they sang hymns and formed groups which took shifts to pray loudly for the young girl's return.

Among the community members were Angel's parents. Her mother, Sbonisa Sibanda, sobbed, inconsolable, one hand to her chest and the other pressed into her pregnant belly. Her father, Thabani Thsuma, clutched a small, colourful plastic photo album with the transparent sleeves inside housing the few photos that existed of the child.

He showed them to me as he described a sweet and loving child; a respectful child who loved attending school and learning. The most recent photo – the last one in the album – showed a small, neatly dressed girl sitting at a table, her plump face beaming at the camera from behind a big chocolate cake. It had been taken on her sixth birthday.

Specialised digging equipment was brought in to help clear debris from the flash flood, and more than 200 people were involved in the search and rescue mission. By Saturday evening, the police announced quietly that this was now being treated as a recovery operation.

It was a fisherman, casting his line in the Jukskei River, who would eventually make the discovery on Sunday morning, more than 11 km from the place where she had last been seen four days earlier, and 10 km from where the waters that flowed through Diepsloot joined with the bigger river. Her body was trapped in a pyramid of rubble next to a pedestrian bridge.

A source had tipped me off that the rescue teams were on route and had sent me a location. It was early on Sunday morning, and I was unhindered by traffic. I arrived shortly after the emergency services, just in time to see them cover the child's body where she lay on the river banks, surrounded by debris that had been pulled out of the water with her. The intensity of the current and the effects of being in the water left her almost unrecognisable; she was bloated and decomposing, her small body was patchwork quilt of brown and pink where layers of skin had sloughed off. She was naked, except for a pair of muddied panties.

The fisherman shook his head. 'I thought she was a doll…but when I looked closer…'

Her family arrived shortly after I did; her body needed to be identified before it could be 'processed' by authorities. This time, Sbonisa did not smile and she did not talk. She sat alone with her head in her hands on a sandbank. A short distance away, Thabani knelt over his daughter's body. I watched the scene through tears. I took a photo.

The rescue workers stood to the side with me. Their work was done. In hushed tones, they explained that the stream flowed to a grate, which stopped debris from making its way into the Jukskei River, but that the grating had been bent during the storm, which allowed her body to be swept further than anticipated.

When I finally left the scene, long after her body had been loaded into the state pathology van, the fisherman was still muttering the same words, over and over. 'I thought she was doll. I didn't know…I thought she was a doll.'

In my radio feature, broadcast the Monday after her body had been recovered, police spokesperson Daniel Mavimbela explained that a water safety campaign would be launched in an attempt to keep the children of Diepsloot safe: 'We would like to start educating children about the dangers of water because it is easy for a little kid to underestimate the power that water carries with it. And we want to appeal to the school authorities that they should assess the situation when it rains and if possible, advise the kids to remain behind at school until it is safe for them to go home.'

He added, however, that it was important to remember that while this was a tragedy, nobody was to blame for this unfortunate incident.

Community activist and ANC ward secretary Godfrey Sinthumule, however, did not agree. The radio feature ended with his belief that Angel's untimely and preventable death was a symptom of a much larger societal problem: 'We urge the government to come and help us when we need help, because we need help. We still have a long way to go to improve our community. As you can see, we're living here with the poorest of the poor…there are thousands of people here who are not working, who are unemployed and cannot afford transport for their children to get to school.'

He sighed. 'The life of a black child here is still cheap compared with that of the children living in the suburbs that surround us.'

It took years of activism, protest and political posturing before a modest pedestrian bridge was constructed in her honour, and in 2019 school children and community members were finally afforded safe passage across the waters that took her.

In the ashes of Alex

These incidents are not isolated – the river is prone to flooding, and journalists are often assigned to cover the aftermath of the disasters that ensue. Cars are routinely swept off low-lying bridges, and informal homes and their residents are swallowed by the rising river after heavy rainfall.

This is especially true in Alexandra township. Known colloquially as 'Gomora,' the mixture of formal residential structures, semi-permanent dwellings and informal structures is considered one of the poorest urban areas in the country. The township is a boiling pot of cultures, ethnicities, and nationalities, and while this makes for a vibrant society on a good day, community tensions sporadically erupt into xenophobic violence. As a journalist, I was often caught in the crossfire as residents and police clashed, while politicians fuelled anti-foreigner sentiments to suit their own agendas and hide their own shortcomings.

In the shadow of the Marlboro Gautrain station, alongside one of South Africa's most affluent regions, the cardboard and hardwood shacks of Alex's Stjwetla informal settlement stand in stark contrast to the mansions of its neighbouring suburb of Sandton. Situated on the banks of the Jukskei River, it was here where I first met Brian Mahlangu, a brick-maker from Limpopo who stepped up to lead the community when formal governance structures repeatedly failed him and his neighbours.

REPORTING ON THE JUKSKEI

It was on the banks of the river that our relationship evolved; Brian stopped being a source and became a friend. We spent many afternoons in the shade of a makeshift gazebo overlooking his brickyard on the banks of the Jukskei, sharing stories and debating life from opposite ends of the rivers of history and experiences that should have separated us. Instead, they became a bridge that connected us.

Those very river banks flooded (and continue to flood) frequently, with devastating consequences. But this is not the only danger this community faces. Despite its proximity to water, fires often run rampant through the community, with hundreds of homes lost before the abundant water can even be accessed to aid in extinguishing the flames.

This is the background to an angry rant that I shared on social media on 5 March 2019:

> I'm going to post something I wrote after I left the 'scene' of a township fire earlier this week. It's long, and it's raw. It's sad and it's angry. But despite my disillusionment – stories are meant to be told, so here goes.
>
> I know, I know – I'm a journalist. I'm supposed to have deadlines and sources, soundbites and boundaries. But what happens when a source becomes a person, and that person becomes a friend? And what happens when a soundbite stops being a soundbite and becomes a story? A story that encapsulates the hopes and dreams of a person you have come to know, to respect and even to love?
>
> What happens when you cross that professional boundary, and 500 shacks become 500 homes to 500 families? When you're not standing at the scene of another humanitarian disaster, but you're standing in the ashes of Brian's home? Brian, who has lost so much already and has now lost so much more. What happens when it's not a community member fighting the fire, soot smeared across his cheeks, but Collen. Collen, who talks passionately about poverty and deprivation, economic freedom and pain and unfairness and justice with the same good humour as he talks about his family and his vegetable garden that he has started to feed Stjwetla's kids. Collen, his usually mischievous and smiling face twisted in anger as he hauls bucket after bucket of water scooped from the river uphill, amid the injustice and indifference and lethargy and lack of response by those entrusted with his safekeeping.
>
> What happens when the media staging area isn't a staging area but a community gathering point where you laughed and cried and learnt and shared – hours lazing in the sun, overlooking the temperamental waters below; hours filled with philosophy, religion, politics, history, happiness, pain, dreams, hopes and longings? When the mass of twisted zink (corrugated roof sheets), metal and smouldering wood isn't just that – a

mass – but rather the memory of a twisting alley that you've come to know as well as you know the streets in your own middle-class suburb a world away. What happens when the ruins aren't ruins but landmarks – taps that you've seen repaired, and tarpaulins erected to ward off the waters from above even as the rain caused the river below to swell; chicken mesh that separated the shebeen yard from the area where the women sold Mopani worms and spicy Foxi Nax chips and the open dirt patch where children played hopscotch while their fathers played cards?

Suddenly, you're standing in the outline of what was once a shack, but it's not just one of hundreds of structures that went up in flames – it's the shack where Faith lived. Faith, the little one who defied the odds, despite being born three months premature. Faith, whose tiny body fitted snugly in the crook of my arm when I first met her on Christmas Day, three months after she entered this world. Faith, who first stirred maternal instincts I never knew I possessed.

I would have visited her when I was in the area again; I always did. I promised I would. I can see it now – her mom would embrace me with one arm while using the other to hand me 'my Christmas baby' with a smile. I'd take her in my arms, and at first, I'd balance on the rickety wooden bench that they'd pull closer for me, before eventually moving to the floor, with the doorway behind my back as I cradle her in my lap. I was standing where that doorway was. Where it used to be.

I don't know where Faith and her mom have gone or where they are sleeping, or whether they still have the stuffed toy I gave her that first Christmas when I met her. They managed to save it after the floods a few months ago; perhaps they managed this time too. Standing in that doorway, I prayed for them.

I don't pray, but I prayed today for the first time in years. I prayed from the moment I got news of the fire, as I sped down the N1 and crossed the bridge; all the way to the area that the police had cordoned off. I prayed as I ran down the uneven dirt path, past the newly erected shacks that had materialised since my last visit and past what was left of Collen's vegetable patch. I prayed past the plastic awning that had once collapsed on me when I took cover during a thunderstorm, and I prayed past the port-a-potties that I'd only braved a look into once.

I prayed into the clearing where Brian makes his bricks – the community gathering area, the media staging area – where I was immediately comforted by familiar faces, smeared in soot and drenched to the bone, reassuring me that they were okay, everything was okay, it would all be okay. I didn't have to worry.

It was only when my arms found their way around Brian's neck that the tears started. He dropped the buckets of river water he was hauling, and we held each other. He repeated what the others had said – it would all be okay. I was standing in a community I had come to love, at the centre of a huddle of EFF leaders who were ideologically opposed to everything I represent, clinging for dear life to my brother who had just lost all his worldly possessions – and he was comforting me.

He took me by the hand, and we stood together in the ashes, our line of sight of the winding waters below now unobstructed by the dwellings that usually obscured the view. He assured me that he had saved his important documents, along with the book of poems that he wrote. He told me that we would be back to philosophising under the shading on the river banks in no time; they would rebuild.

The tears kept coming. The forced acceptance of injustice, the resignation to the pain and suffering and the matter-of-fact manner that the losses were assessed; it all burns more than any fucking fire that could rip through a thousand homes.

Later that evening I laughed for the first time again.

I laughed as I sat in the dark, in the wet soot on the floor of one of the 2x2 brick structures that survived the blaze, its walls still warm from the earlier flames and damp from buckets that preserved it. I shared bread and chicken and Fanta orange with six other people as we spoke and joked about the absurdity of it all. Six people who kept thanking me. Thanking me despite the fact that I had nothing to offer except a 2l Coke and a bucket of KFC that they insisted I share in because I hadn't eaten yet either. Thanked me despite the fact that nothing – no soundbite or award-winning feature or headline – nothing that I'd done in the past months had been able to change what led up to this moment.

I said goodbye long after the sun had set, with laughs and hugs and kisses and reassurances that we would see each other soon. I started crying again the moment I got into the car.

I'm still crying. I'm crying because I'm sad. But more than that, I'm crying because I'm angry. I'm so FUCKING angry. I'm furious.

Furious at that resignation to the pain and that acceptance of what has become inevitable. I'm angry that injustice has become the norm and that there is no humanity in our so-called rights. I'm so angry at a system that has asked so much, taken so much, and given nothing in return. I'm angry at a river whose waters offered no protection and little reprieve against the flames; that with the next rainfall would devastate this same community in a different way. Above all, I'm angry at myself that despite all my big talk about stories bringing change, I could not change what happened.

No story has any impact if it keeps falling on the same deaf ears, regardless of how loudly we shout it. Nobody gives a shit if hundreds of more shacks burn down or wash away and thousands of people are left standing in the ruins of their lives – not unless those people know, like I do, that that ruin was where Faith lived. Or where Collen quoted Malcolm X to me with a mischievous smile on his face. Or where Brian sat when the pain became too much, putting pen to paper to stop the memories of his late daughter, Dineo, from slipping away. She was just 16 years old when she died from a manageable autoimmune disease that went undiagnosed by a failing healthcare system for too long.

What use are our sources and our soundbites and our stories if we just end up standing in their ashes as dreams and hopes and rights disappear in flames and mud along with corrugated iron and wood and social spaces and vegetable gardens, all while the powers that be give us another soundbite – a soundbite to try convince us that none of those things should ever have been there in the first place.

Conclusion

Water is not politically neutral. In South Africa, few things are. We cannot talk about the Jukskei River without acknowledging its role as a divider; without acknowledging how its natural geographic barriers were weaponised to uphold apartheid. In apartheid South Africa, the river was a physical and symbolic barrier between the white and non-white populations. In contemporary South Africa, not much has changed – while the system that existed to segregate the people of the land fell almost three decades ago, the physical barriers like the river and the societal divide it created were never dismantled and prevail to this day.

As a journalist, it has been a privilege and a burden to report from both sides of the riverbanks. Some stories stay with us much longer than others. Some stories cannot be washed away. And maybe, some stories shouldn't.

13 The creaturely life of the Jukskei, and anxious bewilderment of faecal discourse

Jessica Webster

This chapter is a meditation on the material state of the Jukskei, as it is filled with pathogenic sewage. The author explores how aesthetics can help us find symbolic meaning in places where meaning seems lost. The author begins from the point that the bewilderment and shock attending media representation of the Jukskei is also a root cause of apathy and inaction. Furthermore, as much as science-based research can provide the grounds for positive solutions, by itself it cannot provide the impetus to act on human and environmental degradation. Instead, a deeper look at figures of trauma engages those ghostly presences that moments of bewilderment and shock leave in our encounters with the degeneration of the Jukskei. The author suggests that reflection on these sensations, however instinctively unwelcome, can derive deeper kinds of empathy required for shifting modes of discourse from faecal-avoidance, to acknowledging shared vulnerability.

Introduction

This chapter develops an aesthetic theme described in terms of 'faecal discourse': a term for media analysis of the 'discursive construction of sewerage and sewage in relation to Johannesburg's Jukskei River.'[1,2] As explored by Iqani and Webster, various news-based narratives pertaining to the Jukskei, and on the failure of South African sewerage infrastructure in general, are seated in narratives of abject disgust with current politics, and post-apartheid traumatic experience – the profound inequity and careless treatment of impoverished citizens and the kind of environments they are forced to inhabit, like they do at large sections of the Jukskei.

Meanwhile, scientific research on the pathological state of the Jukskei is not yet comprehensive, yet indicators are that it is a river of raw faeces, viral bacteria, and buildings are constructed to face away from the canalised waterway, forming a largely ignored corridor where abandoned building waste and weeds choke off the original biome.[3] The back-facing attitude towards natural features of landscape, themselves left to concrete repression, 'urban disorder,' and disintegration, is a documented character of the unique sense of 'dystopia' of Johannesburg at large.[4] From this perspective, Iqani and I have previously described a 'conceptual abyss'[5] that the river represents: it 'falls short of public perception' – it is generally overlooked – and 'the shit exceeds our symbolic sphere,' in its excessive effect of smelly filth and collapse.[6] I explore in further detail this abyssal condition[7] as at once forming the basis of faecal discourse, while it empties discourse of its turn to comparative cultures, to symbolic meaning, and fresh understanding.

At the same time, it is well-theorised that 'technologies of the self' are embedded in and reproduced by the infrastructures that support – or stymy, as the case may be – human flourishing.[8] So too, do the relational role of infrastructural systems condense and displace, congest and discharge our most intimate relations.[9] The felt dimension of bearing witness to the Jukskei's entropy – emotional qualities ranging from disgust to shame, fear to sadness – is reproduced by media reportage but often exceeds it: as writers and readers we are left with a sense of things being incomprehensible. This incomprehension can become a source of bewilderment – being abandoned in a post-apocalyptic wilderness – without a recourse to proper action.[10] Further, this incomprehensibility and bewilderment resonates backwards in the history of lived experience and memory for each individual, of unconscious perceptions and past traumas in South Africa; and it resonates in its particular confusion and disorder because of that history.

However, it may be where this excess of affect meets the river, as site of disuse, of violent poverty, and of excrement, that significant and shared symbolic meaning may yet be obtained. In the stuff of our sewage lie the antagonisms of pathogenic malnourishment and the brute load of overconsumption; a stinking provocation of how infrastructure and its output inform our relationships to each other. But if we can consider this overwhelming stench in itself, a form of life might yet be elaborated in the service of 'faecal discourse.' I theorise here a faecal aesthetics of the Jukskei; a 'poetics of infrastructure' precisely where it concerns 'relationality as the foundational quality of being in common.'[11] Insofar as shit-in-the-river can contextualise and form a metaphor for South Africa's social, political and economic predicament, so too does the river contextualise experience of South African 'infrastructural citizenship.'[12] Through thinking about the shared basis of citizenship in a poetics of infrastructure, I explore through the notion of 'creaturely life' a reflection on the senses of bewilderment emerging from the material and discursive trauma represented by the Jukskei.[13]

A poetics of infrastructure

In Eric Santner's analysis of 'creaturely life' in European postwar literature (2006), he writes that

> 'Creatureliness' [signifies] less a dimension that traverses the boundaries of human and nonhuman forms of life than a specifically human way of finding oneself caught in the midst of antagonisms in and of the political field.[14]

I situate the Jukskei's creaturely life in the particular relationships which produce the river-as-sewerage and of-sewage in contemporary South Africa – a unique and (even futurist?) condition of traumatic biopolitical existence. The notion of creaturely life is then less an objectifying description or naming of organisms in and on the riverbanks. Equally so, it is not a descriptor of humans themselves –

certainly not those who are forced to live near the Jukskei. Rather, the notion of creaturely life refers to a heightened, even 'transgressive' moment of affect that a scene, in its bewildering confrontation with the degradation of techno-political relations, produces in the viewer.[15] That scene is characterised by Santner as a space of melancholic darkness, of entropy and ruinous landscapes, where 'we no longer possess the key to […] meaning.'[16] Rather, the effigies of reason and meaning – what a colonial modernity of infrastructure once stood for – maintain only the shell of their previous condition, pointing in their decay to the evisceration of misbegotten ideals: the remains of modern history in all its violence.

Art critic Claire Bishop deftly defines the notion of aesthetics as 'an autonomous regime of experience that is not reducible to logic, reason or morality.'[17] Santner's creatureliness is aesthetic because it is drawn from the poetry of Rilke, whose work ties traumatic perception specifically to aesthetic experience; outside of reason. Santner approaches aesthetic perception as holding a particular logic in relation to traumatic memory: in its provocation of absence and anxiety, the creature is an expressive figure eliciting the relation between a traumatic past and ruins of the present. Furthermore, this creaturely figure represents 'a perpetual state of exception/emergency in which the boundaries of the law are undecidable.'[18]

The Jukskei embodies this tension between past and present, law and transgression, and so it reflects much of the social and political state of South Africa. How we see the 'body' of the Jukskei River is far removed from its conventional understanding of flowing water and animal inhabitants making a babbling way through rocky banks. The Jukskei is not only a watery stream (or a collection of streams) but also a sewage-filled rampart; it not only designates a place and a boundary running on a map, but it also represents a historical goldmining site always already prone to neglect and illegal dumping. These tensions in the Jukskei's lack of meaning feel unwelcome, and it is no surprise the Jukskei is ignored. However, the 'state of exception/emergency' aroused by those tensions, the creaturely way in which its presence creeps upon the neck of the perceiver, holds value. Potentially, the traumatic aesthetics provoked by the sewage-filled canal may offer a more intimate pause for the privileged observer, who otherwise views these effects through the portal of media and day-visits to a shock-tainted grotesque, and who otherwise forgets that creaturely bewilderment runs in a deep vein of shared humanity.

Mythical undercurrents in/of faecal discourse

A number of recent critical texts suggest a return to traditions evoking supernatural phenomena as crucially decolonial forms of reinvesting environments with resonance and meaning, especially as it may transcend the normative view of a landscape's economic value and surplus.[19] Indigenous Amerindian ecologist Robin Wall Kimmerer uses the Anishinaabe figure of the 'Windigo,' a monstrous folkloric spirit who roams the forests consuming everything in its path, animal and child alike, as a traumatic metaphor embodying the violent extraction of natural resources wrought by capitalist industry.[20] But the figure of Windigo also retains a significant message from the past, which is that 'Windigo nature is in each of us…that we might learn why we should recoil from our greedy part of ourselves' and thus, rather, choose to embody external qualities of nature which enable a gentle balance between consumption and regeneration.[21]

Where the Jukskei is concerned, however, my interest is less to suggest a return to myth than to explore experience caught in the aftershock of a 'Windigo' monster – the Jukskei bearing the remains of a history of extraction, of social prejudice and incomprehensibly reckless neglect. This place is inhabited by a figure of mourning, a melancholic creature crawling in the very brownfield banks, sewer lines and waste that dominate the river as it exists today. This 'mournful dimension' holds the aesthetic quality of what I am calling the 'creaturely life' of the Jukskei.[22]

In his treatise on 'creaturely life,' Santner's main point of reference are the remnants of world war and the Holocaust, still visible in European city and rural landscapes.[23] He analyses the postwar fiction of German writer W.G. Sebald, whose forms depend on the 'flayed surfaces of urban space' left to ruin in Europe.[24] But we find ourselves with a different set of relations in South Africa, where the ruins of history seem as layers under fresh ruins – the half-dug cabling and open drain-ways left to inorganic putrefaction, the half-begun and careless attempts to restitute the Jukskei. This vein of ruin-on-ruin, a psychological depth of perpetually flayed surfaces and bodies, is explored intensively through Achille Mbembe's notion of 'necropolitics,' where those in power determine life and death, opting for death where it can maintain the lowest ebb of agency for their citizens….Enacted particularly in the postcolony, Mbembe writes, it is where 'sovereignty consists fundamentally in the exercise of a power outside the law…and where "peace" is more likely to take on the face of a "war without end." '[25]

At the receiving end of total sovereignty, those without agency in Mbembe's theory of necropolitics, are historically and at present the black working class in South Africa. In an article for *Mail & Guardian* (2022), psychologist and writer Hugo Ka Canham describes a similar concern for

> the mourning classes [who] are always working class and black. Those unable to turn to insurance, second homes and savings. These are Frantz Fanon's wretched of the Earth whose dazed faces we see searching for their dead, livestock and meagre possessions. Our television screens are filled with their haunted eyes.[26]

And yet, in Ka Canham concept of 'riotous deathscapes,' precisely this class of people are characterised as the protagonists, those with an *essential* type of agency that remains, precisely, in those sites of disorder and disuse so ubiquitous in South Africa.[27]

At this point of melancholic haunting, Ka Canham invokes the potential of the river. Rivers hold sacred significance in Canham's Mpondo traditional personhood, prompting his entreaty to imbibe the 'cleansing and fortifying' role of the natural world as a vital form of relation for people otherwise forced to 'riotousness' and suffering under communal trauma.

On the banks of the Jukskei, the very leakage of faecal matter into the river condenses the necropolis and deathscape, where the waste of both empowered and powerlessness intermingle and merge in polluted waters. This displacement of faecal matter in a river, a perpetual river-of-shit, exposes the perverse relations between power and powerlessness to the eye of the media cameras, the journalist writers, and the purveyors of discourse. The entangled relation of power and manifest vulnerability lies exposed like so many 'torn and opened bodies' of 'wound culture'[28]; spoiling for choice the great and distant eye of TV, a way of mourning which offers only bewilderment in the profane.

If material exchanges and toxic intimacies are relayed at a distance to the purveyor-viewers discourse and media, it is a distance that grips on disgust and 'riotous' sensations. This truly slippery moment is dragged into oblique comprehension by Santner's evocation of 'the creaturely' as sensing a 'state of emergency' where laws are 'undecidable.'[29] Santner links this to the aesthetics of psychoanalyst Jacques Lacan, whose notion of *jouissance* is a term normally reserved for positive sexual enjoyment; a kind of thrilling satisfaction. But in the realm of the creaturely, an aesthetic trigger of 'ex-citement and discharge' is irradiated by at once encountering and being alienated by entropy in/of infrastructure; what I am exploring in terms of bewilderment.[30]

Indeed, bewilderment resonates with the creaturely evoked by Santner as a 'captivated' shock, caught in a 'disenchantment' of 'ex-citation and discharge.'[31] The bewildering affect Santner affords shock in these moments embed perception right down to the viscera of embodied experience. 'Exciting'/triggering an overly intimate recognition of these sights and smells, 'discharge' involves a flickering emptying of immediate threat this river may pose. The moment repeats again and again on the perceiving self, a battle with proximity and distance to thrill and discharge, of lure and repulsion.

These familiar if negative moments hold resonance for thinking a contemporary climate of environmental cataclysm and political strife: the body of the perceiver is situated in relation to 'other' bodies, an aesthetic moment inducing the bewildered 'cringing' of the self in a field of 'shame.'[32] As incomprehensibly terrible this point of cognition is, however, does it not bring the body of you, the perceiver, into a specifically situated awareness, into the ruinous frame of the present moment, where the bodies and lived experiences of others are brought, if only for a moment, into a deeply shared space of re-cognition? Can we indeed recognise the depths by which this end-zone of apocalyptic extraction and socio-environmental injury – the bewildering dialectic of 'excitement and discharge' it engenders – presents a creaturely life-force which is traumatic *but* shared? The sharing of faeces comingled with the river provokes the question of new identities, new forms of infrastructural

Gaping restoration

There's a story that provokes, rather than describes, the creaturely life of the Jukskei River in Johannesburg. In resistance to the tendencies of 'poverty porn' to make spectacular, some artists refuse to create conventional forms of art, opting instead for active participation in and (creaturely) experience of the wasteland. Io Makandal, an environmental artist working in Johannesburg, draws many of her materials directly from the riparian zones of the Jukskei. These generate what she calls 'hybrid ecologies' comprised of everything from concrete debris, old carpets and other junked items; to mud, moss and mould; to precious indigenous seeds still found scattered from the originary biome. Makandal creates socially active artwork which situates viewers as inhabitants of the environment, rather than spectators. They invite reflection on one's position in the dystopian context of Johannesburg and its failing infrastructures. That situatedness in space is also intended to cultivate alertness to the multiple forms of plant, animal and human life that continue above the mortification of other forms, unabated. The present condition of the Jukskei is less a 'wound that needs healing' she says, than a place with a future to which it is worth finding a 'conscious relationship' (Webster in conversation with Makandal, 2022).

Her recent work concerned the slow installation of a 'Listening Garden' (2022–2023). This was placed on the edge of the Jukskei canal, adjacent to a new afterschool care centre started by local resident Lungile Hlatshwayo for indigent children in the area. As Makandal explained (Webster 2022), the children participated in the process of designing the small garden by placing plants and concrete pieces, flower beds and decorations of found objects to create a sitting area. In addition, the children were invited to draw and describe the environment of the canal – part grassy embankment, part brick-and-mortar alley, with the humming stream running below – and their drawings reproduced in perspex signs to draw the attention of visitors from the nearby shopping centre to the space. This was the children's only open play area. It was the artist's intent that it be a more comfortable space for them and visitors, focusing on the presence of the river and the confluence of sensations, both difficult and pleasurable, enabling a quiet space for reflection on problematic water and ecologies within urban brownfields.

While the garden was being established in early 2023, two events occurred which almost permanently disrupted the garden's progress. First, Lungile shockingly died of stress-related illness, and the aftercare was suspended. Then, the shopping centre management sent construction workers into the area for renovations to the centre's external boundary wall without alerting workers to the indigenous grassland and flowers growing there, or the understated sitting area that was functioning as a nuanced form of art. The builders mixed concrete on the garden itself and scattered rubble and waste over the signs and flowers, devastating the site. Makandal has worked to clear the space of unwanted debris and replanted flowers and grasses. But the event of damage led to ideas for installing a more iconic work at the site so that people are made conscious of a set of relationships between matter and the river which construct the area as a purposeful space; while yet maintaining the absence of day-to-day purpose and reason this canal alleyway represents.

Using clay bricks from old gold-mining-era demolished houses, Makandal built a curved bridge linking the haphazard semi-abandoned industrial side of the canal to the commercial centre. Entitled *Ophidian's Promise* (2024) the large-scale yet delicate edifice references the many mythological symbols of the snake (an 'ophidian') in ancient African and European cultures, indicating the potential of fresh 'skins' in the habitat of nature and the river. The dappled and time-eaten bricks of the bridge, once home to migrants from the world over, are elegantly yet somewhat precariously layered to bow over the canal, a spectacular scene which is *as* haunting as it functions as 'an invitation of repair to the more-than-human entities, living beings and materialities that make up the precious and precarious environment.'[33]

Figure 13.1 Ophidian's Promise, *2024. Artist: Io Makandal (public artwork commission by Alserkal Advisory for A Feral Common, curated by Tairone Bastien). Site: Victoria Yards over the Jukskei River culvert. Image credit: courtesy Io Makandal, photographed by Brett Rubin*

Co-habiting disenchantment

From newly-bridged canals of the Jukskei River, crossing to an oceanic island across the globe, degradations of environment often involve the disappearance of supernatural beings whose lost mediumship over body and forest reflect growing disinterest in the welfare of environment and/as identity. In an embracing linguistic study and diary on a remote Papua New Guinea tribe, anthropologist Don Kulick (2019) enlists the multiple forms of 'death' which occur when a native language degrades, dissolves, and finally disappears, under the weight of modernity. The context is, firstly, the physical effects on land and environment arising with the gradual and sudden assumption of colonialist, capitalist desire (for sterile, unwooded landscapes, roads – where there are no cars – and other half-usable goods and products). Secondly, it is amongst the loss of memory attending the loss of a language, used to describe one's culture and its sacred objects. In this context, an elder's recounting of a rainforest (once populated with what Kulick calls 'supernatural beings') stands out:

> These ranged from powerful spirits called *emari*, who commonly took the form of giant crocodiles, to mischievous elflike dwarves who lived in the crowns of trees [...] Raya laughed nostalgically when he remembered that encounter, and then he grew serious. Nobody ever sees forest beings these days, he told me in a quiet, puzzled tone. He guessed that this must be because they have retreated; they've either moved ever deeper into the rainforest, or they've paddled away over sea [...] Perceiving that villagers were no longer interested in them and were no longer paying them any attention or respect, the crocodile spirits and the tree-dwelling dwarves must have packed up their belongings, and left.[34]

If supernatural beings were once spotted moving through the watery vleis and valleys of Johannesburg's landscape, the records have been obliterated by colonial conflict and possession and their concomitant gold rushes. Finally, the 'modernisation' of the springs and river have covered ancient signs and traces in concrete.[35] Rather than any one indigenous social identity, it is the Jukskei River's devastation as ecological and historical site that locates it in a space analogous to the death of a language as described by Kulick.

But a language remains. While there is no longer any single indigenous language spoken throughout the Jukskei area, it is rather the perpetual appropriation of the river concourse as so many watering holes and ox-wagon stops, as gold deposit, as drainage canal and finally a dumping site for displaced migrants, exiles and disadvantaged women and children, that determines its course as a particular form of metaphor and metonymy (substitution). From the river's origins as Edenic proliferation of 'white waters' and gushing springs,[36] to the current concrete of pathogenic ooze and stinking issue, the river dies multiple symbolic deaths... and yet, it runs on. Indeed, it is a strange and estranging form of death because, as Don Kulick equally asserts of the Tayap tribe, it doesn't entail the total loss of life and identity, or the resumption of supernaturality. Instead, it evokes echoes of these histories in the anxious discharge of encountering and re-encountering the creaturely life of the Jukskei.

Faecal matter in the Jukskei negates the river's aesthetic and symbolic function, and therefore the river's social, public reason for being: it points towards 'a broader sense of post-colonial collapse of both infrastructure and trust in those responsible for it.'[37] In this chapter, I have characterised that negation – as it affects matters of trust in authority in a post-apartheid democracy – for the hazardous condition of 'social connectivity' in rivers that the Jukskei in its current state materialises – a state that is antithetical to the forms of connectivity that vibrant rivers are theorised as providing.[38] But paradoxically, perhaps, a certain symbolic sense of social connectivity is contextualised by faecal waste and fear – of collective bewilderment in what the matter of present and future are really comprised of. If recognised, analysed and reflected upon, this form of shared, affective alienation may contain the germ of collective agency, beyond the mirror of brutality in the modern South African landscape.

Notes

1   Mehita Iqani and Jessica Webster, 'Johannesburg's Shitty Little River: Faecal Discourse and Discontent Regarding the Jukskei,' *Social Dynamics Journal* (February 2022).

2   Kousar Banu Hoorzook, Anton Pieterse, Lee Heine & Tobias George Barnard, 'Soul of the Jukskei River: The Extent of Bacterial Contamination in the Jukskei River in Gauteng Province, South Africa,' *International Journal of Environmental Research and Public Health (IJERPH)*. (August 2021).

3   Liz Day, 'Jukskei Rejuvenation Project: Aquatic Ecology Status Quo Report with Conceptual Recommendations,' Report for Emifula Consultants (Johannesburg: Freshwater Consultants CC, 2018).

4   Sandiswa Mapukata, *South African Urban Imaginaries: Cases from Johannesburg*, ed. Richard Ballard (Gauteng City-Region Observatory, 2022), https://doi.org/10.36634/KDEW3665; Landi Raubenheimer, 'Nostalgic Dystopia in Neill Blomkamp's District 9: An Emerging Idiom of Johannesburg as Landscape in Film, Photography and Popular Media, 1994-2018' (PhD, Netherlands, University of Groningen, 2021).

5   The 'abyss' in this sense describes how it is difficult to form an integrated idea of the river because, on the one hand, it has been constructed as a back-faced canal which is easy to ignore, and it is. On the other hand, wherever one does happen to stumble across the river, the stark sight and wretched smells can be overwhelming.

6   Mehita Iqani and Jessica Webster, 'Johannesburg's Shitty Little River: Faecal Discourse and Discontent Regarding the Jukskei,' *Social Dynamics Journal* (February 2022).

7   The 'abyss' in this sense describes how it is difficult to form an integrated idea of the river because on the one hand, it has been constructed as a back-faced canal which is easy to ignore, and it is. On the other hand, wherever one does happen to stumble across the river, the stark sight and wretched smells can be overwhelming.

8   Michel Foucault et al., eds., *Technologies of the Self: A Seminar with Michel Foucault* (Amherst: University of Massachusetts Press, 1988).

9   Steven Robins, Andrea Cornwall, and Bettina Von Lieres, 'Rethinking "Citizenship" in the Postcolony,' *Third World Quarterly* 29, no. 6 (September 2008): 1069–1086, https://doi.org/10.1080/01436590802201048; Charlotte Lemanski, 'Infrastructural Citizenship: The Everyday Citizenships of Adapting and/or Destroying Public Infrastructure in Cape Town, South Africa,' *Transactions of the Institute of British Geographers* 45, no. 3 (September 2020): 589–605, https://doi.org/10.1111/tran.12370; Lauren Berlant, 'The Commons: Infrastructures for Troubling Times*,' *Environment and Planning D: Society and Space* 34, no. 3 (June 2016): 393–419, https://doi.org/10.1177/0263775816645989.

10 My evocation of 'bewilderment' connects to Giorgio Agamben's treatise (2005) on the 'biopolitical life' of citizens being subject to political power to the extent that life experience is wholly defined by reigning politics: in the same way as an animal is theorised as defined by the exigencies of the wild to both protect and expose the animal to numerous dangers and traumas. Indeed, Santer's notion of 'creaturely life' deploys Agamben's philosophy to shift understanding of human/animal subjectivity as a concept underpinned by trauma (Agamben in Santner 2006, pg 12).

11 Brian Larkin, 'The Politics and Poetics of Infrastructure,' *Annual Review of Anthropology* 42, no. 1 (2013): 327–343, https://doi.org/10.1146/annurev-anthro-092412-155522; Berlant, 'The Commons.'

12 Lemanski, 'Infrastructural Citizenship.'

13 Santner, Eric L., *On Creaturely Life: Rilke, Benjamin, Sebald.* University of Chicago Press, 2006.

14 Santner, *On Creaturely Life*, xix.

15 Santner, 22.

16 Santner, 17.

17 Claire Bishop, 'Artificial Hells: Participatory Art and the Politics of Spectatorship,' *Choice Reviews Online* 50, no. 08 (April 1, 2013): 50-4224, https://doi.org/10.5860/CHOICE.50-4224.

18 Santner, 21.

19 Shiri Pasternak et al., 'Infrastructure, Jurisdiction, Extractivism: Keywords for Decolonising Geographies,' *Political Geography*, December 2022, 102763, https://doi.org/10.1016/j.polgeo.2022.102763; Donna Jeanne Haraway, *Staying with the Trouble: Making Kin in the Chthulucene*, Experimental Futures: Technological Lives, Scientific Arts, Anthropological Voices (Durham: Duke University Press, 2016); Robin Wall Kimmerer, *Braiding Sweetgrass: Indigenous Wisdom, Scientific Knowledge and the Teachings of Plants* (Milkweed Editions, 2013); Anna Lowenhaupt Tsing, *In the Realm of the Diamond Queen* (Princeton, N.J: Princeton University Press, 1993), https://press.princeton.edu/books/paperback/9780691000510/in-the-realm-of-the-diamond-queen; Hugo ka Canham, *Riotous Deathscapes* (USA: Duke University Press, 2023).

20 Kimmerer, *Braiding Sweetgrass*, 304.

21 Kimmerer, *Braiding Sweetgrass*, 306.

22 Santner, *On Creaturely Life*, 10.

23 Santner, *On Creaturely Life*, xx.

24 Santner, *On Creaturely Life*, xx.

25 J. A. Mbembe and Libby Meintjes, 'Necropolitics,' *Public Culture* 15 (January 1, 2003): 11–40.

26 Hugo ka Canham, 'OPINION| Wretched Zones of the Damned in South Africa,' *The Mail & Guardian*, May 1, 2022, https://mg.co.za/thoughtleader/opinion/2022-05-01-opinion-wretched-zones-of-the-damned-in-south-africa/.

27 Canham, *Riotous Deathscapes*.

28 Mark Seltzer, 'Wound Culture: Trauma in the Pathological Public Sphere,' *October* 80 (1997): 3, https://doi.org/10.2307/778805.

29 Santner, *On Creaturely Life*, 21.

30 Santner, 15.

31 Santner, 10, 26.

32 Santner, 23.

33 Io Makandal, 'Ophidian's Promise: Global Co-Commission in Partnership with Victoria Yards and Water for the Future' (Johannesburg: Unpublished press release, 2024).

34 Don Kulick, *A Death in the Rainforest: How a Language and a Way of Life Came to an End in Papua New Guinea* (United Kingdom: Hachette UK, 2019).

35 Marian P. Laserson, 'Renovation of the Jukskei River Canal in Bertrams, Lorentzville, Judith's Paarl to Bezuidenhout Valley,' 2018.

36 Willem Snyman, 'Op-Ed: A Return to Source: Saving the Witwatersrand's Ancient Freshwater System to Save South Africa's Rivers,' *Daily Maverick*, November 26, 2021, https://www.dailymaverick.co.za/article/2021-11-26-a-return-to-source-saving-the-witwatersrands-ancient-freshwater-system-to-save-south-africas-rivers/.

37 Azwidohwi Benson Neswiswi, 'Development of Water Quality Index (Wqi) For The Jukskei River Catchment, Johannesburg,' Research report in partial fulfillment, University of the Witwatersrand (Johannesburg, 2014).

38 G. Mathias Kondolf and Pedro J. Pinto, 'The Social Connectivity of Urban Rivers,' *Geomorphology*, Connectivity in Geomorphology from Binghamton 2016, 277 (January 15, 2017): 182–196, https://doi.org/10.1016/j.geomorph.2016.09.028.

PART 4
RIVER LIVING

14 *On the edge: Riverbank living along a Jukskei tributary*

Sarah Charlton

Riverside living along the Braamfontein Spruit in Johannesburg presents a complex narrative of informal living, particularly through the experiences of individuals like Peter, who has resided there for over four years. Utilising rudimentary materials such as plastic for shelter and wood for cooking, Peter's living conditions highlight the precariousness of urban poverty. Daily activities, including laundry and personal hygiene, are conducted in the river, while personal belongings are often hidden in nearby bushes to avoid theft or removal by authorities. This informal lifestyle, while framed here as a form of housing, reflects broader socio-economic challenges faced by residents who often feel invisible to wealthier communities. The dynamics of choice and agency are central to understanding their situation, as many migrants arrive in Johannesburg seeking better opportunities, but encounter unfulfilled expectations. Interviews with park dwellers reveal a spectrum of experiences, underscoring the stigma of returning home without financial success. Economic pressures compel individuals to prioritise remittances over personal needs, while casual work in informal economies becomes a survival strategy. The study critiques simplistic definitions of homelessness, advocating for nuanced interventions that address sanitation and infrastructure, recognising the agency of individuals within their circumstances.

Introduction

Peter[1] points as he says 'I sleep under that big tree. When it is raining, I use a big [piece of] plastic that we collected from furniture shops.' For cooking Peter uses wood to make a fire and pots acquired from a friend. Peter does his laundry in the river and also washes his body there. His belongings are hidden in the bushes. Indicating that he has lived here for more than four years, ever since arriving in Johannesburg, Peter says: 'This is the only place I know.'

Peter is describing the daily practicalities of life along the Braamfontein Spruit, a watercourse wending its way through the affluent, mainly residential, suburbs of northern Johannesburg, heading towards the Jukskei River. At least, this is life for those living informally, often clandestinely, frequently precariously, along the river's banks. Often either invisible to the property-owning classes, or feared, sidelined and targeted for removal by them, this chapter positions their living situation as constituting a form of housing in the city.

The chapter shows how for many park dwellers this form of living does not amount to a disconnected parallel existence on the margins, but instead is entwined with maintaining and sustaining an urban existence, as well as lives beyond Johannesburg. Riverside living constitutes a layer amongst multiple and diverse efforts to live extremely low cost in the city, and can co-exist, or intertwine with other forms of accommodation. The park, and the river within this, facilitate a strategy of living ultra-low budget in several ways: through the physical space it provides, its vegetation for concealment, water for clothes and body washing, and its access to ways of generating income in the prosperous neighbourhoods alongside. While the need to live like this is an indictment on the city's overlay of wealth and poverty, spatial structure and its political economy, comprehending riverbank occupation in this way draws attention to the factors underpinning these practices. Interwoven with this lens is thus how people select this life, or else are forced into it through lack of options and structural circumstances. This debate helps open imagination to interventions better targeted to address the multi-layered drivers of riverside living.

Seeing riverbank living as ultra-low-budget accommodation is not a perspective recognised in policy nor by many fellow city-dwellers, who more typically label this as homelessness. In the first section below, I outline the distinctions I make from the terminology of homelessness, and why this is significant. I go on to discuss how living rough (on the streets or public spaces) can be seen as either a form of freedom and claim-making, or its opposite: the absence of choice. With this as overall framing – the contestation with the notion of homelessness, and the debate on the extent of choice involved – I discuss the data-collection approach underpinning this chapter. Findings from interviews with park dwellers reveal varying degrees and dimensions of personal agency, but demonstrate that the notion of 'choice' in relation to living by the river in Johannesburg is a slippery, complex notion to be used with care. I discuss these findings relative to the notion of street homelessness and the political economy of accommodation in Johannesburg, showing the complex mix of agency and lack of agency in living rough on a tributary of the Jukskei River.

Introducing homelessness vs ultra low cost living

Peter's way of living is, I argue, one of a number of practices in Johannesburg where people prioritise 'living cheaply' in some way. These intersect with a spectrum of shelter circumstances and associated costs, ranging from assembling or purchasing rooms of provisional materials in informal settlements, renting a tiny space in a multi-occupied room or apartment, particularly in the inner city, or renting a room in a yard (backyarding). Occupants' levels of affordability and circumstances vary considerably, but include very limited funds to spend on their shelter and infrastructure. In extreme situations, people cut these costs entirely and live rough, for various reasons. Though often because they literally do not have money to pay for shelter, it may also be because they are choosing to spend such funds in other ways – notably, to send to family living elsewhere.

Additional circumstances which result in living shelter-less are those of informal reclaimers. Apart from very low earnings, the nature of their work requires periods of time living with their goods and cart, during the cycle of collecting, sorting, stockpiling and selling generally high volumes of low value goods. Many reclaimers work the streets of Johannesburg, including its multiple residential suburbs, with some periodically sleeping and sorting in parks and other open spaces such as road reserves.[2,3]

The chapter argues for differentiating these circumstances from amongst a wider grouping of people positioned as street homeless, who reflect a diverse set of trajectories and circumstances, including people with substance abuse or mental health difficulties. Those living rough along the Braamfontein Spruit are often conflated in an undifferentiated grouping labelled 'homeless,' or 'vagrants,' but in fact many of their circumstances elevate other dimensions of the complex matter of pared-down living circumstances (dimensions not necessarily unique to this riverine environment but well-illustrated by it). Later in the chapter I illustrate the ways in which the study's findings contest the notion of homelessness. Into this debate comes the issue of living shelter-less as freedom, or its opposite, and I turn to a brief outline of this next.

Living shelterless as freedom and exertion of rights, or its opposite?

Does living unsheltered in a city represent an expression of freedom and exertion of rights, to access city opportunities, or its opposite – the absence of choice and rights? Does it reflect an inability to exercise agency towards a life of meaning, or is it an embodiment of agency? There are divergent perspectives on this. A capabilities approach concerned with the notion of inequality has been used by Greenwood et al.,[4] who assess homelessness against the ideal of having 'the freedom to do and be' within an environment. Homelessness is understood as caused by, and representing, a deficit of capabilities, where the diverse assets or resources needed for a meaningful life crafted and valued by the individual themselves, have been eroded (ibid). The condition of being homeless is thus 'a situation of extreme unfairness that severely restricts individuals' freedom to achieve their full potential and live a dignified, fulfilling life.'[5]

Taking a different line and from a South African perspective, De Beer and Valley[6] refer to some forms of street homelessness in South Africa as constituting in some way 'an economic choice.' They characterise living in this way as 'insisting on access to the city and its resources.' Seen this way the practice is, for some people, exerting a right to claim a stake in opportunities, though people living in these situations themselves do not express it this way.[7] Critically though, the point is made that any such 'choice' is made within the deep confines of structural conditions shaping society. This perspective nevertheless draws attention to a degree of agency and self-determination in the circumstance, though almost universally unrecognised as this by authorities and fellow city-residents alike.

Part of the significance of these debates relate to what are conceptualised as the core interventions needed in response. For Greenwood et al.,[8] interventions and services should be measured by the extent to which they improve capabilities. Integral to their position is that a 'home' is essential in supporting capabilities, offering 'ontological security, which is the experience of privacy, safety and control over one's environment.'[9] Busch-Geertsema et al.[10] privilege three key dimensions of home which they see homeless people lacking, namely legal security of place, a location for social interactions, and decent physical shelter. Their notion of homelessness is, at its core 'lacking access to minimally adequate housing.'[11]

With these concerns, delivering a home is the priority intervention identified – sometimes in the form of institutionally-run overnight or longer-term shelters, or else other forms of more independent housing. In these debates, the point is made that personal aspects such as relations of power, all influence the extent to which a house becomes a home.[12]

Later I debate this position – of the core understanding of homelessness as being without a home and the key priority intervention needed as provision of a home. But first I discuss how, in this research, we obtained the data from respondents living rough along the Spruit, before presenting findings that relate to the complex matter of choice and agency.

Collecting stories from riverside living

In 2018, our research team explored the stories and motivations of people living rough along the Braamfontein Spruit, in a section before it joins the Jukskei River. Fieldworkers came from the Homeless Writers Project, whose stories provided the foundation for the acclaimed film *Vaya*, and the book of the same name. Madoda Ntuli, Tshabalira Lebakeng, Anthony Mafela and David Majoka, undertook interviews along the Spruit supported by the author and by Homeless Writers' Project's Harriet Perlman, writer and film producer.

For multiple reasons, accessing people living unsheltered, in their place of residence, for an engaged and sensitive discussion about their circumstances is difficult: park-dwellers are often wanting to avoid interactions with strangers who may pose a threat or be exerting a form of authority (perceived or actual); they may feel self-conscious about their circumstances; they may be involved in clandestine or illicit activities; they may simply wish to be left alone.

As their name indicates, the Homeless Writers have all experienced forms of street homelessness and have developed multiple skills through navigating the streets of Johannesburg. This equipped them with the practical abilities and insights to seek out and interact with those they encountered. They received training at Wits University on key ethics issues, interview techniques, and data capture, and we worked through and refined the interview guide together. For all the fieldworkers it was their first time undertaking formal research.

The Writers worked in pairs, with one person leading the discussion, and the other taking notes, as we anticipated recorded interviews would not be welcome. In the subsequent write-ups, interviewers were encouraged to include their observations, feelings and impressions. The write-ups varied in style and length: some aimed to capture some of the actual words used by respondents. In other instances the fieldworker summarised their recall and their own assessment of the respondent and their situation. Some respondents provided quite a lot of detail; others provided only very brief information and did not want to engage in depth.

We used five different access points along an approximately 10 km stretch of river-park. Twenty-eight respondents were interviewed between April and June 2018. The vast majority were men, but three were women. Respondents did not always divulge their age, but data coupled with observation put the age range from early 20s to 62 years old. A number of participants were from the surrounding countries of Lesotho, Mozambique and Zimbabwe, but at least 15 of the respondents were from various parts of South Africa. Some had been living in the park for a few months; some intermittently spent time there but also had other accommodation in Johannesburg; and others had lived there for very long periods (such as for 'more than 10 years,' 18, 21 years, and astonishingly in one case, 32 years.)

Choice and agency on the Braamfontein Spruit

In this section I organise findings from the fieldwork for their resonance with the theme of freedom/choice or its opposite, outlined earlier. The discussion shows how the issue of choice (and agency) or its absence, in life along the riverbank, is complex, with dimensions expressed in multiple ways and at different scales by respondents. Material is organised into three themes: the pull but potential trap of coming to Johannesburg; networks and their navigation; and the difficulty of moving on from riverside living, or the desire to retain a connection there.

The pull but potential trap of coming to Johannesburg

A number of respondents spoke of trying to access Johannesburg as a place for work or opportunity – coming from elsewhere to this big metropolis with the hope of finding work. Although interviewees such as Amos suggest a degree of agency as he 'decided to go and look for work in the city,' it is clear from his story and that of many others that circumstances in their place of origin left no real option but to migrate in search of jobs. The pressure of needing to support dependents was a key driver: 'we are forced to come to Johannesburg to work' as 'we can't stay back home without providing for our families' (Mandla). For Theo the issue of masculinity is explicit in these pressures: 'as a man you have to go out and hunt for the family.'

But although Johannesburg lured them with its evocation of economic activities and jobs, these proved elusive, transitory or meagre. Yet with unfulfilled expectations, going back to their former life was not really an option. Similar stresses to those driving their original migration prevented some of the respondents from leaving their life in Johannesburg, and in particular river-side living, and returning home. Meshak says 'I can't go home and stay there because there are no jobs [there].' Ivan describes how he battles to send any money home, and, knowing he is struggling in Johannesburg his family once wanted to send money for him to travel back home. But he told them to 'use that money for food.' Also making reference to the expectations attached to him he explained that as he's the 'man' he must provide, not be the one taking money from home. But he says, he didn't tell his family he's living 'like monkey in bush,' forced there when he was not paid wages he was owed and, without a financial cushion to tide him over, ran out of rent money.

For others, there is shame in going home without showing material success from their life in Johannesburg: Julius commented that 'he won't go back home because the village will call him names – a loser.' By contrast, at the time of the interview James had decided to go back home to Mozambique permanently at the end of that year. But though he 'would love to be at home with my family….going home without money to support them is a nightmare.' Though he is able to afford to get himself home he comments that 'the saddest part of all is that I will go back without anything while I left a long time ago.'

Networks

Networks and relationships also allude to aspects of choice and agency. On their arrival in Johannesburg a number of respondents relied on networks of family, friends or kin, for information or access to accommodation in the city. Then, in a second stage move, networks also assisted with finding the river-park to live in. These subsequent relocations to the park evidenced varying levels of agency, or lack of it. In a name-echo of the place he would end up living in, Tom's first locality in Gauteng was in the neighbourhood of Spruitview ('view of the stream') in the East Rand (Ekurhuleni) where he had a 'homeboy' connection – a friend who he had grown up with in Lesotho. When the cost of commuting from the East Rand to more central parts of Gauteng became too expensive, his construction-work networks led him to the banks of the Braamfontein Spruit in northern Johannesburg and he decided – made the choice, perhaps – to join the way of living of 'the other guys who use to work with him.' At the time of the interview, he had lived along the river bank for six years, accessing 'piece' jobs and sending small portions of money back to his wife and child (interview with Tom).

In a situation indicating very few alternatives Miriam was 'fetched by her friend from Lesotho to work at Jozi, only to find out it was only three months' work.' When the work ran out her friend couldn't help her with a place to sleep. Miriam found a boyfriend working in recycling and living along the river, where she also now lives.

Pressures from urban families also account for riverbank living. Khotso first stayed in his cousin's house in Alexandra, but left under pressure from his cousin's wife as he

ON THE EDGE

was not working and not contributing to the household. He decided to move out, and joined people he knew from home who were living next to the river. Unemployed Ami also landed there after he was unable to contribute financially after the birth of another child: 'I was not allowed to see my kids until I bring some money.' For all of these respondents, riverbank living provided an alternative when their original plan failed or became unviable or impractical.

Some respondents had a more traumatic displacement from their erstwhile living conditions, and the emergency connections and networks led them to the park. Matt was earning enough to rent a shack in Alex, but in a period of xenophobic violence 'they burn my shack with everything I had.' He fled in terror and never returned, and when his plumbing job terminated in the same month, he followed the example of friends living in a park: 'that's how I started sleeping like this.' Fear of the society around him but also his financial situation shaped his 'choice.' Similarly, Mpho ran away from Diepsloot after finding someone had simply occupied his brother's small shop whilst Mpho was away attending to his brother's burial, 'killed in Diepsloot by tsotsis.' After sleeping at Park Station for a week, friends he made there, also from his home country of Mozambique, helped him buy stock for a new business. Though these friends subsequently left the country during xenophobic violence, 'they are the ones who brought me here,' to the river where he now peddles clothes to other riverside dwellers.

For some people – as with Peter at the beginning of this chapter, riverbank living is all they have known in Johannesburg, or all they anticipated or planned when they envisaged life in the city. When he left home in Lesotho in 2007 Theo 'knew that he was coming to live by the river,' having followed in the footsteps of a friend who had told him how he survives in Joburg. Theo seems at peace with the situation: 'I'm fine here staying with my brothers from home; we know each other.' Reliant on intermittent casual work, Derek arrived some 30 years ago looking for a job. The interviewer notes that 'he chose this place (Riverside) next to the river because he can get piece jobs around the area and also it is for him to wash clothes and himself in the river.' Others have become reconciled to their situation: Although his arrival in the river park was precipitated by a frightening episode, Matt seems resigned to living on piece jobs and has no plans to move away from the riverside.

Stuck on the riverbank or using it intermittently

It is clear that some of those living along the river would like to leave, or to get themselves out of their situation, but are in a sense stuck there. Miriam, working hard with her boyfriend in recycling work, misses her children and family in Lesotho and wants to go back home and live with them, and work once again for very low wages 'in Chinese shops.' However, she needs to assemble the money to get there and is struggling to do so. Her agency in the situation seems highly constrained. Owen has relatives in Orange Farm south of Johannesburg but can seldom afford the taxi fare there: also a reclaimer, it takes him three days to fill up his bag but sometimes

159

he earns only R35 per load of cardboard, 'close to nothing.' His one-way travel cost to Orange Farm is R22. He takes money in December to his wife and children in Zimbabwe, or when he can. The interviewer was struck by the dire conditions Owen lives in, but notes he has no plans – or opportunity, presumably – to move away from the river.

Like a number of other respondents, Tom does not want his family to know how he lives. He works in construction but is distressed that he cannot get a job using the driver's licence his family helped him acquire, as companies want demonstrated driving experience. He feels he has disappointed the family. Not only can Meshak not go home as noted earlier, but 'I can't even consider going to the townships around Johannesburg. We stay here because of seeking for jobs every day.' Financial constraints bind him, coupled with the essential access provided by this part of the river to the prosperous suburbs where there is the hope of a day's work now and then, without having to pay for transport in addition.

In a different pattern, a few respondents move between riverside living and other accommodation at times. Respondent Margaret does so regularly, visiting her children in (relatively) nearby Alexandra township every two or three months. She tells them she's renting elsewhere in between times. But in the words of her interviewer, she is, in fact, 'sleeping in a plastic tent in cold bush land,' earning a living selling home-brewed beer to others living along the river. For other respondents, the riverbank is a fallback position, and they escape it at times: Vicky mostly lives in a shack she shares with a friend, but when she can't afford the taxi fare home, she sleeps in the park. Sometimes when Derek secures short-term casual work, he rents a room in a township close to where he is working and returns to the riverbank when the job finishes. For these respondents, using the riverbank intermittently or at certain periods of time, there is some dynamism in their situation and arguably some strategic choice in their use of the park.

But while its very nature provides opportunity, its official designation as park land increases vulnerability to those contravening its intended usage by living in it. Thus, the riverbank can become a trap that is very difficult to escape from. Police and private security raids on park dwellers frequently result in critical goods and personal documentation being confiscated or destroyed, knocking precarious people further into poverty. Respondent Meshak's story illustrates this, finding one day on returning to the park that his goods had been burnt and his identity document destroyed – by the Metro Police, he learnt. This has impacted on work-seeking as 'Some of the employers want to see your ID. To this day I can't afford to go and register for a new ID document.'

As with Meshak the requirements or the direct cost of trying to replace essential items including crucial personal documentation can be just too difficult to manage. To minimise this risk, vegetation along the river becomes essential for hiding personal goods in. Meshak's comment that 'I have my belongings somewhere in the park hidden,' or variations of this, is a repeated refrain from many of the respondents, who are trying to evade several hazards. Primarily, the threat to goods does not come from fellow park dwellers, but from the Metro Police or private security firms. The latter are deployed at times by surrounding residents or their associations, targeting what they perceive as vagrants and criminals living along the river, in a form of othering that reinforces existing socio-economic disparities (Charlton 2019). But despite this the river course maintains its attraction: Guy, 36, from Limpopo says 'even if they [police] arrest us we will come back ....Here is better because we can look for work easily unlike (in the) township.'

In raids work items are also broken or confiscated. Margaret who brews beer to sell to park dwellers will organise new pots when the metropolitan police, called by residents who forever mistake them with 'criminals,' come to destroy everything and take her pots. A similar tale comes from 59-year-old Vicky. With 9 children and 13 grandchildren in Kwa-Zulu Natal, she used to work as a low-paid live-in domestic worker until her employers moved, and now sells fruit and vegetables to people in and around the park. 'The challenge is when the metro police come and take all my stock, telling me to leave this park or else I will get arrested. I would tell them that I'm not working, and I have children to support but they will [not] care less.' Unlike some other respondents, Margaret and Vicky are not trying to escape the park, but rather to retain their connection to it, as their businesses depend on it, and they have 'chosen' to make a living here.

In the various examples cited across the three themes above, of coming to Johannesburg, networks in the city and the river-park, and potentially being stuck there, the lack of choice is starkly illustrated. At the same time there are also various examples where a degree of choice is evident. Thus, collectively, these themes show variations in the extent to which selection and personal agency factor into becoming a riverside dweller. This complexity also raises questions about the notion of homelessness. In their riverside living the respondents are indeed living shelterless and not in a home, but they are not necessarily without a home in their lives. In the next section, I discuss how the circumstances of riverside dwellers add to debates that caution and offer limits to the notion of homelessness in a Global South context.

Cautions and limits to the notion of homelessness

The fieldwork findings complexify a straightforward understanding of homelessness as lacking an acceptable shelter on a long-term basis. Some respondents had ongoing or intermittent alternative accommodation, within the city, and many had homes outside of the city with which they maintain a relationship. Many of the respondents are earning money, albeit precariously and often intermittently. Eleven participants were doing casual and intermittent work – piece jobs – related to building or renovations (on construction sites or private homes, including tiling, plumbing or painting). Two others previously did this work but have found more regular income through reclaiming recyclable goods. A further six were also involved in reclaiming, and three earned a living selling to other people along the river (trading in beer, clothing and groceries).

Thus, in line with several authors writing about or from the Global South,[13] a differentiation can be made amongst those who are homeless and living on the street, that enables the particular circumstance of people *working* and living shelterless to come into focus. Speak[14] notes that assuming that most homeless people are 'destitute beggars' is incorrect, and that, in fact, many people living shelterless in developing countries are generating income in various ways, often in the so-called informal economy. Examples might include transport workers, street vendors and porters carrying or loading/unloading goods, but also people whose work is not literally in public spaces, such as construction workers, waiters and cleaners[15] – as is the case in this study for respondent Amos, for example, who is a gardener.

Often this work is short-term and precarious: a week's labour on a construction site, assistance in the catering industry during high season, or a few days' work as a painter.[16] While this labour is 'low paid, often temporary, insecure, unskilled,' access to this work may also not need 'a formal residence, address or bank account'[17] and thus is feasible for those without these trappings of urban life. Beyond the Global South, these situations are also recognised in places like California, where researchers note that a key driver of homelessness is low-wage jobs.[18]

Speak's[19] continuum of homelessness in developing countries distinguishes between 'rough sleeping' and 'pavement dwelling.' The former, she summarises, is 'literally lying down on the street, under a bridge or in a public place to sleep at night,' though this can be a repeated and long-term condition. In pavement dwelling 'a regular "pitch" is used over a longer period of time and some very rudimentary shelter of card, cloth or plastic is erected.' Other authors build on Speak's, and Tipple and Speak's work undertaken over the years, with Busch-Geertsema et al.[20] referring to four sub-categories of 'people without accommodation' who sleep 'in places not intended for human habitation.' Their four-part typology also draws on the type of shelter or its absence (for example, distinguishing between roofed shelters such as bus stations, and open public spaces).

At least some of this work leads to a focus on *housing* as the main response. While noting distinctions between living conditions, the work of Busch-Geertsema et al.[21] and others is concerned with finding commonalities amongst homelessness across diverse contexts, spanning both global north and south. In part a political project, it seeks to elevate the issue in forums such as the United Nations, and cautions against contesting the term 'homeless,' arguing:

> we would agree with Tipple and Speak (2005, p.351), that we should not be 'quick to abandon the term homeless' in favour of more 'neutral' terms such as 'houseless' or 'shelterless,' as homelessness has a resonance for lay people and an implied moral and policy imperative that we would seek to preserve.[22]

However, in my research I have come to question the utility of the 'homeless' label, including through the stories from Braamfontein Spruit. In earlier work with students focused on informal reclaiming in the streets of Johannesburg, respondents reported a considerable variety of night-sleeping arrangements which spanned several variations of street homelessness.[23] But the research *also* identified the rhythmic or temporal nature of some people's alternation between different circumstances, including living shelterless at times but in housing at other times, similar to that described by some respondents on the Braamfontein Spruit. It has also emerged that people working informally and living shelterless can in fact *at the same time* be recognised home-*owners*, with a house in another part of the city![24] The primary reason underlying this is economic – the inability to earn an income in the vicinity of the house and the need to live cheaply at the alternative work location.

A focus on economic activity as the lens thus disrupts a shelter-categorisation of street homelessness, as some people are clearly traversing different typologies in a more dynamic manner than usually recognised. Here, a label of 'homeless' is arguably unhelpful, doing more to conceal than it does to reveal – overly emphasising the shelter circumstances, whilst obscuring the spatiality and circumstances of the earning practices.

Increasingly the intertwining of economic practices with ultra-basic living circumstances is recognised in South Africa, though extensive research on this is still scarce. De Beer and Valley[25] refer to the 'working homeless.' Examples of this and a set of reasons related to the spatial economy of Johannesburg are provided by Charlton and Rubin[26] in the same volume, highlighting the problem of people 'who do not earn enough to rent a home or pay for transport to commute to work.'[27]

An important part of the overall story is often the issue of remittances, or support to family living elsewhere, highlighted in research from multiple parts of the Global South.[28] Similarly the Braamfontein Spruit study shows many respondents prioritising sending money home to children and other family members over spending scarce funds on their own living circumstances. Multiple respondents such as Owen, Tom, Theo and Margaret spoke of their concerns and obligations to people living elsewhere, and their efforts to support them financially.[29] As Speak[30] puts it, 'in the developing world, the immediate priority of most homeless people is not housing, but income generation. Housing, even shelter, is secondary to this.'

In South Africa, as in many other places, income-generating work is extremely scarce, and unemployment and joblessness play directly into homelessness. In Tshwane unemployment is cited as the biggest single cause of homelessness,[31] with De Beer and Valley noting the particularly high unemployment figures amongst young people 'who just cannot find work.'[32] Under these circumstances of precarious and very low earnings the form of shelter most practical for many people may be 'flexible, temporary and virtually free accommodation,' but as Speak[33] notes: 'With the exception of a few emergency night shelters, no such accommodation is included in urban housing policies.'

From this discussion it is clear that highly significant structural conditions underpin key aspects of street homelessness. In Johannesburg these include the extensive unemployment, and the very low wages paid for short term or casual work: including so called piece-work, which may be paid by employers in prosperous parts of the city but which are insufficient to sustain rental payments. Also critical is the absence of any significant welfare support for unemployment. Further key factors are the high costs of transport, and often long distances between places of earning and places where it is possible to find low budget accommodation.[34]

In this contest 'the choice' to live as cheaply as possible, to the extent of living rough in a park, is one both pushed by the lack of affordable accommodation or decent earnings (representing no choice) and selected because it enables maximising what opportunities there are in a highly constrained environment (some choice). Various practical benefits of riverside living enable cost-savings: vegetation used for shelter, concealment, firewood, and to hang clothes on to dry. The river water is itself of course significant, for washing clothes and bodies, as it is in many other contexts.[35] The Braamfontein Spruit is used for this even by those not living along its banks: fieldworkers reported that 'Madala told us that he is sleeping somewhere in Linden, he only comes by the stream to wash his clothes once a week.'

Respondent Derek says he chose his location next to the river both because he can get piece jobs around the area but also because he can wash clothes and himself in the river. In literature on homelessness, keeping body and clothes clean is recognised as an essential part of trying to connect to income earning opportunities, and a difficult one to achieve. Becoming displaced from one's accommodation and resorting to sleeping in a public place it is easy to quickly become scruffy, unwashed and dishevelled, and this appearance along with odours quickly means one is shunned by others and marginalised as a homeless person.

Several respondents spoke of not using river water for drinking though, as it is 'dirty and poisonous' (respondent Derek). Park dwellers get clean water from petrol stations in the area or other places such as churches, from security guards or from domestic workers or gardeners working at houses. Fieldworker observations noted in relation to Theo the following: 'in that part of area we went on Sunday, some of the guys look decent, clean and they were washing their clothes, and some were cooking. They were using clean water to wash and cook [food], from garage and shops. They are known where they fetch water.'

Conclusion

This study shows that living along the river reflects an effort to reduce the daily costs of living, of social reproduction, as much as possible. It shows how the river resources, as well as resources and interactions with surrounding neighbourhoods, are used to facilitate this strategy. It highlights how straightforward conceptualisations of this as street homelessness can be misguided. These can lead to interventions focused on family reunification, skills development, or housing, or placement in shelters aimed at social rehabilitation or as stepping stones to other (largely non-existent) forms of cheap but more long-term accommodation. But these responses may not be addressing the reasons underlying riverside living as demonstrated in this chapter.

The chapter positions riverside living as an extreme form of low-cost living, placing it in a spectrum of housing options that in our Johannesburg context needs a much finer-grained and nuanced understanding, of the forms of accommodation accessed 'at the bottom of the housing ladder.'[36] This range of accommodation should not be seen as a horizontal assemblage of roughly similar dwellings – backyard rooms, shacks in informal settlements, for example– but as each constituting particular dimensions that enable or constrain survival in the city. These dimensions, separated out, include the extent of rental cost, including as in this case of living on the Spruit, no cost; the quality of shelter (how safe and secure, how protective from the elements; how comfortable), that includes, as in this case, almost nothing offered by conventional dwellings but which may nevertheless offer a form of safety (from persecution, from attack, from authorities); the location of housing (how close to work and other amenities; to transport to work; and with what cost), that includes, as in this case, walking distance.

This is not to make the case for living alongside the river as decent or acceptable living circumstances; rather it is to place these ways of life within an analytical lens that acknowledges the political economy, spatial patterns, unemployment and social support/limits of the city. It draws attention to the complex matter of 'choice' or its absence, in determining an existence along the Spruit. It opens up potential to draw attention to the constituent elements of daily life, where significant improvement interventions could be targeted that are different to a housing intervention: for example, towards the collective sanitation infrastructure argued by Speer[37] to be the key need in her Californian example of encampments and street homelessness.

The chapter also demonstrates some of the manifold dimensions of competing claims, conflict and contestation over forms of public space in Johannesburg. In this river park, opportunity is seized for informal or unauthorised trade, as it is in multiple other places such as sidewalks, squares and taxi ranks throughout Johannesburg. Here natural resources of water, wood and vegetation are used to sustain daily life, in contravention of regulations and permissions. Here activities of fire making, washing, storing, sleeping and sorting goods defy what is allowed in parks – though other forms of these activities might be permitted (picnics, sitting and lying in groups for recreation and so on).

For some respondents, living unsheltered along the river represents a falling out of or a displacement from their previous more sheltered living circumstances, though these were not necessarily formal or more secure. For other respondents, riverside living was expected and planned. Or, though not anticipated in dreams of coming to Johannesburg and early experiences of the city, became a calculated move when the cost of transport and/or accommodation became unmanageable.

Thus, in a number of cases, river edge dwelling needs to be seen for what it is… as ultra budget living that makes most use of available resources to make daily accommodation costs as low as possible – to take away the burden of housing costs in order to facilitate other expenditure, or simply survival. It is more accurate to understand it as part of the distortions in income generation, spatial ordering and economic power of contemporary urban living than as a manifestation of homelessness.

Notes

1 Pseudonyms are used throughout.

2 J. Mzingaye, The management of homelessness in Public Spaces: Lessons from the George Lea Park Intervention (BSc Honours in Urban and Regional Planning Degree, 2018, at the University of the Witwatersrand).

3 M. Ndovela, Learning from Skeemsaam's Involvement in Mediating for the Homeless Informal Recyclers in Suburban Parks: A Case Study of James and Ethel Gray Park and Albert's Farm Park (Masters of Urban Studies Degree, 2019, University of the Witwatersrand.

4 R. M. Greenwood, R. M. Manning, B. R. O'Shaughnessy, M. J. Vargas-Moniz et al., 'Structure and agency in capabilities-enhancing homeless services: Housing first, housing quality and consumer choice,' *Journal of Community & Applied Social Psychology* 32, no. 2 (2022): p. 326.

5 Greenwood et al., *Structure and Agency in Capabilities*, p. 316.

6 S. de Beer & R. Vally (Eds.), *Facing Homelessness: Finding Inclusionary, Collaborative Solutions* (Cape Town: AOSIS, 2021).

7 De Beer and Vally, *Facing Homelessness*, p. 16.

8 Greenwood et al., *Structure and Agency in Capabilities*.

9 Greenwood et al., *Structure and Agency in Capabilities*, 318, with reference to Padgett, 2007.

10 Volker Busch-Geertsema, Dennis Culhane and Suzanne Fitzpatrick, 'Developing a global framework for conceptualising and measuring homelessness,' *Habitat International* 55 (2016): 124-132.

11 Busch-Geertsema, Culhane and Fitzpatrick (2016), 125.

12 Deb Batterham, 'Homelessness as capability deprivation: A conceptual model,' *Housing, Theory and Society* 36, no. 3 (2019): 274-297.

13 See, for example, Tipple, Graham, and Suzanne Speak. *The Hidden Millions: Homelessness in Developing Countries*, Routledge, 2009; Speak, Susan, 'The state of homelessness in developing countries,' In *Annals in Expert Group Meeting on Affordable Housing and Social Protection Systems for all to Address Homelessness* (England: Newcastle University, 2019); Charlton and Rubin, 2021.

14 Speak, *The State of Homelessness in Developing Countries*, 2019.

15 Tipple and Speak, *The Hidden Millions*, 2009.

16 Speak, *The State of Homelessness in Developing Countries*, 2019.

17 Speak, *The State of Homelessness in Developing Countries*, 8.

18 Flanigan, Shawn, and Megan Welsh, 'Unmet Needs of Individuals Experiencing Homelessness Near San Diego Waterways.' *Journal of Health and Human Services Administration* 43, no. 2 (2020): 105-130.

19 Speak, *The State of Homelessness in Developing Countries*, 1.

20 Busch-Geertsema et al., *Developing a Global Framework*, 125.

21 Busch-Geertsema et al., *Developing a Global Framework*, 121.

22 Busch-Geertsema et al., *Developing a Global Framework*, 127.

23 Sarah Charlton, 'Informal recyclers in Johannesburg.' in *Changing Space, Changing City: Johannesburg after Apartheid*, ed. Philip Harrison, Graeme Gotz, Alison Todes and Chris Wray (Johannesburg: Wits University Press., 2014).

24 Sarah Charlton, 'Spanning the spectrum: infrastructural experiences in South Africa's state housing programme,' *International Development Planning Review* 40 (2) (2018): 97-120.

25 De Beer and Valley, *Facing Homelessness*, 15.

26 Sarah Charlton and Margot Rubin, 'Facing Homelessness: Scales of spatial exclusion' in *Facing Homelessness: Finding Inclusionary, Collaborative Solutions*, ed Stephan de Beer and Rehana Valley, AOSIS Scholarly Books, 2021, 2.

27 De Beer and Valley, *Facing Homelessness*, 15.

28 Speak, *The State of Homelessness in Developing Countries*, 3.

29 See also Sarah Charlton 'Down by the river: park dwellers, *Transformation: Critical Perspectives on, Southern Africa Public Space and the Politics of Invisibility in Johannesburg's Northern Suburbs,*' 101(1) (2019): 127-150. 9.

30 Speak, *The State of Homelessness in Developing Countries*, 9.

31 Mabone, W., 'Unemployment is fuelling homelessness in Tshwane, report finds,' *Daily Maverick 168* (2023), 1-7 April 2023.

32 Compare De Beer & Vally 2015, 62–63, in De Beer and Valley 2021, 13.

33 Speak, *The State of Homelessness in Developing Countries*, 6.

34 For further on this see Charlton and Rubin, 2021.

35 See, for example, in Ethiopia, Getachew Gebeyaw, Messay Gebremariam Kotecho, and Margaret E. Adamek, "No Matter How Harsh, We Are Alive': Coping Strategies of Rural-Urban Migrant Homeless Older People in Ethiopia,' *Health & Social Care in the Community* 30, no. 6 (2022): e4442-e4449; in San Diego, Shawn Flanigan and Megan Welsh, 'Unmet Needs of Individuals Experiencing Homelessness Near San Diego Waterways,' *Journal of Health and Human Services Administration* 43, no. 2 (2020): 105-130; and in California, Jessie Speer, 'The right to infrastructure: A struggle for sanitation in Fresno, California homeless encampments,' *Urban Geography* 37.7 (2016): 1049-1069.

36 See also Shapurjee in Charlton 2014.

37 Speer, *The Right to Infrastructure*.

15 *Mamlambo in Waterfall City*

Ujithra Ponniah

This chapter is an exploration of the Jukskei River within the context of Waterfall City, a gated community in South Africa. It serves as a reflection on the author's fieldwork, emphasising the importance of fieldnotes in anthropological research. The initial research questions revolved around the narratives that shape private property and the socio-political dynamics surrounding land ownership, particularly in a post-apartheid context. The myth of Mamlambo, a river goddess, is employed as a lens to examine the river's significance, intertwining indigenous knowledge with contemporary socio-technical arrangements. The narrative reveals the stark contrasts between the affluent lifestyles in Waterfall City and the impoverished realities of surrounding areas like Alexandra township. It highlights the ongoing legacies of colonialism and apartheid that continue to influence land and water access, illustrating how elite actors manipulate urban spaces to reinforce socio-spatial inequalities. The chapter also critiques the commodification of water, showcasing how the river is both a resource for the wealthy and a site of neglect and pollution.

Introduction

This chapter captures my fieldnotes of the Jukskei River in a gated city called Waterfall. Fieldnotes are raw accounts that researchers use to contextualise, make meaning, and travel back to their field. On a good research day, fieldnotes provide a cathartic release. At the time of doing my fieldwork, my research questions were half-baked. I was interested in unearthing the stories that go into the making of private property. I use the myth of Mamlambo to read the riparian life of Jukskei in Waterfall City, by bringing together indigenous knowledge and techno-social arrangements, to reflect on the inherent fragility and mutability of the private property regime. Going beyond the individualist, developmental, and capitalist readings of water as a resource to be harnessed, controlled, and dammed, this approach provides an agentive reading of water.

Fieldnotes capture a researcher's first impressions of the field. What fieldnotes 'are' is a long-standing debate in anthropology. Are they inscriptions, transcriptions, translations, narrations, or textualisations?[1] Each of these metaphors captures a different type of power relation that a researcher has with their field. At the time I wrote these fieldnotes, I had been in South Africa for just about a year. To everyone's relief, the COVID-19 pandemic was on its way out and lockdowns were easing internationally. My 'outsider' status was fresh, as is evident in the fieldnotes and the perhaps disarming effect it had on my interlocutor. The field is always new, exciting, and overwhelming. Capturing things in vivid details requires an immersion, even a surrender. Every detail is significant, for one doesn't know what will make the final cut. Fieldnotes, on a good research day, can provide a cathartic outlet. The authorial voice is one of looking rather than showing. However, for narrative coherence, readability and to capture the progression in my thinking since I was first in the field, these fieldnotes have been edited to look and show.

When I started my fieldwork, my research questions were half-formed. I was interested in learning how elite actors mould urban space by making private property. What were the genealogies or stories used by property elites to construct private property as a 'self-evident' institution?[2] Across settler-colonial contexts, the right to own land and property has been used to legitimate social differences and control enfranchisement rights; South Africa is no exception. The political subjecthood of the black working class has been made and unmade by regulating their relationship to land and property ownership, and infrastructural access, by English mining capital and Afrikaner commercial agricultural interests during the colonial and apartheid periods.[3] The post-apartheid neoliberal city has done away with regressive legal interventions; however, the legacies of racial, colonial-apartheid, and patriarchal logic in moulding land, water, and infrastructure inequalities continue in visible and invisible ways.[4]

Given this context, Waterfall City presents a befitting case study for my research on the making of private property. Continuing the northern peripheral expansion of Johannesburg, private spatial planning, and gated luxury living, the City is an iteration and amplification of existing socio-spatial and infrastructural inequalities in urban living. The Jukskei River runs through Johannesburg and Waterfall City, acting as a connecting tissue, bringing unequal landscapes of people, property, infrastructure, meaning, value, actors, and institutions together. I prepared for the field by reading academic texts and secondary material on Waterfall City. The field has a way of unsettling one's neat schemas, and my field did the same, by introducing the myth of Mamlambo. The serpentine goddess is known to be gender fluid and addressed with the pronouns her/they in the text.

Anthropologists have long had an interest in conceptualising the role of myths in social life. Kluckhohn argues that myths are 'cultural products, a part of the social hereditary of a society.'[5] Emmet sees myths as an 'expression of social relations, reinforced norms, and heightened morals.'[6] In using the myth of Mamlambo to read the riparian life of Jukskei in Waterfall City, I bring together indigenous knowledge and techno-social arrangements, to reflect on the inherent fragility and mutability of the private property regime. Going beyond the individualist, developmental, and capitalist readings of water as a resource to be harnessed, controlled, and dammed, this approach provides an agentive reading of water, by considering it a sentient being.

Mamlambo – The river goddess

Figure 15.1 *Sketch by author*

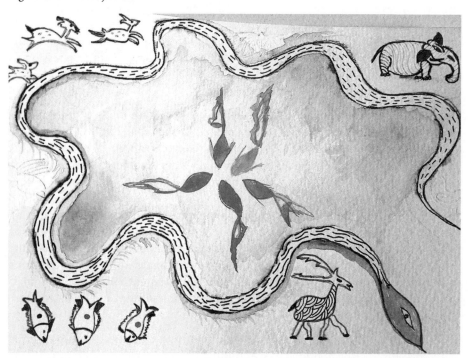

'She has come to talk about Mamlambo,' the kids screamed as they ran behind their rolling tyre on Alexandra's streets, jumping over potholes and open sewage drains. They had overheard me speaking to Paul about wanting to see the river. This was the first time; I was introduced to Mamlambo – the river goddess. I made a mental note to ask more about the serpentine goddess. I was in Alexandra township, a poor and densely populated township through which the river runs before entering Waterfall City. It was World Environment Day, and the Ministry of Agriculture and Sustained Development had planned an event at the Heritage Precinct, with a non-profit organisation responsible for cleaning the river. It was a cold morning, and men stood in circles talking around lit fires. The poster from the event read – 'Only One Earth.'

I had taken an Uber to the location shared by Paul, who worked with the non-profit organisation. Paul was thin with caved cheeks, far from the big and gregarious man the tone of his messages had led me to imagine. The Precinct was dilapidated and had a pile of chairs in the corner of the room. I lent Paul a hand as he carried the hot water flask and cupcakes inside. Paul continued talking as we worked to set up the place for the event. He had a background in tourism and wanted to restore the river to its old glory. He said the river in the 1960s was full of life: fish, frogs, and a place for grandmothers to do their rituals. Paul mentioned a litter trap that had been set up to catch the refuse in the water. We were interrupted by another gentleman.

I did not quite catch his name, as I was focused on his woollen cap and long black coat. He introduced himself as the CEO of the organisation and spoke emphatically like a political leader making a pitch for investment in the river. He said, 'cleaning the Jukskei is like cleaning the image of Alex. We do not want people to think that Alex is a place of violence; we want to attract investments and jobs here, and cleaning Jukskei is a step in that direction.'

It appeared Paul had heard this pitch many times. He interrupted his CEO to introduce me to Vusi – my guide for the day. This is when I heard the kids scream Mamlambo's name. Vusi was dressed in a tattered blue t-shirt. They asked me if I wanted to Uber to the river, and I said I wanted to walk and see the neighbourhood. Vusi looked nervous, and Paul laughed and said, 'she is the same colour as us, she should be fine.' I thanked Paul and started walking with Vusi, who spoke incessantly. His ancestors, the Zulu king, and the corrupt and 'chowing' ANC government were strung together in the same sentence. I was distracted though, for I wanted to learn about Mamlambo. I managed to piece together snippets of information and learned that the river goddess was a large serpent, feared, who brought fortune to whoever accommodated her but at a heavy price. Mamlambo was long, had the head of a horse, the lower body of a fish, short legs, the neck of a snake, sported a green sheen at night, and was a goddess. The river was full of garbage and sluggish. The newly installed green litter trap was struggling to hold the broken TV. Vusi said people also discarded dead foetuses in the water, and I recoiled. The river seemed to hold everything without discretion.

At the end of a long day of walking around the Jukskei River in Alex, I came home and looked for material on the serpentine goddess. I learnt that the river in Xhosa is called *Mlambo*. As Mamlambo resides in deep water, it is known as the mother of the river.[7] The snake is a shapeshifter and becomes a man, a woman, a mermaid, a heterosexual, or a gay person depending on the situation.[8] Mamlambo is part of oral literature emerging from the rural parts of the Eastern Cape, especially in the Transkei region. Niehaus traces the belief in Mamlambo, to when the migrant labour system developed in the region.[9] Individuals struggled to sustain themselves using traditional means and were economically dependent on white-owned mining and commercial farming enterprises. Mamlambo presents a socio-economic critique that brings together the contradictory pulls of desire and disgust for wealth.

With the expansion of market-based capitalism, the interplay of magic and market forces has become a defining feature of occult beliefs and practices in Africa.[10] Jean and John Comaroff use the term 'occult economies' to explain the usage of magic for material ends.[11] Mamlambo facilitates access to material benefits through occult forces, as opposed to the agents of the market. For the marginalised in whose oral accounts Mamlambo is first found, the market carries the magic and enchantment that is made familiar to them through their occult beliefs and practices. The affluence Mamlambo offers is unstable like the contemporary economic trends.[12] It is an indigenous cautionary tale against over-accumulation of wealth. When a neighbour or a former lover got wealth suddenly and through unexplained methods, it was attributed to Mamlambo. Or if someone's kin suddenly died after they made money, it was said that Mamlambo had been paid. As per the myth, the snake goddess facilitates the unchecked accumulation of wealth but at an expensive price. At times it is a material sacrifice, but Niehaus in his accounts found that it had to be a human sacrifice, usually of close kin.[13] Participation in the market comes with its own threat of reducing humans into commodities by stripping away their essence.[14]

Going forward, I chose to rechristen the Jukskei River as Mamlambo in my fieldnotes. The sluggish and highly polluted river that Paul and others wanted to clean to promote tourism, the water that Vusi said carried discarded foetuses, and the water features that increased the property value of the wealthy in Waterfall City, had their own whims that betrayed the efforts of the Homeowner's Association (HOA) consisting of property elites in Waterfall city.

Mamlambo and her caretaker in Waterfall City

'The river enters Waterfall through a 30 cm diversion'…(Ashley[15] was frozen on the Zoom call with an animated expression). I stared at the screen, waiting for him to resume. 'Sorry, you were saying the river is diverted,' I said, wondering about the infrastructure used by the developers to divert Mamlambo to suit the City's needs. Ashley was the City's sustainability manager, and he spoke non-stop for 7 minutes, complaining about the river. I had found his details from the bi-monthly magazine produced by the estate and I set up a Zoom call. Ashley had a thick Afrikaans accent, brown-black hair, was wearing a formal shirt, and appeared to be in his late 30s. I wore my yellow shirt and foregrounded my foreigner identity. He had not heard about Mamlambo, and we concluded our Zoom call with a promise of a guided tour of the river's entry into the estate.

On the agreed day, I met Ashley at his office and got into his white *bakkie* (light pick up truck). We transferred from his car to a green golf cart. He rolled up his sleeves, and I gripped the handle to my right. As discussed on the Zoom call, we were driving to see the entry of the river within the estate. 'Waterfall Homeowner's Association' was typed on the right side of the golf cart. We drove on a bridge and Ashley stopped the cart to tell me that the river looks its best at this point (Figure 15.2). Having seen the river at Alex, I knew by best, he meant the cleanest. Mostly, Mamlambo in the estate looked lifeless, with an uninviting muddy colour. I noticed that the banks had been cleaned, trees trimmed, and there was a smell of fresh-cut grass in the air.

Mamlambo geographically oriented the estate by dividing it into Country Village (north) and Country Village (south). We passed a big commercial building, cluster houses, and the retirement village all built to have a view of the river. The closer the proximity of the property to the river, the higher the property value. We drove along well-laid out trails. There were boards that cautioned – 'Keep Calm, Don't Rush' and 'Look Ahead' – with a depiction of binoculars to accompany it. A lady in neon pink tracksuits jogged with her dogs, as I looked at the opulent houses, tailor-made

Figure 15.2 *Mamlambo in Waterfall City, photograph by author*

to accommodate the landowner and developers designed building restrictions and wealthy individual idiosyncrasies. A house stood out with its all-glass exterior. Ashley said that this homeowner was particularly difficult. He was paranoid about anyone driving or walking around his house and kept calling security. A wealthy, scared man in a house of glass living in a gated estate – it all seamlessly came together.

Next, Ashley drew my attention to the Kikuyu grass on Mamlambo's banks. He said, 'it was a bad decision on the developer's part to plant Kikuyu. We are reviewing to remove this as well.' We stopped to inspect the banks and Ashley said, 'the angle of the river has to be smoothened here, you do not want a sharp fall, you want to make it at an angle, in such a way that there is least resistance, and the river can just pass through.' I wondered what Mamlambo felt about this policy of forced least resistance. We stopped to look at weeds like Black Jacks and the pretty pink pompoms; the bent Bush Willow tree with its beautiful red leaves touching Mamlambo. The tree did not seem to mind the few pieces of blue garbage stuck around its roots. 'None of this is indigenous, we will be taking it all out, along with the Bush Willow tree,' Ashley said with an air of certainty.

Mamlambo in a holding dam and ozone plant

Ashley stepped out of the golf cart, walked ahead, and stopped in front of an open area where the water was forming a thick foam. This part of the river looked like her other self at Alex. Although the river was carrying white Styrofoam food containers and coke bottles, and was frothing there too, there were more seagulls flying at Alex than in Waterfall. 'The residents complain, but I am told that all the foam is not from detergents. It also comes from a change in temperature and that is not a bad thing,' Ashley said anticipating my question about the homeowners' relationship to the river.

We then approached the river in a small lake. Ashley called this a holding dam. I learnt that Mamlambo was directed to the holding dam through underground pipes and two pumps. I was eager to see the river at the source, but for now, we paused to gaze at the clear water that reflected the cloudy blue sky, and the black ducks floating in it.

'You would not be able to stand here, if it was not for the two bricks of bio-enzymes that have been kept at the point where the water enters the holding dam.' We walked to inspect the bio-enzyme bricks, but I could not see them.

'Do you live in Waterfall City, Ashley?' I asked while we continued to stare at the water.

'Oh no, I could not afford these two million and above worth properties. It would be nice to be able to play with my son in all this free space that they have.' We paused and looked at four kids who had parked their bikes next to the holding dam and were throwing stones in the water. The ducks staged their exit and Ashley continued, 'but you know these people are not happy. If I were to buy a property this expensive, I would know that the Jukskei causes trouble. They keep complaining about the smell and the refuse.' Ashley continued, 'In 2016, there was a big flood, and the water was so close to the property. When the river flooded it carried with it all the rubbish that was floating in it.' Millions of rand worth of property next to water swelling with garbage – I was beginning to see the mischievous side of Mamlambo, that had drawn me to the myth.

Next, we walked to the interconnected thick blue pipes that forms the ozone plant (Figure 15.3). Ashley continued, 'the work of the ozone plant is not enough for all the needs we have, but again without it you would not be able to use the dirty water. The residents have their own borewells for freshwater.' The wealthy had multiple uses and, more importantly, diverse sources of water at their disposal. I asked Ashley, 'why is the municipality water not used to make up for the gap in supply?'

Figure 15.3 *Interconnected blue pipes of the ozone plant, photography by author*

'I do not think the municipality would even give permission' Ashley said as we walked from the ozone plant back to the golf cart.

'Would it also be very expensive?'

'Oh yes, they would ask whatever they feel like. In any case it is going to land in the pockets of a few people, so why get the municipality involved.' Ashley said as we continued our drive on the paved road, this time greeting a man on his mid-morning run while attending what appeared to be a work call.

'Yes, but by keeping the municipality out, you also affect public revenue.' I persisted. Ashley was distracted by the guinea fowl, and I left the matter to revisit later.

Mamlambo's entrance in the city

Our next stop was the one I was anticipating – a sight of Mamlambo as they entered the city. We drove towards the electric fence and barbed wires (Figure 15.4). The river flowed straight, and through a small diversion, they were made to run underground, towards the holding dam. A rather unceremonious entrance, I thought, as I looked at the refuse in the water being held back through sieves in the fence. Mamlambo's life began in Waterfall City, as she left her former Alex self behind. She entered the City through fences and barbed wires, with a tower to her right manned by a security guard with a rifle.

The security guard came down asking Ashley for his identity proof and details. Ashley looked upset and irritated for having his authority questioned. I continued to gaze at the river and the politician's house adjacent to it. The house was built not on

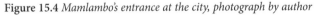

Figure 15.4 *Mamlambo's entrance at the city, photograph by author*

one but two stands and was massive. The security guard was satisfied with Ashley's identity proof and went back to his tower.

Ashley was clicking pictures of a gourd that he had not seen growing in the area before. I was worried he was going to claim that the gourd needed to be removed.

'See it is barely a diversion,' Ashley said pointing at the paved path for the river, starting at the fence.

He was right, it was 'barely' a diversion, but without this diversion, Mamlambo would not be serviced to irrigate the lawns of the wealthy, and public spaces in Waterfall.

Mamlambo charges her rent

On our drive back to the estate's entrance, Ashley stopped by the Club House, which had its own lakefront. I saw workers using specialised equipment that could trim the grass to as close as 0.5 cm from the ground. The invisible hands worked carefully to plant the saplings in an equidistant manner around another water feature, that decorated the entrance of the Club House.

In the myth of Mamlambo, the keeper must make sacrifices to keep the goddess of fortune pleased. So far, I had seen the technocratic power of the developers. Mamlambo was diverted, and run through underground pipes, only to resurface in a holding dam, and then sent to an Ozone plant. Her smell was made bearable through bio-enzymes, the plants that grew on her banks were handpicked, and a team of 18 workers cleaned the refuse that managed to escape from her previous self at Alex. Apart from occasionally flooding and damaging property, I had only seen Mamlambo increasing the property value of the wealthy. How did Mamlambo charge their rent?

Figure 15.5 *Mamlambo charges her rent, photograph by author*

As I looked at the lake, Ashley pointed to a mini-island in the centre of the lake with tall trees. I had assumed that the lake was natural but learnt that it was made from the runoff water collected and diverted to form the lake. Ashley explained the difficulty of transporting full-grown trees to the mini-island by helicopter, because his incompetent boss, had not listened to his advice to smoothen the banks of the island. To add to the farcical situation, the trees needed to be irrigated manually through water pipes attached to the island. Workers in pairs, used a canoe to reach the island, and water the trees. Ashley, in a slightly lowered voice said, 'a worker drowned in the lake last month. He did not have his lifejacket on and did not know how to swim.' Workers had planted a tree to commemorate the 23-year-old Africa Chauke's life (Figure 15.5). I offered a small prayer as I read the metal plate on the tree. Mamlambo had charged her rent, even if, once again it was the working class that was being made to pay for the wealthy.

Notes

1   Pachirat, Timothy, *Among Wolves: Ethnography and the Immersive Study of Power* (New York: Routledge, 2018).

2   Ranganathan, M, and A Bonds, 'Racial regimes of property: Introductions to the special issue.' *Environment and Planning D: Society and Space* 40 (2) (2022): 198.

3   Nightingale, C.H, *Segregation: A Global History of Divided Cities.* (Chicago: The University of Chicago Press, 2012).

4   Crankshaw, O. *Urban Inequality: Theory, Evidence, and Method in Johannesburg* (London: Bloomsbury Publishing, 2022); Lemanski, C. 'Infrastructural citizenship: (de) constructing state-society relations,' *International Development Planning Review* 42 (2022): 115-125.

5   Kluckhohn, Clyde, 'Myths and Rituals: A General Theory,' *Harvard Theological Review* Vol 35: No 1 (1942): 45-79.

6   Emmet, Dorothy, *A Study in Social and Religious Philosophy* (London: Palgrave Macmillan, 1998).

7   Wood, Felicity, 'Wealth-Giving Mermaid Women and the Malign Magic of the Market: Contemporary Oral Accounts of the South African Mamlambo,' in *Vernacular Worlds, Cosmopolitan*, ed. Stephanos Stephanides and Stavros Karayanni (Leiden, Boston: Brill Rodopi, 2015).

8   Wood, 'Wealth-Giving Mermaid Women and the Malign Magic of the Market: Contemporary Oral Accounts of the South African Mamlambo,' 63.

9   Niehaus, Isak, 'Perversion of Power: Witchcraft and the Sexuality of Evil in the South African Lowveld,' *Journal of Religion in Africa*, Vol 32, (2002).

10   Wood, 'Wealth-Giving Mermaid Women and the Malign Magic of the Market: Contemporary Oral Accounts of the South African Mamlambo,' 60.

11   Wood, 'Wealth-Giving Mermaid Women and the Malign Magic of the Market: Contemporary Oral Accounts of the South African Mamlambo,' 63.

12   Wood, Felicity, 'Kinship, collegiality, and witchcraft: South African perceptions of sorcery and the occult aspects of contemporary academia,' *Tydskrif Vir Letterkunde*, 51 (1) (2014).

13 Niehaus, Isak, 'Perversion of Power: Witchcraft and the Sexuality of Evil in the South African Lowveld,' 290.

14 Wood, 'Wealth-Giving Mermaid Women and the Malign Magic of the Market: Contemporary Oral Accounts of the South African Mamlambo,' 69.

15 This is a pseudonym.

16 The river talks

Sibusiso Sangweni

To tell of my relationship with the Jukskei River, I must go back to my childhood. I grew up in a small town called Mkhondo, in Mpumalanga. It used to be called Piet Retief and it is near the border with eSwatini. When I was a newborn, I cried a lot and couldn't breastfeed or sleep with my mother. The family was worried that perhaps we had been victims of witchcraft, so I was sent to family near eSwatini for a few years. When I was sent back, I lived with my grandmother, who looked after me and my two siblings. I loved my gogo so much; she was very precious to me, I even slept in her bed. I loved school and I was good at it. I always knew the answers to the teachers' questions. They moved me from kindergarten to primary because I could answer questions meant for bigger children! School went well, but I got sick in my stomach in Grade 5 and I had to take six months off to get better. It was a long time to be sick. My gogo looked after me. The community advised that I take traditional medicine, from plants that grow near the rivers. I took it and after some time I got better and went back to school.

Mpumalanga is a beautiful place. There are many mountains that you can see in the distance, and there are also rivers. There are some small rivers that run through Mkhondo. As a child, it was known that the rivers are dangerous and that children should not go there on their own, especially not to play. There was talk in the village about witchcraft that could put curses on babies and children that would put their lives at risk if they played near the river. There was talk of a big snake that lived in the river and would eat the brains of drowned children or trap their bodies under rocks so that their families could not get them back to give them a proper burial. So, the elders would always warn us to keep away from the dangers of the river. It was only if you had a reason to cross the river that you should step near it. If the adults saw a child near the river, they would chase us away. They did not want a child to be lost to the river. They told us stories of evil river spirits who would capture people and drag them down under the water. If we secretly went into the river, and we got back home the adults would see that our skin was ashy because we didn't take Vaseline to moisturise after swimming, and they would ask us what we were doing, and even give a whipping to teach us that we were not supposed to go near the river.

My mother was in Johannesburg working as a cleaner for a company called Prestige that serviced offices, and she was staying in Alex. She worked and would send money on a monthly basis so that we could buy food. Sometimes we would come to visit her during the December holidays. We used to go to the public pool in Alex, where it was safe to swim and there were lifeguards. I loved that. We couldn't swim

JOHANNESBURG FROM THE RIVERBANKS: NAVIGATING THE JUKSKEI

in the river, but we could swim in the pool, even though our bodies weren't used to the chlorine. It was a marvellous experience, to go in the water without anyone questioning you.

I came to Alex after I matriculated. I came for two reasons: one, to further my studies and second to try find a job or become an entrepreneur. I studied tourism at Southwest College, where we did six months theory, and six months practical. I also graduated as a provincial tourism guide. I went to the City of Joburg tourism information centre, and I saw that they had no information there for tourists about Alex. I had a job placement with Alex Bicycle Tours where I started to see that there was potential for bringing tourists to Alex, and to give them tours about our heritage. I know how to handle tourists; I like to meet the people from different countries, and I can tell them stories about the history of Alexandra. Any question they have I can answer it. In our family we are known to be clever. I wanted to get a job as a tour guide, but there were no jobs; no company even came forward to offer internships. So, I realised I must try to create my own job, by offering tours. I can now offer tours in Alex, and The Cradle of Humankind. I can teach visitors about our heritage and environment.

In 2019, a lady called Pat Naidoo said I must go and meet Paul Maluleke, so I went to his place and called him, and he came out and I introduced myself. Then we started to talk about doing tours of Alex. We saw that if we take visitors around Alex, on every street corner there is dumping. So, we had to think about the right way to solve this problem. We started planning and then we were hit by coronavirus. We are working on environmental issues, not only on water. We do work to help different organisations and people understand the importance of the environment. There are many struggles in Alex, and sometimes the people want to shut things down with violence. Like Operation Dudula – we are trying to work with them to help move things forward, show them that they can go to a government department, rather than do rioting.

My work in Alex Water Warriors means that I go to the river about twice a week. We implemented a litter trap, and my job is to go into the river to clean it out. This trap catches a lot of rubbish. Everything that flows down the river is trapped there. It is hard work. I have to wear special overalls to protect me from the water, which is polluted, and I use something like a rake to pull the litter out. Then the other workers waiting outside on the bank put it into rubbish bags, and others take it to designated sites. When I am working in the river, I feel like I am part of the ecosystem of the river. The river talks. When I am standing in it, I can hear the harmonic sounds that are made as the water runs over the stones. It takes me deep into my thinking, about the future, about what happened long ago. From when I started working in the river, I have changed. I don't like alcohol anymore or going to the taverns. The river talks, and the mountains talk, and the trees talk. The river sometimes talks to me in my dreams. One time I was supposed to host a traditional ceremony at my place in the coming days. But I was broke, I did not have even one Rand to supply my guests with

THE RIVER TALKS

what was needed for the ceremony. I went to bed with nothing in my pocket. In my sleep, I heard a voice tell me to go there to the river and wash my face. The next day I went there, and I splashed my face, then I looked in the water I saw there were all these copper cables. The voice said the river is so clean because of you guys. Then I could take the cables and I burned off the plastic, and I could sell the copper and I got three hundred and eighty rands, which I could then use for the ceremony, to buy food and beer for the guests. The ceremony went well. The river helped me. In my family history, with our clan name, we are known to be healers.

I've been staying in Alex since 2007 and it seems like every year a child must die in the river. It's like the river has a magnetic energy, the children always want to play in the open space near the river. But it is a dangerous area, there should be lifeguards on duty. If the ball goes into the water, the children will go and fetch it, and maybe one child will not come back. We have to chase the children away from the river because we want them to be safe. Recently, 17 people drowned in the river in Alex. There was a pastor who took his congregants to the river to baptise them, and then a flood came and washed them away. One child is still missing. If a family follows a culture, they have to do a process to bury their loved one, and they need the body to do the proper burial. People still say that there is a snake in the river, it lives under the rocks, and it holds on to the bodies of those who have drowned and disappeared. Then the families must ask a healer or prophet to come and help them commune with their loved one, to ask the snake to release it, so that they can see if their person is dead or alive. Families need to know that their dead will not come back to haunt them, so they have to follow up to find the body and bring it home. So, it is really, really necessary to do a follow up. Especially for someone who died in the river.

My vision of the river in the future is that we will put more litter traps, and it will become cleaner. If we keep throwing things like used diapers inside the river, it will stay polluted and it will become angrier. But if we clean it, then it can be safe, and those who live near the river can use the water. Even now you can see that with the river being a bit cleaner after our work, there are people who go there in the morning and walk alone or with their dogs. I want the children to come play here and for it to be safe and neat and clean. As it is getting cleaner, people are using the space and they are appreciating it. In our culture, we are very connected with our ancestors, and the river can be a spiritual place for us to commune with them. The ancestors talk with you, they guide you. They tell me what to do and how to run away from danger. They are strongest in the course of the rivers.

To be near a beautiful river is a spiritual experience; you can get some spiritual sense just going near the water. We can't live without that river. In the future we can create hiking trails along the river for everyone to enjoy. I want people to come and do their yoga next to the river, to meditate, to activate their seven chakras, or just to eat breakfast or lunch and chill.

17 What elites think with the Jukskei: Property, race, and blame in totemic thought

Renugan Raidoo

This chapter joins others in this book by claiming that rivers are good to think with. Drawing on insights from the classical anthropological literature on totemism as well as 26 months of ethnographic fieldwork, it engages the discursive, ideological, and moral orientations that residents of an elite golf and residential gated community have to the river that bisects their estate. Just as the river serves as an orientating device for thinking Johannesburg as a whole, the relationship residents have to the river, in true totemic fashion, structures important aspects of their social worlds, from property to race to environmentalism. As evidenced in engagements throughout the piece with philosophers who use rivers as productive metaphors, the author also argues that rivers are universally useful to think with, considering that they embody a number of contradictions. Embracing such contradictions, the piece concludes with a hopeful reflection on fragile and dangerous but nonetheless present possibilities afforded by this urban river flowing through capitalist ruins.

Thinking with rivers

Rivers are good to think with. What Claude Lévi-Strauss said of 'natural species' in *Totemism* – that they are chosen as totems 'not because they are "good to eat" but because they are "good to think"'[1] – has been re-worked for different subjects so many times that it has become 'almost meaningless, something between a tautology and a cliché.'[2] I nonetheless use it for several reasons, not least because, although mine is not a strictly structuralist account, some of Lévi-Strauss's arguments are relevant to the present discussion.

Taking my opening statement at face value, many philosophers (the professional thinkers) have employed rivers as conceptual metaphors. Some are referenced in this chapter. Whether or not as totems in the conventional sense (which Lévi-Strauss demonstrates at any rate lacks coherence), the relevance of rivers real and imagined, agencies associated with them, and creatures inhabiting them to cosmologies around the world is testament to the fact that everyone – professional thinker or not – thinks with rivers. Philosophical engagements with rivers, I contend, serve a similar purpose to 'primitive' cosmological ones, and to the elite engagements with rivers that I document here. As in *Totemism*, here the distinctions organising thought about rivers are simultaneously about other things well beyond rivers: race, post-apartheid governance, property, history, and 'good' environmentalism among them.

While this book is about rivers in general and the meanings/distinctions they generate universally,[3] it is also about *the Jukskei*, a river especially useful as an organising device for thinking the city of Johannesburg. To hear visitors speak of Johannesburg, they (not incorrectly) find it oppressively enclaved, walls often separating the most starkly contrasted extremes of destitution and opulence. Like no other feature of the urban landscape, the Jukskei flows through and past the vast range of the city's urban forms: neglected inner city, stormwater infrastructure, township, prison complex, municipal park, and luxury gated estate among them. Although at various points the river's course is manipulated by infrastructural intervention, is made to pass through mesh nets to catch rubbish or must bypass various security barriers that prevent humans from following the course of the river, the water originating below Ellis Park stadium still inevitably runs to the sea, making the river an unavoidable connection between the city's extremes.

Property and aesthetic anxieties on the banks of Dainfern

Dainfern Golf & Residential Estate, where I lived for 26 months conducting ethnographic fieldwork from 2019–2021, is located on the northwest edge of the city in an area called Fourways. The 1235 homes in the estate are arranged in 'villages' around the 18-hole golf course designed by sporting icon Gary Player. Amidst the pristine greens of the course and the homes are 15 nature trails and areas managed by the Dainfern Nature Association (DNA) and Turfnet, a company contracted for landscaping and natural resource management.

'The golfing challenge on the Par 72 course (Rating 71) was developed around the meandering Jukskei River with its undulating terrain and is a truly spectacular layout,' boasts the estate's website. 'The river is in play on six holes with the rolling terrain providing a challenge to both amateurs and professionals and affords breathtaking views of the surrounding landscape. Dams, water features, rocky outcrops, weeping willows as well as abundant birdlife provide a tranquil country ambiance.'[4] For golfers, the course provides a space for recreational leisure, and for non-golfing residents prestige and the sublime of expansive green space. Never mind that it remains green throughout the year, even while the highveld grassland is brown and dry. The terrace of the clubhouse restaurant overlooks the river, so residents and golfers can take in a panoramic view of the valley as they enjoy a drink or a meal.

Figure 17.1 *A map of nature trails displayed outside one of the estate's communal spaces.*
Image credit: Sujen Moodley

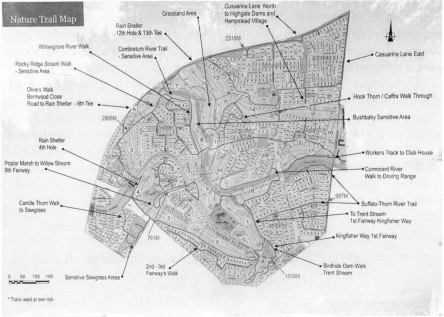

The golf course speaks to the changing values of (settler post)colonial aesthetics, and since 2005 the homeowners' association and the DNA have endeavoured to incorporate more native vegetation (although some is native only to the country, not necessarily the highveld, and landscapers are well aware that not all plants hailing from elsewhere are necessarily invasive). The DNA undertook the project of re-wilding areas of the estate for human consumption by adding and managing paths, dams, benches, flora, and fauna. Although paved paths, planned flower beds, and benches in some of the nature areas evince their histories of human intervention, most try to efface that history. A DNA brochure and species list suggests that residents might wonder 'why there is "just bush" in the middle of smooth mowed [invasive] kikuyu.' Several trails – Willowgrove River Walk, Combretum River Trail, Cormorant River Walk, and Buffalo-thorn River Trail among them – meander alongside the river (Figure 17.1), the banks of which were modified through the addition of gabions to prevent erosion, lest the paths and viewing terraces wash away. Olivia Denny, a former resident and the primary force behind the creation and maintenance of the nature areas, recalls fondly in the 21st-anniversary edition of the estate magazine: 'When [residents] see us working along the trails, they stop to tell us stories of the Jukskei River, which runs through the Estate (and has its own story to tell) or of some of the little creatures that they have encountered.' One Saturday each month the DNA hosts a bird walk. Besides (inter alia) ducks and geese floating on the water, darters drying their wings nearby, kingfishers waiting for an opportune moment, and sacred ibises feeding *en masse* on the shore, a common morning site is legavaans (water monitor lizards) basking on banks, rocks, or gabions.

Whether influenced by the DNA's efforts, estate advertisements, prevailing global interest in environmentalism on the eve of climate catastrophe, or something else, residents *are* enthusiastic about the river. Not only do they submit photographs to a monthly competition to be on the cover of the *InFocus* magazine (advertising in which provides the primary revenue stream for the DNA), but they also regularly post images that feature the river on the estate Facebook group and private social media accounts. The rise of Web 2.0 and user-generated content has profoundly affected our attitudes to the natural world, and to interventions into it;[5] the circulation of overexposed photographs of a mist-draped Jukskei at dawn, or of dynamic wildlife in the stream, on which residents can comment and share further, augment the already powerful efforts by the DNA and estate management to orientate residents' affective sensibilities regarding the environment (Figure 17.2).

I have argued elsewhere that, in the context of ongoing debates about land that hinge on competing autochthonous and Lockean claims to property, attitudes towards nature signal a claim to property that supersedes both the autochthonous argument (that land belongs to its original inhabitants) and the Lockean argument (forwarded by white minority interest groups like AfriForum, that land belongs to those who cultivate it).[6] Residents' 'patrician environmentalism'[7] likely does very little for conservation, yet fosters a strong sense of stewardship as an idiom of ownership,[8] an idiom built on experiences and images of primordial ante-human nature that circumvents the current terms of the South African land debate. The resident's overexposed photograph referenced above is emblematic of this affective orientation: the glowing mist obscures any signs of human habitation or intervention, while simultaneously giving a dreamlike sense of a natural landscape outside of history itself.

What these various forms of value extraction from the river – on the one hand providing real revenue to the clubhouse restaurant, golf club, estate agents, and developers, and on the other providing enjoyment and the objects of affective attachment to foster a sense of ownership and belonging – have in common is their reliance on a sanitised idea of nature enabled by a bourgeois alienation from it. Nature does not, of course, conform to those rosy, filtered visions, but introduces peril into the very attachments that sustain lifestyles on the estate. I thus previously suggested that such attachments, and the senses of belonging and ownership they engender, are inherently anxious; the very relationships that validate us are always liable to sour.

And sour they do. Although I am unsure what stories residents told Olivia of the Jukskei, the stories they tell one another on social media are more often about the river's destructive potential than about its beauty. The highveld is famous for its summer storms, and every year with the torrential rains comes flooding. On a number of occasions, the golf course was rendered 'unplayable' due to flooding. At times, the flooding was so severe that even once the water subsided, several days needed to be set aside to address damage to the course. In contrast to the serene photographs described above, these announcements were often accompanied by videos of violently rushing water.

Under one post of images and videos depicting both the rushing stream and damage it had caused, a resident wrote, 'I'm in awe at the water! So sad we lost part of the magnificent weeping willow.' When the water level rises high enough, it carries litter over the nets and the other barrier technologies meant to filter out debris, leaving piles of garbage on the banks. I will return to conflicts over river cleanup shortly, but the mixture of disgust and concern occasionally extends into anxieties about Dainfern's value when compared to other estates. One man commenting on a Facebook post indignantly compared Dainfern to Steyn City downstream: 'It's a disgrace to see so much rubbish in the estate. It really makes it hard to enjoy. We pay so much in levies, surely the DHA and Turfnet must be able to do something? They say this is a premier estate. Steyn City doesn't look like this.' On any given day, the river may suffuse the valley with unpleasant, though rarely recognisable, stenches. A few times during my two years living in Dainfern, alarmingly large pillows of foam accumulated on areas of the river.

The commoditisation of the river as an aesthetic resource, and the related project of building affective attachments in the interest of property and belonging, require fixing the meaning of the river and our relations to it. While theorists[9] have demonstrated that all matter resists being fixed, rivers are among the archetypal examples of unruliness and non-fixity. It is the fragments on rivers from the pre-Socratic philosopher Heraclitus that have led his interpreters to ascribe to him theories of flux and the unity of opposites. Although translations from the Greek differ, Heraclitus is credited with having said 'You cannot step twice into the same river; for fresh waters are ever flowing in upon you,' or 'We step and do not step into the same rivers; we are, and are not.'[10] On two wadings into a river, neither the water nor the wader are the same; rivers abound with paradoxes: nourishing and threatening, fixed and flowing, calming and disturbing.

Not because it's 'good to [drink]'

But as other contributions to this volume demonstrate, many risks come with stepping into the Jukskei once, let alone twice! If some totems might also be good to eat, that much definitely cannot be said of the Jukskei's being good to drink.[11] What unites the many phenomena that have been collected under the term totemism is that they describe ideological relationships posed between, on the one hand, persons and groups, and on the other individual elements or classes of elements in the natural world (most often animals).[12] These relationships, and the rituals, beliefs, and observances associated with them, define and regulate social order. In this section and the one that follows, it will become clear that my interlocutors made social distinctions based on their relationships to the river and on relationships they perceived others to have (or not) to the river. But inasmuch as such distinctions are shot through with racialised assumptions about civilisation and worth, I also follow Lévi-Strauss's adamance that totemism is characteristic of universal modes of thought, and that our attitudes to nature do not separate us into primitive and modern, savage and civilised.

When residents complain about the smell and pollution, they sometimes rename the at-other-times-picturesque Jukskei the 'Yuckskei.' One morning after one of the DNA's monthly birdwalks, I sat with a group of other birdwatchers on the clubhouse verandah. The view of the river sparked conversation about recent flooding. One woman said, 'You know, I saw a maid down there the other day with a small boy. She was letting him near the water! I went down straight away. I had to take her aside and explain that the water isn't safe. I was worried he might drink it.' Setting her cappuccino down next to her pair of Swarovski binoculars, another woman responded, 'That was good of you. But you know, in the homelands, they're used to just drinking water straight from the river. I'm sure she didn't know.'

A similar story was recounted on the estate Facebook page a few months later. Someone wrote, 'Earlier on we encountered a young man who was having great fun playing in the water next to one of the low bridges, right beside the waves and gushing torrent of the flooded river. We chatted to him and discovered that he's unaware of the concept of a flash-flood and its potential dangers should it arise. And he was also unaware that the Jukskei has a high bacteria count and that the water can make one ill when ingested. Maybe it's a conversation we should all have with our children, to ensure that they stay away from the river when it's in flood or when storms might be occurring upstream?'

An issue of the estate newsletter, likely as a result of a complaint from a resident, (an assumption I'm comfortable making after interviewing the often-frustrated staff members who write the newsletters), encouraged residents to educate their staff about how to treat the animals in and around the river: 'We would like to remind all Residents that we have the privilege of sharing our Estate with an abundance of wildlife. Legavaans are one of the special creatures that call Dainfern home. These large lizards may look like prehistoric monsters however, are actually harmless, peaceful reptiles. We have received reports that employees of Residents are killing them in fear. Please educate your staff that they are not to kill or harm them in any way and that we are to care for all animals on the Estate.' Such warnings echoed concerns I had heard from residents and members of the DNA about the need to protect jackals from being killed for food or sport, and owls out of superstition. I found no resident who could corroborate an instance of one of these animals being killed in the estate; most justified their concern with claims about black South African's beliefs, or stories of animals found dead in Diepsloot or elsewhere.

A conservation-orientated respect for the river and the creatures that inhabit it, combined with knowledge of pathogen count and flash flooding risks, would appear to define an appropriate relation to the Jukskei. Although we do not know the race of the 'young man' in the Facebook post, the anecdote's similarity to the previous one suggests a paternalistic outlook on labourers that puts them on par with children: both sets of people must be educated into civilised relationships with nature.

History, blame, and variations of patrician environmentalism

In 2016, an article in the *Fourways Review* reported on Dainfern's problem with the river and with government water management. General manager of (neighbouring) Dainfern Valley Estate, Dave Weyers told *Fourways Review* that the residents were getting a raw deal from Joburg Water. 'The Jukskei flows through the Dainfern Valley Estate – and numerous surrounding estates, as well as many homes and businesses further upstream,' said Weyers. 'We have noticed raw sewage flowing down the river for a number of weeks and, obviously, this comes with an unbearable stench. All this then finally ends up in the Hartbeespoort Dam.' He shared with the newspaper pictures of used condoms, tissues and other sanitary items flowing in the river. 'We have made numerous calls to Joburg Water, attempted to get hold of the water department and also involved the Blue Scorpions.[13] All we get are reference numbers and a promise to investigate. As a last resort, we have turned to Caxton Newspapers to please assist with getting these departments to respond,' said Weyers.[14]

The river picks up material residues of poor state urban planning and service delivery over its course. Alexandra township bears the brunt of the blame from residents. For some, this is a sign of indifference to the environment on the part of the urban poor. 'I don't understand how people live like that,' one woman told me. 'Why aren't they using their bins? It's disgusting, and *we* are the ones who face the consequences of *their* filth.' Others held a more nuanced view, acknowledging the structural production of the waste problem. The propensity for Alexandra township to flood – as a result of poor drainage and high population density – combined with reportedly poor refuse removal means that anything not fastened down, including entire homes, can be washed away with heavy rains.

The latter explanation was what I heard when I went to a river cleanup with three Dainfern residents on a Saturday morning in December 2020, organised by an organisation called Live Life Always that received a lot of media attention for its cleanup efforts around Fourways. Gwen, the Dainfern resident whom I'd accompanied to the cleanup, was disgusted that – even though it was a drizzly (and early) morning – more residents hadn't come to the clean up which took place at a church upstream from Dainfern. Gwen, her husband, their neighbour Amanda, and I were the only people to show up. Gwen double-checked that no one else from Dainfern was there, looking for familiar faces among those of us who'd congregated awaiting safety instructions. 'Everybody complains in the estate about the rubbish

WHAT ELITES THINK WITH THE JUKSKEI

and the river, but no one is willing to do anything about it. The fucking entitlement and failure to take responsibility is the problem.'

Figure 17.2 *From the 21st-anniversary commemorative edition of the Dainfern estate magazine, a deck overlooking the river from Willowgrove Village*

Gwen had been trying for over a year at that point to get a river cleanup going on the estate but was met with red tape at every juncture. When she contacted the Dainfern Homeowners Association, they were concerned about liability issues and told her that she'd need to get participants to sign waivers and that she would be held *personally* responsible for anything that happened and for making sure that everyone had proper safety equipment. For estate management, it seemed, it was much easier to hire occasional workers from Turfnet to clean up the litter around the river than it would be to take on the liability of residents themselves cleaning it up. 'I thought it would be a great opportunity to get Dainfern College and maybe some other schools involved. We could even make a whole day out of it, with food and activities.' In her mind, Gwen wanted to model this cleanup after similar events encouraging environmental stewardship, like Spruit Day, in the area. But beyond liability, she couldn't get kids involved because the golf club refused to pause golf for even one day. 'They say we can do it on a Monday, when golf is normally closed. But any time there's a holiday on a Monday, then golf stays open. They'll never give us a Saturday or a Sunday, even just for a few hours, because they say they lose too much revenue. They'll complain about the rubbish, but they won't even support people who want to do anything about it.' The DNA was unwilling to support Gwen. 'All they want to do is look at fucking birds, as if that helps anyone.'

When Amanda posted the pictures of the 'Dainfern team' – those of us who had gone to the cleanup that Saturday – online, commenters commended our participation, even while they decried the irresponsible environmental citizens of Alex, disavowing any responsibility they themselves might have to clean up the river.

Philosopher Maurice Merleau-Ponty, in a discussion of the perception of time, challenges the notion that time is like a river, noting that our perception of past and future events on the course of the river – a bottle tossed in Alex yesterday, its floating through Dainfern today to enter Hartbeespoort Dam tomorrow and eventually the ocean – tacitly assume observers tied to places and times.[15] But the sense that events are connected in a flow of perception is an effect of subjective experience. 'Time presupposes a view of time.' While he denaturalises the river's hold on how we imagine the passage of time, he must do so precisely because it is clearly a powerful metaphorical organising device. The glimpses of the past and future – however distant or proximal – are held together by the logic of the river's flow, so deceptively commonsensical as to make each resident certain of their view of how the river came to be the way it is as it runs through Dainfern.

As we cleaned the bank that morning, the four of us, along with the community members, found puzzling things. Most surprising to me was the polystyrene shrapnel that was mixed through all the silt and soil on the banks. While I had half expected to just be picking out large pieces of litter, so numerous, and so small, were the shards that they were impossible to miss or pick out. Whole carpets, shoes, hub caps, and pieces of furniture were testament to the problem upstream and suggested that it was more than just people negligently or carelessly discarding litter. As we walked back up from the banks of the river to the church that was hosting the event to listen to music and eat the boerie rolls donated by a local butchery for the day, Amanda asked me, 'Did you ever watch that film on Netflix? With Ewan McGregor? It was about that English family that was caught in the tsunami and were split up. How they found those kids I have no idea. It was based on a true story.' I didn't know the film she was talking about. 'A few weeks ago, when the river was really pumping, it reminded me of that film. Could you imagine what speeds that water must be going at? And that poor family, I can't imagine what it must have been like being split up in a tsunami like that.'

It made sense that the rushing water might force this thought into Amanda's stream of consciousness (a term psychologist William James used, likening consciousness to the uninterrupted flow of a river[16]) but I did not see the film until a few days after the cleanup. Although the family in *The Impossible*[17] is English, the story is based on what happened to a Spanish family during a holiday in Thailand when the 2004 Indian Ocean tsunami hit. The parents and three children were separated into two groups – the father with two very young boys, and the mother with a pre-teen – and the film follows their successful, if improbable, attempt at reuniting in the aftermath and chaos of the natural disaster.

In an essay on disaster cinema, Susan Sontag suggests that the genre is at once a way of coping with collective moral failure through imagining the annihilation of the present order of things, as well as an emblem of the inadequate response to the ills of the present, whether those be enduring urban inequality, poor urban governance, moral indifference, climate change, or something else. Though written in 1965, the essay could be about Johannesburg today, 'an age of extremity…under continual threat of two equally fearful, but seemingly opposed destinies: unremitting banality [like life in a gated community?] and inconceivable terror.'[18]

Conclusion

Rivers are good to think with – as they were for my interlocutors and thinkers beyond the handful of philosophers I have referenced here – because they coherently embody so many contradictions. Although my treatments of various philosophers is cursory, I draw on their river metaphors for the same reason that Lévi-Strauss brings philosophers together with ethnological source data: to demonstrate that things in the natural world are common objects of fascination that organise the world beyond themselves, and that the often racist arguments made on the basis of relationships to nature are unsound.

Given the many contradictions of rivers, it would seem remiss to leave the reader with a sense only of doom. They feature centrally, of course, in cleansing rituals, rites of passage, and liberation imagery. Black American spirituals like 'Deep River' and 'Roll, Jordan, Roll,' songs of both sorrow and hope, bondage and liberation, poignantly illustrate rivers' ambivalent potentialities.[19] In an article on the Jukskei,

Sean Christie[20] introduces us to Steven Baloyi, found 'sitting under a willow tree, scouring a golf ball using river sand and a bit of a greengrocer's bag.' Steven explains to Sean that he's looking for golf balls in the stretch of the river from Heronbridge to Buccleuch. In two days, he had covered about half of that area and found 32 balls. Steven expected to sell them collectively for 100 to 150 Rand on Cedar Road, which services entrances to both Dainfern Golf Estate and Steyn City. Although inside the gates of Dainfern I have unsurprisingly never encountered any golf-ball hunters, on numerous drives up and down Cedar Road I have seen hawkers trying to sell collections of assorted, presumably found, golf balls.

Steven once worked as a caddy, but fewer and fewer caddies found regular work as more and more golfers took to golf carts. 'There are many of us,' Steven explains to Sean, 'I can't even count them. We call ourselves golf-ball hunters.' Sean responds by suggesting that perhaps they were less hunters than they were prospectors. Pieter Jacob Marais, credited with finding gold on the Witwatersrand in 1853, had done so on the Jukskei less than a kilometre from where Sean found Steven. I like the framing of 'prospecting' especially because it emphasises chance and aspiration in Steven's activities. It points to possibility and hope in the 'latent commons': unpredictable, fleeting, and difficult-to-exploit opportunities for accumulation that emerge amidst capitalist ruins.[21]

It is important not to be overly romantic; Steven isn't getting rich from selling golf balls. Violent forms of capitalist accumulation persist, and the physical enclaving of the riverbanks in Dainfern, Steyn City, and Waterfall City make it more difficult for Steven to gather the balls. As he told Sean, 'The security guards in Steyn City threaten to beat me if they find me in the river, so I have to walk around now.' But such difficulties are precisely what authenticate Steven's activities as creative endeavours at the margins of capitalism. Golf courses and gated communities – garish displays of wealth emblematic of postagricultural late capitalism – both constrain and make possible Steven's economic activities. And the encroachment of automation has made Steven obsolete. We might rightly be concerned for Steven's safety. But treacherous as collecting them may be, Steven's golf balls call our attention to opportunities that buoy up in the wake of capitalist destruction, perhaps giving cause for us to modulate our cynicism, even if only a little.

Notes

1   *Totemism*, Beacon Paperbacks No. 157 (Boston: Beacon Press, 1963), 89.

2   Marjorie B. Garber, *Loaded Words* (New York: Fordham University Press, 2012), 96.

3   See Veronica Strang, 'Common Senses: Water, Sensory Experience and the Generation of Meaning,' *Journal of Material Culture* 10, no. 1 (March 1, 2005): 92–120, https://doi.org/10.1177/1359183505050096.

4   See https://dainfern.co.za/golf/ [accessed October 27, 2023].

WHAT ELITES THINK WITH THE JUKSKEI

5   Bram Büscher and Jim Igoe, 'Prosuming' Conservation? Web 2.0, Nature and the Intensification of Value-Producing Labour in Late Capitalism,' *Journal of Consumer Culture* 13, no. 3 (November 1, 2013): 283–305, https://doi.org/10.1177/1469540513482691.

6   Renugan Raidoo, 'The Unruly in the Anodyne: Nature in Gated Communities,' in *Anxious Joburg: The Inner Lives of a Global South City* (Johannesburg: Wits University Press, 2020), 132–151.

7   Mike Davis, *City of Quartz: Excavating the Future in Los Angeles*, 1st Vintage Books ed. (New York: Vintage Books, 1992), 171.

8   See also David McDermott Hughes, *Whiteness in Zimbabwe: Race, Landscape, and the Problem of Belonging*, 1st ed. (New York: Palgrave Macmillan, 2010).

9   For example, Jane Bennett, *Vibrant Matter: A Political Ecology of Things* (Durham: Duke University Press, 2010).

10 Bertrand Russell, *A History of Western Philosophy* (New York: Simon and Schuster, 1945), 57.

11 Scholars of anthropology will know that examples of what has been called totemism impose strict rules on the use and consumption of totems, many prohibiting consumption entirely. Ritual engagements with rivers are somewhat different and do often require submersion and consumption. In this chapter, elite horror at how the river came to be defiled reveals a tacit set of taboos that define Dainfern residents' relationship to the river, analogous to those that define and ritualise other totemic relations.

12 Lévi-Strauss, *Totemism*, 17.

13 The regulatory body in charge of water within the Department of Waste and Sanitation.

14 Mswazie Dube, 'Atrocious Smell Engulfs Dainfern,' *Fourways Review*, August 24, 2016, https://www.citizen.co.za/fourways-review/241795/atrocious-smell-engulfs-dainfern/.

15 Maurice Merleau-Ponty, *Phenomenology of Perception*, trans. Colin Smith, Routledge Classics (London; New York: Routledge, 2002), 477–478.

16 Jane Hu, 'Stream of Consciousness,' in *Routledge Encyclopedia of Modernism*, 1st ed. (London: Routledge, 2016), https://doi.org/10.4324/9781135000356-REM1103-1.

17 *Lo Imposible*, Drama, History, Thriller (Mediaset España, Summit Entertainment, Apaches Entertainment, 2013).

18 Susan Sontag, *Against Interpretation, and Other Essays*, 1st Picador USA ed. (New York, N. Y.: Picador U.S.A, 2001), 224.

19 W. E. B. Du Bois, *The Souls of Black Folk* (Chicago: A. C. McClurg and Co., 1903).

20 'Searching for the Soul of the Jukskei,' *The Mail & Guardian*, January 2, 2014, https://mg.co.za/article/2014-01-02-searching-for-the-soul-of-the-jukskei/.

21 Anna Lowenhaupt Tsing, *The Mushroom at the End of the World: On the Possibility of Life in Capitalist Ruins* (Princeton: Princeton University Press, 2015).

PART 5
URBAN RIVER MANAGEMENT

18 *The river is our resource: Alex Water Warriors*

Paul Maluleke

I was born and brought up in Alexandra. My granddad came from Gazankulu, in what is now Limpopo. He came to Joburg to represent the Tsongas and Vendas and he arrived in Alex in the 1930s. My granddad had six children (my father was the youngest son) and he was a community leader, an advisor for the ANC, and a businessperson, with a general dealership. My granddad was a Christian, and my grandmother was a traditional healer. She and other healers would use the river for performing some rituals. They had a garden and cultivated plants for food and medicine, using water from the river. After urbanisation, there was a lot of influx and development in Alex. My grandparents did a lot of community work. If God has touched you to become his servant, then with those blessings you can become a community leader. In my community work that I am doing, I am carrying on my grandfather's legacy.

My relationship with the river began a long time ago at the house I inherited from my grandparents; it is maybe four hundred metres to the river. It's not far and I walk to the Jukskei River most of the time.

In Alex, we grew up having a lot of challenges, so I would always belong to a lot of youth development organisations. We needed opportunities for personal development. But we also had to try to address a lot of issues in our community. The biggest one for me, was the environmental impact and sustainability. We were not taught about the environment growing up, but I could see all the pollution around us in Alex. We need more people to take up the role of environmentalists. During the COVID-19 pandemic, I realised we must go full force to clean the Jukskei River. We must follow what God wants us to do. Something gave me the courage to come every day to try and clean the river. I was asking myself, 'How are we going to emerge from the COVID-19 pandemic?' The answer was that we will use the Jukskei River to emerge from the COVID situation and the river could unite us. Then we declared that the environment will be our largest employer. I saw that we must create employment around our community and this was something that is needed. Cleaning the river requires a lot of work and people needed job opportunities.

We are talking about climate change and global warming, and this is now the biggest problem for our community. Alexandra Township is situated in between two motorways, the N3 and the M1. So even now, for our greening project, it's a challenge, because you'll find in one street there are 3 000 people sharing four to five trees. This is a problem for quality of life. We want to make sure that we have a clean environment, but there are still a lot of businesses in Alex who are producing waste and the waste is not being managed properly. There are also problems of drug and alcohol abuse, so there is no straight thinking. There are many people who come to Alex for economic reasons, and they use the environment to generate income, like illegal mining of sand from the river. We rely on City Parks and Pikitup to come and clean our environment and they are not doing it effectively. As a community we were not actually involved in the cleaning of the environment and we thought that the government will do it for us, but we could see it wasn't like that. We have to make sure that we become part of the solution, not the problem. We need to plant more trees. We need to teach the children how to take care of the environment. Most of the parents are busy trying and focusing on finding money. instead of teaching their children about the environment. Our education doesn't give us more opportunity to learn more about the environment, therefore we have a lot of crimes happening at the Jukskei River.

I started my career as an environmentalist when I attended the World Summit on Sustainable Development in 2002. The kind of tourism I am interested in is one that allows us to generate a sustainable income. We registered a project called the Greater Alexandra Greening Route, which wants to create a cultural ecotourism route, and in turn create jobs for this community. We realised we had to start with the rehabilitation of Jukskei River and to try to create a positive impact. I was starting to do some research about the river, and then people in the Alex community came to know this and start sending people to me. Someone from UCT invited me to visit to see how they were trying to clean the Black River. People used to come and say to me that they had dreams about the river, that their grandmother told them to come. And then I started to realise that this thing about the river is serious.

We called our group the Alex Water Warriors. Our Chief Executive Officer is Semadi Manganye, the Chief Administrator is Lifalakhe Mashinini, and the Directors are Mpho Tefo, Kgabo Raphala and Matsidiso Mahloko. Around South Africa there are other water warriors. We met with other activists and community organisations that were working to clean rivers, like the Jukskei River Catchment Forum, Action for Responsible Management of Our Rivers and Water for the Future.

Alexandra is a very political space. It is important that politicians can feel part of a project. And if we present a project to the government authorities, we have to be accountable and make sure that we deliver and invite the officials to give us support. Through word of mouth and coverage from community media, we were able to gain the trust of many people in the community. I have a background in working in government, and experience working with different government authorities and social development departments. This helped me to understand how to interact with the government officials, to be patient, and create good working relationships.

Just imagine the state of the river before we started cleaning. We have gathered around 350 000 bags of rubbish. It was really bad. We were removing a lot of litter from the river. Now we have installed a litter trap. But there is a still a lot of building rubble, some of it was thrown in the river 20 years ago, and the illegal dumping is still happening. We need proper machinery and equipment to remove those bricks and things. We have created consistency with our project and helped teach the community to take responsibility for our actions and stop making mistakes like allowing people to dump in the river at night. It is the problem of employment that causes people who live along the river to take money to allow trucks to come and dump.

There are many myths about the river and some people are scared to go near it. There are parts of the river that are deep and dangerous, and people can get injured. Some people talk about how there is a snake that lives in the river. It can turn into different forms. If a child drowns, some will say that it was the snake that took them, especially if it was a boy. These are the stories of the people who live along the river. They cannot describe the snake, but they say it is there. Some say it is a good snake, others that it is a bad snake. This myth is part of the heritage of Alex. There has also been crime along the river, some robberies and some people were even killed. So, there was also fear of the river because of that. When we started working with the river there was a lot of visibility, so the criminals changed their positions because of this, and it distracted them. We have made the river feel safer.

I am the CEO of the Greater Alexandra Tourism and Heritage Association. The river is part of our heritage, and it is a resource that can create economic opportunities for the people of Alexandra. Tourism can generate jobs, and tourists are interested in Alex because of our heritage. We did a lot of work to bring all the different members of the community, from all political parties, into the river cleaning plan. We drove everything from an organisational point of view and made an effort to approach each and every stakeholder to discuss the opportunity. We got a lot of guidance on how to clean the river, and we shared that information. There are many volunteers who wanted to join the project. We have been raising funds to make sure that everyone who works to clean the river can earn something.

We installed a litter trap. Someone came to advise about installing the litter trap. We got advice from experts on how to clean the river, and how to test the water for pollution. Someone came to advise about alien invasive plants. So, we are building a team of expertise that can help with cleaning the river. There are many problems with the river, including erosion. But we started by removing what doesn't belong in the river. People are throwing old couches and mattresses, or dead dogs into the river. These need to be removed as well. We were advised that the litter we remove from the river might be contaminated and needs to be treated. We need to be very careful when we work, so we have rules and regulations about safety. We must not touch the water. We must not work when the river is at a certain level. We assess our work on an ongoing basis, to simplify it and to ensure all the Water Warriors are safe. So far, we have not had any incident that any volunteer was affected by working with the river. We have had 250 volunteers so far, and with new funding we have secured that allows us to pay stipends, we will be able to employ 500 Water Warriors. When there is remuneration, people will come to do the work.

My vision is that the Jukskei River must generate income through Tourism and Ecotourism Value Chains. When it is clean there can be activities at the river. The river must be able to support life, like fish and frogs, which we do not have now. We need to bring back that life again. Many people have stories about the river, and how they feel when they come here. I can tell you that I know the Jukskei River is alive. It is a very special place. But it is currently complaining; that is why we have to clean the river. More and more people are getting involved in cleaning the river, because we are getting a lot of attention for the river. It has helped a lot that there are different races who are getting involved in our project. When the local community in Alex sees that white people are coming here, and getting involved, they see that there is money in the project and that things can happen, that jobs can be created. A multi-racial image has really helped the project, to show that there is attention from outside of Alex also coming to the river. This helps people see that we can also bring the tourists.

Our biggest challenge is still funding. There are many women who work with the project, but there are not proper restrooms for them to use when they work. We need support to employ security to patrol the river at night to stop illegal dumping. We also need finances to create the jobs to pay people to clean the river. We need resources for uniforms for our people, for transporting the waste to the landfill, for general protective equipment, and for medical insurance for our workers in case they get sick from contact with the river water. Other organisations downstream have come to us to contract us for our river-cleaning expertise, so we have the opportunity to expand our work beyond Alex. We need investment to take on that extra work.

The government spends money to employ security to protect their buildings, and even their nature reserves like the Kruger National Park. But why can they not pay for security to protect our rivers? We must pay to safeguard the environment everywhere, not just at Kruger. The Jukskei joins the Crocodile River which runs through the Kruger. The whole ecosystem is connected. When the factories discharge chemicals into the river, we see the water becomes blue or red, but we don't have the resources to trace who dumped it. Sewage is also pumped into the river. This should be stopped. All the plastic ends up in the ocean, but who provides security for the fish?

I'm a Christian. So I believe that cleanliness is next to godliness. We understand that we don't exist just because it is that way. We belong to God. God himself is a spirit. Spirituality is something which connects me with God and gives my life a purpose. God comes into the world through beauty. For me cleaning the river is about spiritual change. I didn't come to rehabilitate the river for no reason; there is something like a cause that made me to come and do this work. It is a spiritual journey for me. I see some miracles in the river. If we come together, we can stop polluting the river.

19 Temporary or permanent? The built environment and living conditions in Stjwetla informal settlement

Savory Chikomwe

This chapter provides a lens to understand the permanent but impermanent living conditions forced by an inconsistent government policy on the densely populated informal Stjwetla, a riparian settlement in Alexandra Township, bordering the Jukskei River. The study purposed to determine why there are contradictions regarding the provision of basic infrastructure and ambivalence in the upgrading of the 40-year-old riverine settlement. The chapter argues that this status somewhat varies from the conceptual design and definition in the South African informal settlement upgrading policy and programme promulgated in the early 2000s that seeks to upgrade unproclaimed settlements *in situ*. To generate relevant understanding, empirical research employing a qualitative approach encompassing comprehensive secondary and primary data, and case study methodology was used. The primary data source comprised semi-structured key informant interviews purposively sampled from the City of Johannesburg's political and administrative structures, Gauteng Province, National Departments and Stjwetla community. The research gleaned important internal misalignments and dissonances within the city departments concerning the administration of Stjwetla. There are also complex inconsistencies and disconnections across the infrastructure sectors providing permanent electrification, on one hand, and explicitly temporary water and sanitation on the other. The resulting confusion is promoting house consolidation for a settlement threatened with complete removals.

Introduction

This chapter provides a systematic analysis of how the physical and built environments around the Jukskei River are impacting living conditions for the local population in the informal Stjwetla community in Alexandra township in Johannesburg. Just as with many informal settlements in Johannesburg and many other South African cities, the circumstances of the riverine settlement create and maintain poor living conditions. Among the forces driving what is termed riparian urbanism in this book is a state-led settlement upgrading programme that somewhat varies from the conceptual design and definition in the South African policy and programme.[1] The South African informal settlement upgrading policy, a large-scale state subsidisation programme begun in 2004 under the Breaking New Ground (BNG) plan, is widely considered a progressive national policy designed to transform informally developed or unofficial settlements *in situ*. The option of relocation is only in exceptional last resort scenarios.[2] The upgrading is intended to culminate in improvements in the housing and housing-related infrastructural services through the instrument called Upgrading of Informal Settlement programme (UISP).[3] The Department of Human Settlements (DoHS), in conjunction with National Upgrading Support programme (NUSP), frame informal settlements as characterised by illegality, a lack of formal planning, random incrementalism, and high legal-social insecurity.[4]

What this chapter shows about Stjwetla are inconsistencies and variances in the implementation and practice of informal settlement upgrading and how they maintain a state of permanent temporariness and poor living conditions in the settlement. The policy implementation trajectory displays multiple disconnections between residents and state institutions in the execution of infrastructure upgrading initiatives designed to improve living conditions in Stjwetla. Further disjuncture manifests between the state institutions themselves in the water-sanitation and energy infrastructure sectors. This is a feature replicated throughout different levels of government, altogether resulting in the maintenance of a state of 'permanent temporariness' in the settlement. The water and sanitation institutions, on one hand, persist in providing provisional or interim infrastructural improvements of communal water and sanitation services since the inception of the settlement in the 1980s.[5] Yet the energy sector has implemented grid electrification since 2011, which connected individual shack dwellings, confirming speculations of permanency in a settlement that is constantly threatened by complete relocation.[6] The resultant infrastructure conundrum not only brings to the fore uncertainties and contradictions at policy implementation level but also perpetuates a scenario of perpetual temporariness that impacts living conditions in Stjwetla in significant ways. To enable a fuller understanding of the novel urbanism of this environment, challenges and opportunities linked to and shaping the novelty are examined from an infrastructure emplacement and governance framework.

Stjwetla informal settlement is located approximately midway from Johannesburg Central Business District along the western bank of the 40 km long Jukskei River in the sprawling Greater Alexandra Township. Its position encroaching on the riverbanks (and floodplain) illustrated in Figure 19.1 below, subjects the settlement to perennial violent flooding. News outlets have reported that floodwater disasters regularly sweep away temporary housing structures and drown victims in the river.[7] The catastrophic consequences of proximity to the river undermine Stjwetla residents' safety and livelihoods.

Figure 19.1 *The dense Stjwetla settlement sprawling into the off-summer season Jukskei River.*
Source: Author, 2021

Stjwetla is an unproclaimed area, a term developed in electrification guidelines for informal settlements prepared by the Department of Energy in 2011.[8] Another synonymous term used for Stjwetla is Temporary Residential Area (TRA), as it has existed in the 'temporary' mode for more than the past 40 years, since 1982! From its beginnings, the settlement has operated on inadequate temporary communal standpipe water points and shared taps that residents must walk to. Similarly, sewer disposal is done through communal emptiable chemical toilets, a bucket toilet system which is also insufficient and unsafe for the community. Their provision was legislatively recognised in 2000 when the new Comprehensive Plan for the Creation of Sustainable Human Settlements (BNG) was adopted by the City of Johannesburg.[9] An additional important infrastructural service – electricity, was belatedly installed in the 2014–2016 period in line with the Department of Energy policy guidelines for the electrification of unproclaimed areas.[10] The provision of electricity, widely regarded as a key enabler to residents' livelihood improvement, is nevertheless viewed as contradictory to the clearly temporary water and sanitation services. The electrification is perceived by residents as permanent (see detailed discussions below).

Another key feature of the Stjwetla settlement is general uncertainty, occasioned by the state's sporadic and inconsistent efforts aimed at complete eradication of the settlement, ostensibly on account of its general unsuitability for human habitation. At other times, the state has reversed the removals and supplied grid electricity, only to subsequently embark again on settlement eradication, as illustrated in Figure 19.2 below.

Figure 19.2 *Summary of the basic infrastructure trajectory in Stjwetla. Author's own construction, 2021*

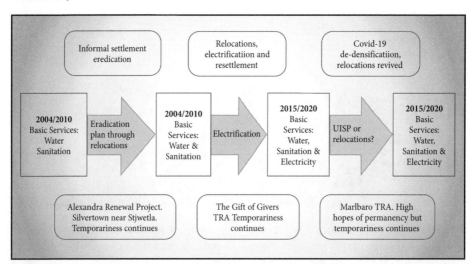

Google Earth imagery show that Stjwetla is currently situated on a 20-hectare land piece which hosts about 5 100 households on a fragile strip of land approximately 100 metres wide, which is a former industrial waste dump.[11] The population estimate converts to a density of 255 households per hectare, but this figure is arguably conservative. Transect walks of the settlement revealed high population densities comparable to extremely densified informal settlements like Dharavi in Mumbai which has above half a million residents in two square kilometres or more than 2 500 persons per hectare, translating to one person per four square meters.[12]

A research approach to Stjwetla informal settlement

This chapter reports findings from my doctoral studies that engaged a plural qualitative approach to understanding the lived conditions of Stjwetla. This included a systematic review of policies and government documents directed at Stjwetla's upgrading and living circumstances, the governance of informal settlements and infrastructure policies in South Africa, done in line with Corbin and Strauss.[13] In addition to this, in 2019 and 2021 purposive semi-structured interviews were conducted with community leaders and a ward councillor in Stjwetla and officials in the City of Johannesburg (CoJ) in the Department of Housing (DoH) and Environment and Infrastructure Services Department (EISD). An interview with the CoJ city manager helped provide overall insights into how the city is managing Stjwetla and other informal settlements. More insights were gained from interviews with City Power and Johannesburg Water officials, responsible for the provision of basic infrastructure of electricity, and water and sanitation, respectively. Interviews were also conducted to get overarching national policy positions for the informal settlements and infrastructure provision from the National Departments of Human Settlements (NDoHS) and Energy (DoE). To complement insights gleaned from interviews, transect walks were conducted to elicit insight into realities of the living conditions in Stjwetla.[14] The walking method enabled gathering records of lived experiences of individuals who live in the community so as to avoid prioritising a top-down visualisation.[15] Findings were triangulated with media reports on Stjwetla.

Permanent temporariness: Perspectives on service provision and living conditions

Against the backdrop of the maintenance of a tacit state of temporariness, undecidedness, and disjuncture (thanks to sectoral policy implementation), it is crucial to try and understand perspectives from within the Stjwetla community about the living conditions in the settlement. One of the community leaders holding the infrastructure portfolio concluded that 'Stjwetla is formalised. There is water and electricity. [City Power] never gave a timeframe for electrification, meaning it was never indicated that the electricity reticulation would be dismantled at a particular point in time.' Another community respondent, Community Leader 2, raised concern about the manner of settlement governance which has thrust Stjwetla in permanent temporariness – a similar TRA condition typically comparable with Yiftachel's[16] grey residential spaces where populations are 'concurrently tolerated and condemned, perpetually waiting 'to be corrected.'" The sentiments about perceived misgovernance follows the first relocations of households in 2010, after which several of the relocated households were brought back by government itself or allowed to come back to reoccupy the vacated spaces after five years. In the administrative lacuna, Community Leader 1 inferred that 'by paying no attention to the reoccupations, this is a confirmation by the Department of Housing [CoJ] that Stjwetla is permanent.' Yet according to various informants, Stjwetla is destined for complete relocation despite the investment in grid electrification and its consequential trigger on the brick-and-mortar construction. Community Leader 3 lamented the logic of CoJ in particular, and the South African government in general, regarding the impact of their strategies on living conditions in Stjwetla and other informal settlements:

> See now. The maintenance of 'transit camp' mentality even for settlements
> that established many years ago for many informal settlements like
> Silvertown, Mamabulo and Vezinyawu in our Ward [109] is a clear
> testimony that the South African Government is not decisive about
> informal settlement upgrading but stuck on maintaining temporariness.

The provision of grid electricity connected to individual shacks suggests permanence, while continuing temporariness is exhibited by the communal but free water and sanitation provisions by Joburg Water, a CoJ municipal-owned entity. According to a Joburg Water official, the lockable and emptiable chemical toilets are designed to serve up to seven households and emptied three times a week. Yet two community respondents commented about the water and sanitation methodologies as follows:

> Three water taps are functional in Silvertown [part of Stjwetla].
> I sometimes personally sort out the broken taps as the CoJ does not do so frequently and the residents do the repairs as the Municipality doesn't do it reliably. On sanitation, it's the bucket system where sewer is collected like once a week. The toilets are always full. I can't say how many families to one toilet as there are people who have vandalised the lock system of the toilets.

> We are using lockable bucket or chemical toilet system…although the locking system has been vandalised and the toilets are very dirt[y] and irregularly emptied, therefore very unpleasant to use.

Dirty unemptied chemical toilets and wastewater effluent flowing down many small rivulets and footways towards the western bank of the Jukskei River are common sights in Stjwetla. These substantial water and sanitation challenges and public health concerns confirm the high risks and vulnerabilities that are typically associated with informal settlements.[17] One consequence of the uncontrolled and barely adequate supply of sanitation provision is the discharge of raw sewage effluent directly into the river, creating environmental hazards. A related environmental malaise is refuse dumping into and around the river. The deposited materials have a huge impact, particularly for downstream water users, with all kinds of trash deposited, including plastics. These two environmental concerns are shown in Figure 19.3.

Apart from public health and environmental concerns in Stjwetla, policy and institutional inconsistencies surrounding basic infrastructure provision and governance frame the living conditions in important ways. The implementation of basic infrastructure programmes by the housing and energy sectors are disconnected from the community. Among the dynamics are the false hopes of permanency in Stjwetla and the consequent intense migration into the settlement, increased competition for residential space, the beginning of permanent brick-and-mortar construction, and amplified infrastructure consumption through informal connections. Brick and concrete consolidations involve active physical construction of permanent housing and business structures. These were triggered by perceptions of permanence after grid electrification in 2016. Such auto-construction and self-production dynamics resonate with resident-led notions of urbanisation elsewhere.[18]

Neither the CoJ nor politicians are communicating with residents about the impending complete relocation of Stjwetla, let alone when and to where. One community respondent justified constructing in brick despite the ongoing talk of a future relocation:

> Permanent house construction started about three to four years ago [2016–2017]. You know it's not nice to have a shack place with a family. There is no privacy. Just imagine you have children, and you want to bath, how are you going to do it? I told everyone to extend shacks wherever there are spaces in front of their shacks. I notified the authorities that we are building in brick to enhance privacy.

This speaks to the level of insecurity associated with the permanent property developments created by desperate communities yet accomplished without decisive guidance of and development control by authorities. The ward councillor quoted next is candid about the future of the brick-and-mortar constructions, which shows that there is a gap in understanding and communication between residents and authorities.

> That is all illegal. Nothing is permanent. All that will be bulldozed. I tell you sewer from those 'double storeys' is discharged into [the] Jukskei River. There are sewage pipes connected from those houses into the river [Figure 19.3 below]. We can't have a settlement like this.

Figure 19.3 *An 'off-site' sewerage effluent disposal into Jukskei through a white PVC pipe and several trash deposits on the riverbanks. Source: Author, 2021*

Forward-backward-forward: Relocation policy and institutional responses to informality

Empirical diagnoses of living conditions in Stjwetla align with ambivalent upgrading policy and disconnected institutional frameworks for informal settlements in South Africa. This is due to the lack of clarity regarding implementation of the two major state-approved upgrading instruments: the Upgrading of Informal Settlement Programme (UISP) and the Integrated National Electrification Programme (INEP). This overall assessment supports Turok's[19] contention that the South African government is making 'all sorts of piecemeal responses' that lack the skills, capabilities, and clear policy directions to improve living conditions in informal settlements. A forward-backward-forward process has characterised governance of Stjwetla settlement, with removal, reversal and then removal again. Historical sequences of Google Earth aerial images show Stjwetla initially maintaining about 14 hectares since its inception in the mid-1980s until 2010 when this ballooned to the current 20 hectares. In what was perceived as targeted eradication of the riverine settlement purportedly to protect residents from flooding incidents, the state implemented extensive clearances in 2010. Both the relocated and those remaining understood the relocations to various housing schemes in the Alexandra Renewal Project in Greater Alexandra Township, Soweto and Diepsloot to have been aimed at the ultimate eradication of the unsuitably located Stjwetla.[20]

The 2010 clearance affected approximately half of Stjwetla. One community leader attested that the created open space was not occupied between 2010 and 2015, until the government encouraged the reoccupation of the area following the re-blocking or replanning processes for grid electrification.[21] The inconsistent reversal of the initial eradication strategy was misconstrued as formalising the settlement in line with renewed commitment to the UISP and INEP, a misperception that has remained pervasive to date. New occupants were encouraged by the prospects of permanence, leading to a general extension of the informal settlement along the whole riverine strip of land. A senior housing official described the challenges with relocations:

> The community of Stjwetla is destined to be moved from this temporary site to the containerised housing units being erected in Marlboro near the commercial hub of Alexander Township. Earlier on the community was supposed to have been relocated and absorbed in an RDP housing project in 2010, whereupon only about 2 000 people were successfully relocated and resettled under the Alexandra Renewable Project....Yet the rest of the people were not moved, this varying from the promise of Government, allegedly due to corrupt allocation tendencies.

The paradoxical resettlement and housing/energy infrastructure policy changes have led to controversies surrounding the conditions of temporariness and permanence that have strong negative bearings on the circumstances of life in Stjwetla. On the surface, developments in the settlement upgrading, including grid electrification, are widely interpreted as signalling permanence and the improvement of living standards. The electrification connecting individual shack dwellings with meter numbers, for example, is widely commended as potentially reducing vulnerabilities and precariousness in the living standards of the community.[22] Yet there are serious disputes over the status of electricity between the energy sector (DoE, CoJ EISD and City Power) officials on one hand, and the housing sector (NDoHS, CoJ DoH, and the ward councillor) on the other. The former's viewpoint firmly aligns with the Stjwetla community position contending the settlement and the electrification are permanent and genuinely improving the living conditions of that community. The latter group of stakeholders argues the developments will have to be reversed, removed or relocated. These contradictory positions keep emerging in informal settlement policymaking, implementation and governance.[23]

To illustrate the contradictions between the energy and housing sectors, a senior official at the Department of Energy (DoE) offers a pragmatic position on electrification, which somewhat differs from the policy guidelines of the *Electrification of Unproclaimed Areas Policy of 2011* and subsequent updates for interim electrification of informal settlements:

> We do not have electrified informal settlements which will be relocated. There are going to be very few [if] any such settlements because of extenuating circumstances. Once grid electrified, the settlement is upgraded automatically. People start building shops, double-storey housing. This [electrification] is surely permanent.

This view was consistent with what was happening in Stjwetla. The electrification increased community confidence in permanence, leading to unassisted but unofficial consolidation processes. The construction of double-storey buildings, albeit poorly built, creates dilemmas as the uncontrolled housing developments are erected near, or incorporate, electrical wiring and poles that pose serious electrocution dangers in some instances. In a consistent affirmation of how electrification contributes to a sense of permanency, a senior official from CoJ's Environmental and Infrastructure Department (EISD) asserted:

> As far as we are concerned, the electricity infrastructure is permanent, and the settlement is also permanent. This is purely a technical assessment given the huge capital investment the CoJ is contributing to the electrification. Yet I do not understand the UISP/USDG and the Department of Housing [CoJ] processes in this regard (CoJ EISD).

The ongoing disagreement about what constitutes permanence was also echoed by officials from City Power:

> There are no interim services with electrification. What we provide is [an] almost permanent service. When we give that electricity and a meter number, that meter has an owner's name, which belongs to that person forever. The electricity may be called interim in that it is

awaiting final connection to a proper RDP house upon *in situ* upgrading that shall take place, but the backbone and the bulk services that take five to seven years to complete are permanent and not temporary at all…To put cables, we need wayleave planning [reblocking]…As such, we can't call the electrification that happens in such an elaborate process temporary. Once we have the approval to install electricity, then it is no more temporary.

Another City Power official argued, 'if [a] settlement is relocated, there is very little recovery of that infrastructure which can only be decommissioned and become scrap. It's not a case that it will be used somewhere else.' Again, this suggests that electrification implied permanence and further brings to the fore complex contradictions and disconnections in the implementation of interim electrification policy on one hand, and water and sanitation on the other, with direct implications for quality of life in Stjwetla.

In contrast to the energy sector viewpoints, the housing sector comprising the National Department of Human Settlement (NDoHS), the CoJ Housing Department and the ward councillor subscribe to the narrative of complete future removal of Stjwetla. This position is based on the unsuitability of the location for human settlement due to, among other reasons, the threat of floods.[24] To demonstrate this point, the NDoHS, for instance, rejuvenated what is widely interpreted as partial forceful removal of residents from Stjwetla in response to the COVID-19 pandemic in the year 2020, according to a CoJ senior housing official. The project, a directive from the then Minister of Human Settlements, Water and Sanitation to 'de-densify' informal settlements in the CoJ and South Africa, targeted Stjwetla for the relocation of 1 600 out of the 5 100 households by constructing yet another TRA constructed of shipping containers on a vacant piece of land in the neighbouring Marlboro industrial area.[25] The construction of another TRA implies continuing temporary living conditions for both remaining and relocated residents. Social movements, however, dismissed the sincerity of government's supposedly benevolent de-densification plan, given the earlier half-hearted attempts at complete settlement eradication. The investigative journalist Dennis Webster feared the de-densification was shorthand for eviction as '[t]here is, after all, no 'de-densification' policy or legislation.'[26] The 'evictions' become an important lens through which to understand sectoral and institutional disjunctures, especially between the DoE and NDoHS, and the maintenance of perpetual precarities.

At the city level, a senior housing official in the CoJ defended the Minister's directive regarding the Stjwetla de-densification but also pinpointed shortcomings left to municipal housing officials to grapple with:

The Minister made herself available over and above in terms of the Housing Act and said to the CoJ: 'you have USDG, and the HSDG [both settlement grants],' and by invoking powers given in terms of the Housing Act the Minister changed the conditions of the grants to emergency housing grants. But the Minister could have been advised more appropriately to make right decisions and still be able to achieve de-densification.

The ward councillor reasserted that 'the electrification, like water and sanitation, is temporary. Nothing is permanent. Government has an intention to redevelop the area [for some other land use] in the next three years.' This comment confirms the popular perceptions of attitudes held in the housing sector.

Implications of Stjwetla for broader policies on informal settlements

Large numbers of the poor rely on informal settlements for housing, given inadequate state responses to housing and poverty. This creates a management issue for state actors. While it is a seemingly rational and progressive response, the concept of TRAs is increasingly varying from its original justification by the Emergency Housing Programme of the NDoHS.[27] Stjwetla is a typical example of how the government has made exceptional policy, financial and administrative commitments, yet remained ambivalent to bringing them to fruition. The conceptualisation and implementation of TRAs has created permanent-temporary sites of marginalisation and high social vulnerability.[28] In close resonance to Turok's[29] argument, the government is ambivalent about how to address informal settlements and lacks 'the skills and capabilities to work with disaffected communities on joint problem-solving.'

South Africa has paid lip service to designing and aligning informal settlement upgrading and participation policies in line with global frameworks. In reality, it has fallen short of putting into action mutual interactions, inter-organisational networking and stakeholder interdependencies.[30] Instead, the implementation and governance of what appear to be progressive infrastructure policies, laws and regulations has induced deep constraints to residents' livelihoods.[31] Accordingly, it is clear that, in line with Turok,[32] South Africa has a 'policy neglect that is based on the assumption that squatter settlements will gradually disappear as people find better housing options.' In this line of argument, Anheier's[33] policy governance analogue becomes relevant, contending that there are generally 'no realistic, visionary grand solutions to guide…to improve governance and, ultimately, policy outcomes….Some innovations would likely do more harm than good; others appear unfeasible, too self-serving, or fraught with unknown consequences.'

Notwithstanding the fact that governance conundrums owing to disagreements between different stakeholders and disconnected infrastructure policy at implementation make immense contribution to the permanent temporariness challenges in Stjwetla, there are many other contributing factors. The poor living conditions in Stjwetla informal settlement can also be analysed as exerting serious 'challenges, including public health risks and other vulnerable living conditions.[34] The net effect is the maintenance of high environmental fragility, high susceptibility to vagaries of violent flooding and catastrophic consequences thereof owing to absence of controls to development servitudes.[35] Furthermore, the density of the built environment and the use of cheap, readily available, but often flammable materials such as cardboard, plastic and untreated wood to construct dwellings make Stjwetla informal settlement susceptible to devastating fires.[36] There are also high security concerns evidenced in continuing settlement informalisation, lack of proper planning and control, and various forms of violence, including muggings, sexual assaults, and killings.[37] The settlement is difficult and dangerous to police because its housing is spontaneous in nature, with, inter alia, no street or house numbers and no street lighting. The security concern is further exacerbated by the long distances travelled outside the house to access basic communal services, exposing residents to other security risks and incidences of violent attacks and/or sexual harassment.

Conclusion

The case study of Stjwetla informal settlement represents a complex riparian urbanism of special importance to policymakers, practitioners, and academics regarding the absolute lack of coherent, concerted and politically engaged policy and governance processes. The disengagements and inconsistencies in the implementation of state-approved programmes for informal settlement upgrading and electricity infrastructure provision of UISP and INEP are a case in point. The paradoxical removal of residents from Stjwetla on account of the inappropriateness of the settlement for human habitation, and the subsequent reversal, resettlement and grid electrification is highly incoherent. Different city or government departments constantly contradict one other. The several dynamics and temperamentalities occurring in the settlement – including shack dwellings built very closely to the Jukskei River – are outcomes of the disconnected infrastructure policy frameworks.

In sum, the implementation of the infrastructure programmes was neither well thought out, nor carefully coordinated. The energy sector, comprising the DoE, CoJ's EISD and City Power has taken realistic and pragmatic positions reflecting an understanding of 'what makes sense' for those living in Stjwetla. This is contrary to the bureaucratic treatment by the housing sector that has been dogmatically pro-relocation, seemingly indifferent to the need for permanent settlement upgrading to accommodate human habitation. Worryingly, the latter have flipped between the paradoxical decisions of removal, reversal and removal again.

The sticking question that remains is whether Stjwetla should be maintained and upgraded for *in situ* housing developments, given its proximity to and environmental impact on the Jukskei River. What policy and governance measures will be necessary to establish Stjwetla or part of it as a township and improve its living conditions? To date, state and city governance has been inconsistent in policy planning, formulation, coordination and implementation. As Anheier[38] concluded, arbitrariness in infrastructure investment and innovation should be avoided as it leads to consequences that are unfeasible and costly, ultimately leading to poor living conditions. To achieve positive outcomes, the state must honestly engage democratic and inclusive governance processes with all stakeholders and community beneficiaries. The state should also decisively deal with horizontal and vertical inter and intra departmental disconnections and make its infrastructure policy implementable without confusion. In that process, the total policy mayhem, corruption, disingenuousness, and lack of real commitment to the poor can hopefully be addressed.

Notes

1   Marie Huchzermeyer, 'The New Instrument for Upgrading Informal Settlements in South Africa: Contributions and Constraints,' in *Informal Settlements: A Perpetual Challenge?* ed. Marie Huchzermeyer and Aly Karam (Cape Town: UCT Press, 2006), https://doi.org/10.58331/UCTPRESS.39; Marie Huchzermeyer, 'The Struggle for *in Situ* Upgrading of Informal Settlements: A Reflection on Cases in Gauteng,' *Development Southern Africa* 26, no. 1 (March 2009): 59–73, https://doi.org/10.1080/03768350802640099.

2   Department of Human Settlements, 'Breaking New Ground: Comprehensive Plan for Housing Delivery'; Huchzermeyer, 'The New Instrument for Upgrading Informal Settlements in South Africa: Contributions and Constraints.'

3   Department of Human Settlements, 'Breaking New Ground: Comprehensive Plan for Housing Delivery.'

4   Department of Human Settlements, 'National Housing Code, 2009'; Huchzermeyer, 'The New Instrument for Upgrading Informal Settlements in South Africa: Contributions and Constraints.'

5   Visagie and Turok, 'Getting Urban Density to Work in Informal Settlements in Africa'; Chikomwe, 'Governance of Infrastructure Provision in Informal Settlements: The Electrification of Unproclaimed Areas in the City of Johannesburg.'

6   Maphanga, 'City of Johannesburg to Relocate 1 600 Residents from Densely Populated Settlement in Alexandra'; Chikomwe, 'Governance of Infrastructure Provision in Informal Settlements: The Electrification of Unproclaimed Areas in the City of Johannesburg.'

7   Swart, 'Jukskei Drownings.'

8   Department of Energy, 'Policy Guidelines for the Electrification of Unproclaimed Areas.'

9   Department of Human Settlements, 'Breaking New Ground: Comprehensive Plan for Housing Delivery.'

10   Department of Energy, 'Policy Guidelines for the Electrification of Unproclaimed Areas.'

11   Webster, 'Relocation Rears Its Head.'

12   Satterthwaite, 'Upgrading Informal Settlements.

13   Bowen, 'Document Analysis as a Qualitative Research Method.'

14　Papanek, *Design for the Real World*; Facer and Buchczyk, 'Walking the City: A Method for Exploring Public Pedagogies.'

15　Facer and Buchczyk, 'Walking the City: A Method for Exploring Public Pedagogies.'

16　Yiftachel, 'Theoretical Notes On "Gray Cities."'

17　Chant, 'Book Reviews'; Zerbo, Delgado, and González, 'Vulnerability and Everyday Health Risks of Urban Informal Settlements in Sub-Saharan Africa'; Gibbs, Govender, and Jewkes, 'An Exploratory Analysis of Factors Associated with Depression in a Vulnerable Group of Young People Living in Informal Settlements in South Africa.'

18　Caldeira, 'Peripheral Urbanisation'; Moreno et al., 'Self-Construction in Informal Settlements.'

19　Turok and Borel-Saladin, 'The Theory and Reality of Urban Slums.'

20　Mvulane, 'Settling on Water Pathways: A Case Study of Setswetla Vulnerability to Flash Floods.'

21　South African National Treasury, 'Scaling Up the Upgrading of Informal Settlements: A Scoping Study of South African Good Practices and Innovations.'

22　Bekker et al., 'South Africa's Rapid Electrification Programme.'

23　Turok and Borel-Saladin, 'The Theory and Reality of Urban Slums'; Chikomwe, 'Governance of Infrastructure Provision in Informal Settlements: The Electrification of Unproclaimed Areas in the City of Johannesburg.'

24　Chikomwe, 'Governance of Infrastructure Provision in Informal Settlements: The Electrification of Unproclaimed Areas in the City of Johannesburg.'

25　Webster, 'Relocation Rears its Head.'

26　Webster, 'Relocation Rears its Head.'

27　Levenson, *Delivery as Dispossession*.

28　Levenson; PlanAct, 'An Urgent Call to Rethink De-Densification as the Dominant Proposed Strategy in the Context of COVID-19.'

29　Turok, 'Informal Settlements.'

30　Rhodes, 'The New Governance.'

31　de Visser, 'Developmental Local Government in South Africa'; Fieuw, 'Deep Rooted Knowledge?'

32　Turok, 'Informal Settlements.'

33　Anheier, '2013.'

34　Chant, 'Book Reviews.'

35　'Informal Settlements and Human Rights in South Africa: Submission to the United Nations Special Rapporteur on Adequate Housing as a Component of the Right an Adequate Standard of Living.'

36　'Informal Settlements and Human Rights in South Africa: Submission to the United Nations Special Rapporteur on Adequate Housing as a Component of the Right an Adequate Standard of Living'; Mvulane, 'Settling on Water Pathways: A Case Study of Setswetla Vulnerability to Flash Floods.'

37 'Informal Settlements and Human Rights in South Africa: Submission to the United Nations Special Rapporteur on Adequate Housing as a Component of the Right an Adequate Standard of Living.'

38 Anheier, '2013.'

20 Converging currents: Urban ecological design strategies towards a resilient river system

Dieter Brandt

This chapter explores innovative approaches to urban ecological design for the Jukskei River, emphasising the need for sustainable river management amidst urbanisation and climate change. The chapter highlights the environmental challenges and opportunities associated with the river's urban context, including declining biodiversity, pollution, and flood risks. It outlines climate action responses where city stakeholders implemented initiatives to manage drainage and enhance water quality. Also presented here is the 'Isitiya soLwazi' concept, which integrates agroecology and urban agriculture to foster community resilience and economic development in Johannesburg. This framework leverages green infrastructure and nature-based solutions to restore ecosystems and improve urban living conditions. Through cross-disciplinary strategies, the chapter advocates for reimagining urban landscapes, promoting climate resilience, and enhancing community well-being, ultimately proposing a model for sustainable urban development and transboundary climate resilience in Southern Africa.

Urban ecologies: Urban development and sustainability along the Jukskei River

Having worked and lived in Braamfontein, I became familiar with the Witwatersrand Ridge system. The ridge is a well-known geographical divide between catchments that drain into the Atlantic Indian Ocean system.[1] My understanding of this landscape was brought to life when I witnessed drilling along a Juta Street servitude: water jetted into the air as the ground was punctured. It was a powerful demonstration of the hydrological pressure beneath our feet. My connection with the river was enriched after discovering a derelict dye factory in Bezuidenhout Valley. Located on a park below the Observatory Ridge, directly adjacent to the canalised section of the Jukskei River, this neglected property provided a unique opportunity for our collective, to give this industrial site a new purpose as an event and production space. The property evolved into vibrant studios for the creative industries, with the old heritage buildings accommodating a string of film and music productions. Site challenges included proximity to a municipal solid waste collection point, a polluted river, and the attendant issues of rats and unpleasant odours. During winter, smog and smoke intermingle with urban smells. Witnessing local environmental changes over a decade, one is confronted with the urban and ecological interplay of the Jukskei River. An unseen change is that the surrounding urban fabric disguises the loss of the indigenous grasslands that have since transformed into an urban ecology dominated by invasive and exotic species.[2] Urbanisation adversely impacts species diversity and grasslands, with landscape changes from human activity affecting the indigenous fauna and flora.

Understanding the interaction between the urban growth of Johannesburg and the reliance on the Jukskei River requires knowledge of its system trade-offs. The Jukskei River, a freshwater resource and tributary of the Crocodile River, drains water into the Limpopo River catchment before discharging from Mozambique into the Indian Ocean. However, minor river channels, like the local Braamfontein Spruit, first feed into the local floodplain of the Jukskei River, where underdeveloped, low-lying settlements are vulnerable to flood risk during heavy rainfall. Upstream watersheds in more built-up areas, with less natural land cover than downstream areas, increase the risk and severity of flash floods. For example, precipitation not absorbed into the ground is typically higher in built-up areas.[3]

Evaluating criteria for sustainable urban development and improving these interlinkages through an integrated approach can support inclusive principles for river management. As part of a climate action response for managing drainage and improving water quality, city stakeholders implemented a Sustainable Urban Drainage System (SUDS) initiative to manage drainage and enhance water quality. Residents maintain streams, semi-vegetated channels, soakaways, and a miniature bio-retention area, thereby reducing surface water and improving water quality.[4]

Declining biodiversity, drought, and flood risks due to urbanisation, putting additional strain on local ecosystems and water availability, are not unique to the Jukskei River catchment. According to Cullis et al., 'Urbanisation, Climate Change and Its Impact on Water Quality and Economic Risks in a Water Scarce and Rapidly Urbanising Catchment,' droughts can lead to increased concentrations of pollutants from settlements, where water demands during drought events coupled with decreased water delivery due to climate change can elevate the impact of pollution. The impact of urbanisation on rivers includes stormwater from developed areas, runoff from informal settlements, and discharges from wastewater treatment plants.[5]

Pollution from urban industries, like the old dye factory, can impact endemic species and degrade original habitats such as the Soweto Grasslands. With a river's natural biodiversity deteriorating, invasive species typically reduce indigenous flora and fauna. Upstream activities can alter the natural vegetation and impact lower wetland areas, allowing invasive species to affect the river ecosystem. As a result, invasive species infiltrate natural landscapes and impact the Jukskei River's functions like flood drainage, filtering water, supporting biodiversity and maintaining ecology.

Planning can minimise environmental impact, and conservation policies can help local communities and municipalities design and develop solutions for sustainably integrating natural and urban landscape systems. Policies for implementation can incorporate compact mixed-use eco-developments, the introduction of Urban Green Infrastructure (UGI), Nature-based Solutions (NBS), and the protection of river edges. Supporting a process where urban development considers ecological health through careful planning is therefore vital. Along the transects of our river systems, townships continue shaping the urban ecology and the well-being of local communities.

Bridging vulnerability and resilience: Examples for limiting flood risk in economically stressed communities

A study by Munyai et al., 'Vulnerability and Adaptation to Flood Hazards in Rural Settlements of Limpopo Province, South Africa,' revealed how tropical cyclones and continental tropical lows have raised flood vulnerability,[6] with a significant flood event in Thohoyandou in 2019 due to extreme precipitation.[7] Flood vulnerability levels in the community of Ga-Kgapane Masakaneng indicated that the area is highly susceptible due to economic factors. The study reveals that financial limitations exacerbate flood vulnerability, as most households in the area are unemployed or earn low incomes.[8] It was recommended that further attention be undertaken to addressing economic factors to mitigate flood vulnerability in the community. Flood adaptation strategies in rural settlements provided valuable insights for the research into adaptation actions to cope with flood hazards. Where damages were caused by floods, including flooded houses and disrupted infrastructure, strategies were employed by the communities' using sandbags, including constructing raised porches known as 'Le-guba' and building furrows around homes.[9] In severe cases, communities relocated.[10] Because economic circumstances can hinder our ability as a community to respond to climate-related challenges, sustainable livelihood practices and healthier interactions across the urban-rural landscape, both up and downstream, are needed to address these challenges.

In a concept note, 'Sustaining transformative climate resilience by closing the agro-processing gaps in a water-scarce mining region of Limpopo, South Africa,' it was proposed to climate-proof and scale the Mogalakwena Sustainable Development Incubator.[11] The aim was to close the rural-urban value chain to benefit both formal and informal markets within the agricultural and agro-processing sector and to target emerging farmers to enhance self-reliance amongst its members. Situated in a UNESCO-designated Biosphere, the region has some of the country's highest poverty levels, with growing unemployment and inadequate education. The proposal would establish a new fresh produce centre in Mokopane, an economic hub, with the objective that the development of agri-businesses would catalyse the integration of communities into the formal economy, while protecting the environment. For longer-term financial sustainability, a proposal was made to connect the incubator to the Agri-Park development framework,[12] thereby integrating the programme for a local agri-value chain into a larger national network. It was written within the Green Climate Fund framework for enhancing livelihoods, food security, health and well-being. Firstly, a baseline assessment would set out to understand the interactions and boundaries of the local systems. This would include identifying their climate-driven vulnerabilities by using tools to quantify water regulation and supply, floral and faunal diversity, pollination services, and flood and soil regulation. The baseline would map the rural-urban linkages, socio-economic divisions, formal-informal markets, and relational practices. Finally, it was to be tracked by an action plan for increasing the adaptive capacities of impacted communities, thereby reducing climate risks by future-proofing the incubator, supporting cost-effective, drought-adaptive action for targeted land and ecosystem services, and closing the agri-loop cycle by promoting fresh produce sales.

Crossing the urban-rural divide: Transferring knowledge from Mogalakwena to Johannesburg, a framework for climate-resilient urban spaces

Isitiya soLwazi, a concept note in 2020 for the City of Johannesburg, promotes the local economic development of parks and open space systems like the Jukskei River through a more balanced, mixed-use approach, with the inclusion of agriculture, agro-enterprises, and forestry together with goals for restoring and rehabilitating ecosystems to improve human and environmental health. For Isitiya soLwazi, meaning 'Knowledge Garden' in isiXhosa, lessons were transferred from the rural Mogalakwena Incubator in Limpopo to the Siyakhana Food Gardens, an urban incubator in Bezuidenhout Park in Johannesburg.[13] The Jukskei River system in Bezuidenhout Valley edges Bezuidenhout Park before crossing Johannesburg's administrative boundary into the City of Ekurhuleni. It eventually courses into the countryside to join the Crocodile River. Due to the financial pressures of the COVID-19 health crisis and the additional economic strain put on city parks by biodiversity loss and climate impacts such as flooding, heat stress, drought, and ground and surface water depletion, the need to efficiently use public resources has become greater.

Open spaces like the Jukskei River and Bezuidenhout Park are vital to the public and the environmental health of urban centres. As they are green spaces, open space systems cool urban micro-climates and manage the impact of urbanisation on water retention, by reducing heat gain and mitigating stormwater runoff. By restoring parks and rehabilitating riparian corridors for improved flood regulation, green infrastructure can also help improve urban biodiversity and mitigate flooding. Additional climate benefits include air purification and sequestrating (capturing and storing) carbon into the ground.

The Isitiya soLwazi proposal to establish new food production channels within Johannesburg's parks (distributed across the city) can enhance livelihoods for vulnerable communities. This is through supporting enterprise development that revitalises urban and township trade and establishes commercially viable enterprises.

Isitiya soLwazi, interlinked with its environs, is a set of knowledge reservoirs for learning, education, and training for scaling agroecology, indigenous knowledge, and community-based adaptation. It is scaling up sustainable urban agricultural practices to promote a circular economy within the food and agro-processing value chain, to link formal and informal markets within a compact radius of urban parks.

The vision combines public and environmental health to co-construct climate-resilient, healthy, and financially self-sufficient communities along urban river catchments. The design framework continues to expand on practice-based research and to develop new site-specific urban ecologies, climate-resilient strategies, and technological innovation. This approach leverages architecture, ecology, and technology for climate-resilient urban development to mitigate climate change impacts and biodiversity loss. This conceptual framework, tested at the intersection of riparian systems, parks, and transport interchanges, includes proposals for flexible land uses on flood-prone river edges, increased access to green spaces at urban nodes, and sponsoring urban agriculture and small-scale farming amongst settlements like Stjwetla in Alexandra, or informal settlements in Ekurhuleni like Mpilisweni, Tamaho, Crossroads, and Union townships. Adaptive solutions are to be affordable and should facilitate both healthcare access in public spaces and infrastructure for promoting food security at public transport interchanges. Initiatives, such as primary health support units and fresh produce market stations, are designed to be functional, addressing immediate healthcare and food security needs in public spaces. These interventions focus on designing urban spaces that balance economic development with landscape restoration, enabling nature to thrive within urban environments. Sustainable micro-farming practices can bolster climate resilience, food security, and the local economy. Isitiya soLwazi envisions micro-farming practices that strengthen climate resilience and food security and contribute to local economic development. The objectives are to manage flood risks through ecosystem regeneration, improve access to primary health through an adaptive architecture, and strengthen local economies through sustainable agriculture and small-scale farming.

Rivers without borders: A journey through a climate crisis and towards transboundary climate resilience in Southern Africa

In Praça da Independência, under a gentle drizzle and the echo of a 21-cannon salute, Joaquim Alberto Chissano was inaugurated as president of Mozambique for a second term, in 2000. Chissano welcomed the crowd and the rain as divine blessings at the start of a year that would soon become marked by a catastrophic event. That same year, a devastating flood caused by intense Cyclone Leon-Eline, submerged many parts of Mozambique. It emerged as a frightening forecast of the havoc that climate impacts would continue to wreak worldwide in the 21st century. The flood coincided with an unprecedented spike in global ocean temperatures,

CONVERGING CURRENTS

accelerating cyclone occurrences and spurring urgent calls for strategies to develop climate resilience.

During that period, I visited Maputo for an architectural rendezvous and took a detour to Inhambane. A tour by boat along bioluminescent currents to the peninsula's tip became an ordeal. In the face of Cyclone Leon-Eline, my travelling companions and I were forced to return, only to find the land underwater. Wading through flooded streets, we boarded the bus to confront a storm-battered mainland and the ensuing cyclone. We crossed the Limpopo River mouth near Xai Xai on our journey back to Maputo. Its banks breached as the water levels rapidly rose above ten meters. While I found lodging in Catemba, the storm escalated. Amidst the rising floodwaters, I had to seek refuge on higher urban ground. The storm paralysed Maputo, disrupting core services, destroying homes, and isolating the city. I was fortunate to get on to one of the last flights out of the city before the rising waters landlocked the remaining exit routes. Back home, the remnants of the low-pressure cell from Mozambique caused significant rainfall in Johannesburg and quickly increased the water levels of the Jukskei River. This water would eventually return to Mozambique, exacerbating the floods in the lower Limpopo Valley and engulfing the town of Xai Xai. In the aftermath, images of famine, poverty, and disease dominated international media,[14] cementing the memory of a catastrophe and its lingering effects for years to come.

International and cross-border cooperation on shared water resources, conservation, and flood management is critical. Advanced Environmental Design Initiatives (AEDI) has tried to define a lens through which it can broadly position its work. The Basin Adaptive Systems Integration Network Complex (BASINc) is an overarching framework for ordering environmental design initiatives. Positioning initiatives within the BASINc framework allows for the identification of social and ecological systems and their related challenges across the selected catchment landscape. Considering the major river basins on the continent of Africa, it integrates 63 African transboundary river basins across its 54 political countries. This acts as a mechanism for challenging the status quo, by reinterpreting the meaning of borders, through prioritising catchment basins as complex adaptive systems over more confined geopolitical interests. This perspective allows for the redefinition of rivers as systems without borders, the elevation of urban-rural linkages, the deepening of regional integration, and the promotion of a network of interdependent social and ecological systems. The biophysical boundaries of river catchments define new territories for understanding the context in which ecological urban design initiatives can be located. Rivers are transboundary actors, which materially demonstrate the connections between what we do in Johannesburg and what happens in Maputo.

Climate policy and action must be co-designed to empower local communities to become custodians of rivers to help protect, enhance, and benefit from these majestic river catchments that contribute to our physical well-being and urban ecological health.

Notes

1   The systemic interaction of the 'Atlantic Indian Ocean system,' primarily through the Agulhas Current Retroflection in the South Atlantic Ocean, not only contributes to Atlantic Meridional Overturning Circulation (AMOC) but is a major influence on weather patterns across Southern Africa. Paola Castellanos, Estrella Olmedo, Josep Lluis Pelegrí, Antonio Turiel, and Edmo J. D. Campos, 'Seasonal Variability of Retroflection Structures and Transports in the Atlantic Ocean as Inferred from Satellite-Derived Salinity Maps,' *Remote Sensing* 11, no. 7 (January 2019): 802, https://doi.org/10.3390/rs11070802.

2   The park area around the studios, originally Soweto highveld grasslands, has since been transformed into Kikuyu parkland, now dominated by invasive and exotic species. See C. L. Cook, *Preliminary Ecological Assessment for the Proposed Expansion of the Bezuidenhout Valley Clinic & Parking Area; Gauteng Province* (Ecological consultant: Specialist faunal consultant, 2017), compiled for Royal Haskoning DHV.

3   Mawasha, Tshepo Sylvester, and Wilma Britz, 'Simulating Change in Surface Runoff Depth Due to LULC Change Using Soil and Water Assessment Tool for Flash Floods Prediction.' *South African Journal of Geomatics* 9, no. 2 (2020): 282–301. https://doi.org/10.4314/sajg.v9i2.19.

4   City of Johannesburg, *Climate Action Plan*. EISD, City of Johannesburg, March 2021.

5   James D. S. Cullis, Annabel Horn, Nico Rossouw, Lloyd Fisher-Jeffes, Marlé M. Kunneke, and Willem Hoffman, 'Urbanisation, Climate Change and Its Impact on Water Quality and Economic Risks in a Water Scarce and Rapidly Urbanising Catchment: Case Study of the Berg River Catchment,' *H2Open Journal* 2, no. 1 (August 2, 2019): 146–167, https://doi.org/10.2166/h2oj.2019.027.

6   Generated from excess latent energy over the Mozambique Channel, mostly because of moisture advection and convergence from the Atlantic and Indian Oceans, Tropical-temperate troughs (TTTs) are responsible for much of South Africa's summer rainfall. See Neil C. G. Hart, Chris J. C. Reason and Nicolas Fauchereau, 'Cloud Bands over Southern Africa: Seasonality, Contribution to Rainfall Variability and Modulation by the MJO,' *Climate Dynamics* 41, no. 5 (September 1, 2013): 1199–1212, https://doi.org/10.1007/s00382-012-1589-4.

7   Rendani B. Munyai, Hector Chikoore, Agnes Musyoki, James Chakwizira, Tshimbiluni P. Muofhe, Nkosinathi G. Xulu, and Tshilidzi C. Manyanya, 'Vulnerability and Adaptation to Flood Hazards in Rural Settlements of Limpopo Province, South Africa,' *Water* 13, no. 24 (January 2021): 3490, https://doi.org/10.3390/w13243490.

8   For example, the demographic of residential plot farming providing basic food security is mostly older women. Micro farmers, including vegetable producers, had some of the highest levels of land productivity, being able to produce the whole year around. While micro-farming is important for food security, it does not alleviate poverty. See Hubert Cochet, Ward Anseeuw, and Sandrine Freguin-Gresh, 'The Interlinked but Continuously Divergent Production Systems of the Catchment Area of the Nwanedzi River (Limpopo Province),' in *South Africa's Agrarian Question* (Cape Town: HSRC Press, 2015), 88.

9   Rendani B. Munyai et al., 'Vulnerability and Adaptation to Flood Hazards in Rural Settlements of Limpopo Province, South Africa,' *Water* 13, no. 24 (January 2021): 3490, 16, https://doi.org/10.3390/w13243490.

10 In a case study for Ekurhuleni Metropolitan Municipality, the Atlasville community identified weaknesses in the system and took alternative actions to address the problem of dealing with urban flood risk. The community's perceptions and response to urban flood risk, as discussed by Christina Elizabeth Fatti and Zarina Patel in 'Perceptions and Responses to Urban Flood Risk: Implications for Climate Governance in the South,' found that they had little confidence in the municipality's ability to address flood risks effectively. As a result, the community took proactive measures, including upgrading the Atlas Spruit stormwater management system, to enhance their resilience to flood events. See Christina Elizabeth Fatti and Zarina Patel, 'Perceptions and Responses to Urban Flood Risk: Implications for Climate Governance in the South,' *Applied Geography,* Special Issue: Constraints and Opportunities in Urban Development in Sub-Saharan Africa 36 (January 1, 2013): 13–22, https://doi.org/10.1016/j.apgeog.2012.06.011.

11 Jessica Thorn and Dieter Brandt, 'Sustaining Transformative Climate Resilience by Closing the Agro-Processing Gaps in a Water-Scarce Mining Region of Limpopo, South Africa,' concept note, Advanced Environmental Design Initiatives (AEDI), 2018.

12 The case study for the catchment area shows how only a fraction of the farmers integrate with high-value agri-business chains to access the market. A solution to this divide is the Agri-Park model developed by the Department of Rural Development and Land Reform (DRDLR) to provide access to shared resources and support services to help micro to medium-scale farmers access resources to increase productivity. See Department of Rural Development and Land Reform, *Agri-Park Model for Integrated Agricultural Development,* 2019.

13 Jessica Thorn, Dieter Brandt, and Michael Rudolph, 'Isitiya soLwazi, an Enterprise and Knowledge Garden: Re-Thinking Community Urban City Parks in a Post-COVID World,' concept note, Advanced Environmental Design Initiatives (AEDI) in partnership with Siyakhana Growth and Development (SGD) NPO, the Centre of Ecological Intelligence (CEI), and the University of Johannesburg (UJ), 2020.

14 As captured by the United Nations Office for the Coordination of Humanitarian Affairs situation reports and media, see 'Mozambique Provinces Affected by February 2000 Flooding,' ReliefWeb, 10 March 2000, https://reliefweb.int/map/mozambique/mozambique-provinces-affected-february-2000-flooding.

21 *The river deserves love: Water for the future*

Romy Stander

It always seems impossible until it's done. – Nelson Mandela

Hardly visible from behind the fence, and definitely not accessible, it wasn't so much a river as it was a no-go zone, surrounded by chop shops and other buildings in disrepair. I remember standing at the locked gate looking at this filthy, forsaken trickle, to which all the surrounding buildings had turned their backs, and I realised it was the Jukskei River. From this very first time that I saw the river, I felt drawn to its water.

At the time, in 2017, I was working for Nando's co-founder, Robbie Brozin, on Nando's philanthropic and other special projects, mostly in Mozambique. I would be sent to various locations to explore and research creative approach to project spaces, which included Nando's peri-peri farm and agricultural academy, and the training centre for Goodbye Malaria. My role was to support the beautification of those spaces, integrating local design, art and crafts. The goal was to provide functional, uplifting and culturally relevant work environments.

It was a Friday, one of those bright winter afternoons in Johannesburg when it takes your eyes several minutes to adjust to the sunshine when you step outside. Robbie had asked me to attend a site walk around a neglected piece of land across from our offices. Brian Green, who subsequently developed the space into the mixed-use development Victoria Yards, led me and the trailblazing South African design promotor, Tracy Lee Lynch, on a tour. During the walk we admired Brian's plans to integrate an urban agriculture space with restaurants, shops and artist studios, similar to his remarkable success with the 44 Stanley development. Very naively I thought about how wonderful it would be for the Jukskei, which seemed so awkwardly out of place, to be cleaned up enough to be part of the development.

When I got home that evening, I jumped into the well of information that is the internet. I couldn't stop thinking about the river, and I spent the whole weekend reading up about it. I came across Sean Christie's piece 'Searching for the soul of the Jukskei' in the *Mail & Guardian* newspaper (2nd January 2014). Christie had explored the river for years in a strange, meandering journey. His article mentioned Paul Fairall, a wetlands expert who had been chair of the Jukskei River Catchment Area Management Forum, among many other roles and duties in the subject area. He had been advocating for South Africa's rivers for decades. I was able to find his phone number and I summoned the nerve to call him. I simply said, 'I'm [Author] and I work for Nando's. I think our offices are here at the Jukskei.'

Paul was excited to hear from someone with fresh interest in the Jukskei and he was an incredible source of knowledge and information. In 2017 he was living in a retirement home in Johannesburg and was in a wheelchair with the words 'African bullfrog' written on its side. The name was in honour of another passion of his, rescuing African bullfrogs, and reflected his mischievous sense of humour.

Around the same time, I crossed paths with eco-artist Hannelie Coetzee, who creates profound environmental and urban art projects. We had met several years earlier when we were both working on community projects related to the use of waste materials in art and crafts. Hannelie was producing a series called Watermense/ Water People, creating portraits of people that she encountered during her walks along Johannesburg's spruits. The portraits took on various forms, including engravings on discarded doors, stencils on found-maps, and other wood-based work. I told her about my ideas for the Jukskei and she came to visit the overgrown culvert section with me. Her curiosity amplified mine and we decided to work together to do something meaningful.

The two of us visited Paul as often as we could. He would always offer us some more whiskey or biscuits, while he talked at length and in depth about the Jukskei River. The two of us had a lot to learn about what an environmental remediation project required. Paul provided much-needed guidance not only on the environmental issues but also about how and where to get additional information. At times the City of Johannesburg Metropolitan Municipality's bureaucracy and siloed departments seemed as tricky to navigate as the Jukskei.

During that time the only ones working to get the cleanup underway were Hannelie, Sanele Ngcobo and Trust Ndlovu (two gardeners who were employed by Victoria Yards), and me (often referred to as the 'chicken and chips lady' because of my affiliation with Nando's). A lot of people thought our goals were delusional!

I presented our ideas for the cleanup and restoration of the Jukskei to the executive committee of Nando's and the board of Victoria Yards. Both parties agreed to provide seed funding, most of which would be used to take the first step: commissioning studies to analyse the extent of the problem.

By then Hannelie and I both felt devoted to the river. We felt compelled to do something to help it. The Jukskei had been neglected and abused for too long. It deserved love and care. I had a vision of a green corridor along this urban river: a natural space where the community could connect to their natural surroundings and to each other. Why did we accept that there weren't safe, beautiful, natural spaces in Johannesburg where anyone could go for a walk?

A few months later, we hosted a roundtable discussion where the scientists who had evaluated the condition of the river and its surroundings presented their findings. Other environmental experts, civil servants, artists and potential funders were invited to give input. That day it felt as if our vision was going to be flushed downstream along with the litter, building rubble, industrial waste and sewerage that was already in the water. The dismal and demoralising findings described the levels of pollution in the soil and water, and the extent to which alien invasive plant species were suffocating the native habitat. Almost all the meeting participants were saying that our ideas would never work, that there was nothing that could be done.

Jane Eagle, Acting Director for Water and Biodiversity for the Environment and Infrastructure Services Department for the City of Johannesburg was one of the attendees. She raised the point that the city didn't have current data about how the headwaters – the river's water sources – were behaving. The most recent data they had were from the 1980s. I decided to interpret this as a counter point to the argument that the river was hopeless: how could we decide to write off the project if there was still so much we didn't know?

I was not ready to give up my belief in nature's power to recover and heal itself, and the power of beautification to instigate change and uplift people. Perhaps it was simply that my naivety left room for my imagination.

To give ourselves an institutional framework and substantiate the legitimacy of our work, Hannelie and I founded a non-governmental organisation (non-profit), called Water for the Future. Gradually word of our project spread, and some individuals reached out to offer their expertise pro bono. Paul McKenzie took the reins of the finance and compliance aspects of the organisation and established meticulous recordkeeping and financial oversight measures.

We began receiving small grants from the environmental and private sectors. We were able to hire a small team, and with the help of some volunteers, we started removing invasive alien plants, and taking steps towards rewilding the culvert section of the Jukskei. People began to see a clear difference in the part of the river that Water for the Future was cleaning up, and they became more interested. We were proving the viability of our vision!

The area around the culvert was just the start. To make further progress, however, we needed additional information, much of which was in the filing cabinets and computers of the municipality. The political manoeuvres inside the city of Johannesburg can be difficult to keep up with. (For example, we presented to three different mayors over the span of two years.) The breakdown of infrastructure and lack of accountability often leaves residents to come up with their own workarounds or to go without services. Fortunately, there are citizens, including dedicated civil servants, who collaborated with us. Jane Eagle commissioned the Upper Jukskei Catchment Management Plan, and Water for the Future was invited to participate in stakeholder sessions. We were learning so much along the way, and it was affirming and encouraging to be asked for our input and engagement on key reports and future policies.

Dr Simon Lorentz, a principal hydrologist at SRK Consulting, offered to collect and report additional data about water sources, quality and flow. Faculty members at the

University of Johannesburg's Process, Energy & Environmental Technology Station contributed expertise and funding for an environmental management plan. These efforts were key in helping us to determine where to start the work, and what the most impactful and cost-effective strategies would be.

In 2020 Hannelie resigned to focus on her work as an artist. I will always be grateful for her enthusiastic work and profound contribution to the project. The onset of the COVID-19 pandemic meant that I was able to spend a lot more time physically working on the river project, and to meet more people in the community where I lived and worked. One of the most exceptional among these individuals was Lungile Hlatshwayo, a social worker, activist, arts advocate and photojournalist. She helped to set up a soup kitchen and a non-profit called Safe Study for children in the surrounding area.

Lungi and I spent a lot of time together sharing ideas and supporting each other's work. She agreed to become a director at Water for the Future. Much of her work focused on making the Jukskei project relatable to the people who worked and lived in the area, especially children. She knew that the river's well-being was powerfully connected to the local community's well-being. In order for the project to succeed and be sustainable, it needed to offer tangible benefits like employment and ways to enjoy the natural resources.

I am so grateful for the many, many people who have contributed financially and also with ideas, expertise, time, resources and hard work: from the older residents of the community to artists, local business owners, and even pre-school children. Nando's and Victoria Yards have continued to support us. Nando's chose to keep their head office in Lorentzville and further invest in the community rather than move to a glitzier office space in Rosebank or Sandton. I feel very fortunate to have established a network of caring experts, like the incredibly knowledgeable Stuart Dunsmore [co-author of Chapter 5], to whom I can reach out to check facts and help to validate decisions. We've partnered with other organisations and groups like the Alex Water Warriors in the downstream township of Alexandra, and undertaken projects including street cleaning and clearing stormwater drains.

Water for the Future has received funding and incredible support from global organisations like the Goethe Institute and Bloomberg Philanthropies. Financial backing has also come from South African endeavours like the Social Employment Fund (SEF), through local initiatives like the Johannesburg Inner City Partnership (JICP) in partnership with the Industrial Development Corporation (IDC) and the President Stimulus Fund. One of the most important opportunities we received was from the SEF-JICP: it enabled us to hire 110 people for a 9 month period. These individuals received useful and marketable skills training, such as how to remove invasive alien plants safely and turn the biomass into fencing or firewood. Other skills included learning how to use a chainsaw, how to plant trees and establish native plants, and even mushroom farming. We recently received approval for a 10-month extension of this training and employment programme.

I'm also encouraged by the shift in some people's understanding of how nature and the environment can benefit them. Economic opportunity can be created in caring for nature and keeping it clean. The areas that we've revitalised have stayed clean! The green corridor is taking shape.

I believe that hyper-local interventions are integral in making cities more climate resilient. Small projects can be scaled up and linked to extend their impact. We have to forge collaborative efforts, always include local people, learn from each other and build networks.

The Jukskei has become a huge part of my life; mostly because of the community that lives around it, and that this project has built up around it. The river has some sort of hold on me. If I haven't been to the river in a while, I physically miss it. I feel compelled to go there for a walk and to see Io Makandal's beautiful artwork, *The Listening Garden*. I see the bird life that is changing, the trees we've planted growing, and the grasses thriving, and my optimism swells.

While the project never felt impossible to me, it does sometimes feel overwhelming. Paul Fairall's sudden death in 2018 was among the first of many wounds that the river washed up at my feet. I'm deeply grateful for the knowledge he shared with me, and the gifts of documents and reports, which have informed our work. At times the work has pushed me to my physical and emotional limits, especially since my amazing friend, inspirational colleague, and co-director of Water for the Future, Lungile Hlatshwayo, passed away in 2023. This work is harder and lonelier without her.

Our team's vision of rejuvenating the river continues to grow into something more beautiful and real. As I always experience through my work, when love, care and attention are given to a space, it lifts people's spirits. I have seen people stop to contemplate the rejuvenating culvert section. Sometimes they turn to tell me it reminds them of home.

Acknowledgement

This chapter was produced with the editorial assistance of Karen Huxham.

About the authors

Nina Barnett is an artist using drawings, papermaking, immersive installations and experimental filmmaking to engage with questions of geography, infrastructure, materiality, and experiential knowledge. Her most recent exhibitions, entitled *The Ballast and the Pine* (POOL x Field Station in Greenpoint Park, Cape Town, 2023), *The Weight in the Air* (Origins Centre, Johannesburg, 2022*)* and *On Breathing* (Adler Museum of Medicine, Johannesburg, 2022), reflect on the futures of colonial material flow, extraction and radioactivity in the elemental atmospheres of Johannesburg and Cape Town. She is a currently a PhD candidate at the University of Johannesburg.

Antoinette Bootsma holds a master's degree in environmental science from the University of South Africa (*Cum Laude)*. She has worked as an ecologist for 18 years and has been involved in a very wide range of projects. As a specialist consultant in the environmental sector, she has worked nationally and internationally as a wetland ecologist. She is particularly passionate about restoration and rehabilitation of aquatic ecosystems and she has contributed to this field through published research, mentoring, contribution to environmental impact assessments and support of special interest groups.

Dieter Brandt is a leading architect and transition design expert with over 20 years of experience. Graduating with distinction from the University of Cape Town, he has led significant projects like the Freedom Park Museum and the Mathematical Sciences building in Johannesburg. In 2018, Dieter founded Advanced Environmental Design Initiatives (AEDI) in Berlin, focusing on climate action and sustainable strategies in Africa. He is a senior researcher for the Centre of Ecological Intelligence at the University of Johannesburg. Known for his innovative solutions in sustainable development, Dieter collaborates across borders to promote urban-ecological resilience and address climate challenges through adaptive architecture and regenerative design.

Sarah Charlton is Associate Professor in the School of Architecture and Planning at the University of the Witwatersrand, Johannesburg. She has extensive experience in low-income housing policy and practice, including in homelessness and the institutional spaces of local government and the non-profit sector. Her research includes the interfaces between urban infrastructure and people's practices, state development initiatives and matters of governance. She has a long-standing collaboration with colleagues at the University of Sheffield, Glasgow, and Cardiff, and joint work has included research on housing, youth and mobility with partner organisations in Mozambique and Ethiopia.

Savory Chikomwe holds a BSSc Degree (GZU, Zimbabwe), a Master of the Built Environment (Wits University, Johannesburg), a BSc Special Honours Degree in Urban Studies (LSU, Zimbabwe) and a PhD (Wits, Johannesburg) in 2012, 2014, 2016 and 2022 respectively. He has extensive spatial planning practice in the built environment (1996–to date), University Teaching experiences at GZU (2016–2019 and 2024 to date), and an assistant lectureship at Witwatersrand University (2020–2021). Recently, he worked as a Deputy Director of Infrastructure Planning and Development in the Office of the President and Cabinet, Zimbabwe. In 2024, he was appointed a Lead Planner Consultant to prepare a Rural District Master Plan for the Chivi district of Zimbabwe.

Sean Christie is a Zimbabwean-born journalist and the author of the non-fiction book, *Under Nelson Mandela Boulevard – Life Among the Stowaways* (Jonathan Ball Publishers, 2016), which was awarded the 2017 Recht Malan Prize and shortlisted for the *Sunday Times* Alan Paton Award. He is currently working on a non-fiction book that surfaces forgotten Johannesburg histories, styled as a journey down the Jukskei River.

Abri de Swardt is an artist whose work connects interrelated concerns between queerness, decoloniality, and the more-than-human to imagine forms of affiliation that are critical, fluid, and reparative. De Swardt positions his work as an expanded form of collage, moving between photography, video, sculpture, fiction, sound, costume, historiography, and performance in a convergence of the elemental and theatrical. Solo exhibitions include POOL x Field Station, Cape Town (2024), as part of the *World Weather Network*; POOL, Johannesburg (2018); MOT International Projects, London (2013); and *blank projects*, Cape Town (2011). He has taught at the Wits School of the Arts, Rhodes University, and Stellenbosch University.

Stuart Dunsmore is a registered professional engineer (RSA & UK) and a Chartered Water and Environmental Manager (CIWEM, UK). He has over 30 years of experience in the water sector, mainly in river engineering, flood management, catchment analysis and stormwater management. He specialises in sustainable engineering solutions. Over the last decade, Stuart has been particularly active in urban surface water solutions, collaborating with local and provincial governments in the application and implementation of sustainable drainage practices, nature-based solutions and urban catchment recovery. He is co-author of the *City of Johannesburg Stormwater Design Manual* (2019) and *Design Flood Estimation Guideline for Municipalities in South Africa* (2023). Stuart has developed the pilot catchment management plan for the water resources of the upper Jukskei River in Johannesburg, a river highly impacted by urban development. He is also a consultant to the World Bank on surface water management and nature-based solutions.

ABOUT THE AUTHORS

Nicky Falkof is a professor of Media Studies at the University of the Witwatersrand in Johannesburg. Her books include *The End of Whiteness: Satanism and Family Murder in Late Apartheid South Africa* (2015), *Anxious Joburg: The Inner Lives of a Global South City* (2020) and *Worrier State: Risk, Anxiety and Moral Panic in South Africa* (2022).

Dunja Herzog, an artist, creates installations in which a larger spectrum of stories in their complex interrelationships of matter, material and their transformation and relationship to people, is made tangible and enables new perspectives. Working with natural materials is integral to her practice. Having worked on the African continent for the last twenty years, Dunja's practice is rooted in different forms of exchange and collaboration. Inherent in her projects is an awareness of her own position and carefully addressing the complexities of the deeply unequal post-colonial societies in which she works.

Lungile Hlatshwayo was a social worker, community activist, arts advocate and photographer. She was a director of the NGO Water for the Future at the time of her passing, in 2023. She was deeply committed to challenging inequality through community work. She started and ran vegetable and soup kitchen projects in schools and established entrepreneurship programmes for abused women and rape survivors in Durban. She initiated projects with homeless youth recyclers in Johannesburg and Bez Valley. She was a key contributor to Timbuktu, an NGO in Lorenztville offering services to local children and youth. She was a co-founder of Safe Study SA, a creative arts enrichment initiative for children and young people, in Troyeville. She was also a talented photographer, and a keen urban cyclist who would often be seen using her bicycle for transport around the city.

Kousar Banu Hoorzook is a programme manager in the Water and Sanitation focus area at the University of Johannesburg's Process Energy Environment Technology Station (PEETS). She earned her doctoral degree in Biomedical Technology from UJ Water and Health Research Centre and specialised in microbial and molecular biology techniques for detecting bacterial pathogens in water. Her expertise lies in *Escherichia coli*'s virulence and antimicrobial resistance, water quality, water pollution and management. Dr Hoorzook's work is published in national and international journals and continues to impact water quality research and education. She is currently Y2 rated by National Research Foundation. She currently manages and leads several projects to fulfil the PEETS mandate. The mandate is to contribute towards improving the competitiveness of industry and SMEs through the application of specialised knowledge, technology and facilitating the interaction between industry (especially SMEs) and academia to enable innovation and technology transfer to grow the green economy.

Mehita Iqani was appointed as Chairholder of the South African Research Chair in Science Communication (SciCOM) at Stellenbosch University from January 2022. Prior to this, she was Professor in Media Studies at the University of the

Witwatersrand, where she taught, researched and collaborated for almost eleven years. She is the author and editor of several books on media, consumer culture, luxury, waste, and the Global South, the most recent of which include: *African Luxury Branding: From Soft Power to Queer Futures* (2023), *Garbage in Popular Culture* (2021), *Consumption Media and the Global South* (2016), *Media Studies: Critical African and Decolonial Approaches* (2019), and *African Luxury* (2019). She has published widely in cultural studies journals and is currently leading the SARChI research programme under the theme, 'science communication for social justice.'

Jamaine Krige is a multi-award-winning South African journalist, author, filmmaker and trainer. Her career, which spans almost two decades, is underpinned by a passion for social advocacy and an unwavering belief in the transformative power of storytelling. She started her journalism career at the South African Broadcasting Corporation (SABC) as a radio reporter covering a variety of beats. Her work has appeared in national, regional and international news publications like the *Mail & Guardian*, *Al Jazeera*, *BBC*, *Healthline*, *GroundUp* and more. She holds a BPhil Honours degree in Journalism from Stellenbosch University and an honours degree in Psychology from UNISA.

Io Makandal is an interdisciplinary artist based in Johannesburg, South Africa. Working with drawing, photography, organic matter and installation, her practice is concerned with feminist and environmental embodiments of process, entropy, urban ecology, and hybrid environments during a time of environmental shift. She has exhibited both locally and internationally and her work is a part of several private, public and institutional collections.

Paul Maluleke is one of the founders of the Alex Water Warriors, a team of volunteers who get together to clean up the Jukskei River. The Alex Water Warriors began with a dedicated cadre of 250 volunteers and has grown exponentially into a powerful force of 1 500 individuals. Paul was born and raised in Alexandra, and has been an active community leader for decades. He was instrumental in the establishment the Greater Alexandra Tourism & Heritage Association, driven by the aspiration to revitalise the Jukskei River and envision it as a thriving tourism attraction.

Refiloe Namise explores the making and preserving of a place, Alexandra. Through various sites in Alex, her work *re-members*, re-articulating particular moments and histories. These engagements develop ways of *writing*, recording, storing and sharing social knowledge, heritage and culture. Though much of these concerns are reflected in the present configurations of Alex, a deepened understanding of its existence as a place often demands a return to its past. Namise grapples with the notion of 'return,' through poetic gestures in which she [re]enacts certain past moments. Her work is multi-disciplinary, incorporating image, text, sound, video and performance. She is based in Johannesburg and completed her MFA in Creative Research and Practice at the University of the Witwatersrand.

ABOUT THE AUTHORS

Ujithra Ponniah is a Senior Researcher at the Southern Centre for Inequality Studies (SCIS). She works with the 'Wealth Inequality and Elites' research stream at SCIS. Her research interests include economic elites, caste, race, and gender in India and South Africa.

Renugan Raidoo is a lecturer in social anthropology at Stellenbosch University. His current monograph project concerns lifestyle estates in the Gauteng city region, their political economic origins, and their social and spatial consequences. Previous work focused on secrecy and homophobia in urban Sierra Leone. His research has been funded by awards from various sources at Harvard University (where he completed his PhD), an Emslie Horniman Scholarship from the Royal Anthropological Institute/ Sutasoma Award, and the Fulbright-Hays programme. He holds an MPhil in social anthropology from Oxford University, where he was a Rhodes Scholar, as well as a BA in anthropology and a BS (with honours) in chemistry from the University of Iowa. Previously, he taught at Harvard University and Brandeis University. His academic work can be found in the edited volume *Anxious Joburg: The Inner Lives of a Global South City* (Wits University Press, 2020) and in the journals *GLQ* and *Africa*.

Landi Raubenheimer is an academic and artist living in Johannesburg. She teaches at the Faculty of Art, Design and Architecture at the University of Johannesburg. She is author of the forthcoming monograph entitled *'District 9': Johannesburg as Nostalgic Dystopia* (2025). Her publications are on art, media and spectatorship, and she is interested in the intersections between landscape, media technologies and aesthetics.

Sibusiso Sangweni was one of the most dedicated members of the Alex Water Warriors. He passed away in July 2023 at the age of just 35 years old. His work for the Alex Water Warriors was remarkable – every week he would spend two days as a volunteer, fearlessly stepping in to the river to remove litter. He also oversaw the litter trap that was installed by Alex Water Warriors. He was born in Mpumalanga, and moved to Alexandra after school.

Atheesha Singh, a Senior Lecturer and Researcher at the Water and Health Research Centre, University of Johannesburg, earned her PhD in Microbiology from UKZN. Her expertise includes microbiology, environmental biotechnology, pollution management, and water quality. She focuses on water challenges, pathogen survival, and WASH (water, sanitation, and hygiene). Widely published in international journals, Dr Singh's work significantly impacts water quality research and education. She has trained students in WASH methodologies and has supervised many post-doctorate fellows, doctorates, and master's students. Dr Singh is involved with the Royal Society of Biology, the International Water Association, and the Legionella Action Group.

Romy Stander is a director and co-founder of the NGO, Water for the Future, which currently focuses on rejuvenating the Jukskei River at its source. She is also the

Special Projects Manager at Nando's, one of the main funders of the rejuvenation project alongside Victoria Yards. Her career background is in managing large scale interior design roll outs for blue chip companies around the world, with a particular passion for integrating product development of handmade African crafts, for international market appeal. Romy is committed to understanding how things are made and how this process benefits the maker, immediate community, and environment. She was hired by the founders of Nando's to work on special projects: their flagship peri-peri farm outside Maputo that is being turned into an agricultural academy for women and a malaria-combatting spray training centre on the border of Swaziland. Her role is to assist with improving the working and guest experiences through considered and sensitive beautification projects, approaching them from the ground up. Since the pandemic, her focus has been the remediation of the daylight point of the Jukskei River, a special project which she embarked on in 2017, directly behind the celebrated head office of Nando's, known as Central Kitchen.

Kyle van Heyde is a final-year PhD student in Environmental Management at the University of Johannesburg (UJ). He is also a project manager at the UJ Process, Energy, and Environmental Technology station. Kyle obtained his undergraduate, honours, and master's degrees at the University of the Witwatersrand in Johannesburg, specialising in geography, archaeology, and environmental sciences. His research and work are focused on aquatic environments and pollution, assessing their health, undertaking testing and analyses, and implementing solutions to solve these issues. These are focused mainly on the greater Johannesburg region and the pollution issues faced within the aquatic ecosystems around the city.

Ernita van Wyk is a senior professional officer at ICLEI Africa (Local Governments for Sustainability – Africa Secretariat). Following initial training in ecology and conservation, Ernita's interests and work have focused on research and implementation in the fields of adaptive management, biodiversity mainstreaming and environmental stewardship across a range of ecosystems. She has a particular interest in social-ecological systems and approaches that incorporate biodiversity into urban planning and governance in developing country contexts. Ernita holds a PhD in Environment and Development.

Jessica Webster (PhD, Wits) is a research fellow with the South African Chair of Science Communication at Stellenbosch University. Her background straddles academia and practice-based research in the arts. It is directed towards an 'ethics of communication,' construed as a critical awareness of social and scientific discourses which are specific to South African history and contemporary experience. Webster observes the evolution of threats that already cause intense suffering to South Africa's disadvantaged majority and natural ecologies. Her critical writing and action-research projects are engaged with the psychologies of agency and collectivity in the face of climate change and trauma.

Index

References to tables are **bold**. References to illustrations are *italic*. References to footnotes are exceptional.

A
aafA 38
Acacia caffra, see Senegalia caffra
Acacia karoo, see Vachelia karoo
action plan 217
activation *109*
activism 1, 136
adaptation 48
Adler Museum of Medicine 73
Aeromonas hydrophilia, see AH
aesthetics 143
Afrikaans 121, 123, 124
Afrikaners 122, 123, 126
Agbodohu, Yao 65
agency, *see* choice
Aggregative adherence fimbriae, *see* aafA
Agricultural Journal of South Africa 2
agricultural runoff 41
Agter Elke Man 122
AH **38**
AL **38**
Alcock, GG 118
Alex Action Committee 76
Alexandra 4, 6, 11, 40, 69–70, 76, 80–81, 94,
    136–140, 180
Alexandra Renewal Project 94
Alex Water Warriors 6, 11, 180, 196–197, 225
algae 84
Alsace 63
Aluminium, *see* AL
AMP **38**
Ampicillin, *see* AMP
ANC 122, 138, 187, 211
ancestors 181
Anthropocene 7, 11, 91
anthropology 168
antibiotic resistance 43–44
anticlockwise INGWEMBE 76
apartheid x, 2, 8, 91, 93, 122, 123, 125, 140,
    168
Aquatic and Urban Rescue Unit 134, 150

Arsenic, *see* AS
art 10, 68, 77, 99, 146
ArtBakery 62
Artemisia afra **24**
artists 63, 68, 225
AS **38**
Australopithecines 17
awareness 64

B
Ba **38**
bacteria 37, 76, 116
bacterial contamination
    agricultural 45
    industrial 45
    Jukskei 37
    sources 41
    study 37
    test results 42–44
Baloyi, Steven 192
Barium, *see* Ba
Barnett, Nina 10, 68, 227
Basel 65
baseline assessment 217
Basin Adaptive Systems Integration Network
    Complex 219
BASINc, *see* Basin Adaptive Systems
    Integration Network Complex
beehives 65, 66
beekeeping 65
beeswax 65
bell 63
benchmark sites 18, 19
Benin bronzes 64
Benin City 62, 63, 64
Benin Kingdom 64
Bertrams 11, 16, *108*
bewilderment 142, 145, 149
Bezuidenhout Valley 4, 30, 40
bfpA **38**
biodiversity 18, 215

Birs River 65
Bishop, Claire 143
bleeding 78
Boetzkes, Amanda 98
Bolen, Jeremy 73
Bolhuis, Mike 133–134
Bono 121
Bootsma, Antoinette 9, 227
botany 9, 17
Braamfontein Spruit 10, 40, 91, 153
Brandt, Dieter 11, 227
brass 62, 63
Bredenkamp, George J. 19
bridges 80
bronze 62
Brooker, Vicky 130, 131–132
Brozin, Robbie 222
Bruma 4
Bundle forming pilus, *see* bfpA
bus 70
business sector 57
Bus ya ko 7: The Inauguration 70
Buti, Sam 81
buzzing 66

C
Cadmium, *see* Cd
Cameroon 62
Campbell Scientific 107
Canham, Hugo Ka 144–145
Cassinopsis ilicifolia 19
casting 63, 65
catchment 40, *49*, 50–51, 113
Catchment Management Plan, *see* Upper
    Jukskei Catchment Management Plan
Catha edulis **24**
Cd **38**
cdtB **38**
Cefoxitin, *see* FOX
Centella asiatica **24**
CFU/100 mL **38**
channel 22
Charlton, Sarah 10, 227
Chartwell 130–131
Chauke, Africa 177
chemicals ix
Chikomwe, Savory 11, 228
children 225
Chile 113

Chissano, Joaquim Alberto 218–219
CHL **38**
Chloramphenicol, *see* CHL
choice 155, 157, 158, 161, 164, 165
Christie, Sean 3, 10, 222, 228
Chromium, *see* Cr
City Deep Mine 116
city dwellers 16
City of Johannesburg x, 202, 217, 223, 224
City of Johannesburg Environment and
    Infrastructure Services Department 49
classification of watercourses 21
cleaning up x, 28, 33, *109*, 195, 197, 222, 223
climate change 6, 191, 195, 214–215, 218
Clostridium perfringens, *see* CP
CMP, *see* Upper Jukskei Catchment
    Management Plan
Coetzee, Hannelie 3, 10, 88, 97–98, 223
collaboration 75, *105*
collage 71, 81, 85
collective 76
colonialism 89, 92, 123, 168
Colony forming units per hundred millilitres,
    see CFU/100 mL
colour 76, 79, 86
community 6, 11, 56, 57, 58, 103
compositions 66
condensation 73
confluence 40, *86*
contaminants 37, 45
conversation 70
Conversation with Joel Thamba 70
copper 64–65
corruption 32
Cotyledon orbiculata **24**
cover abundance 19
COVID-19 5, 117, 195, 225
CP **38**
Cr **38**
crack 74
Cradle of Mankind 17
creaturely life 142, 144
Crocodile River 2, 4, 30, 40
Crystal Lagoons® 113–114
culture ix
culvert 29–30, *104*, 224, 226
CURE 89
cut-outs 85
cyanobacteria 76, 84

INDEX

Cyclone Leon-Eline 219
cymatics 64
Cytolethal distending, *see* cdtB

D
Dainfern 11, 115, 183, *184*, *188*
Dainfern Nature Association 183–185
Dainfern Valley 4
dams 79, 80, 86
darting 132
Datura stramonium 16
decolonial perspectives 99
deity 63, 64
democracy x
Denny, Olivia 184–185
Department of Agriculture and Rural
    Development 131
design framework 218
De Swardt, Abri 10, 68, 228
Diaz, Natalie 79–80
Diepsloot 136
Dikobe, Modikwe 78
discussions 68
diseases 116
dissolved oxygen 42
Ditshwantsho tsa Rona 70, *71*
DNA, *see* Dainfern Nature Association
Doornfontein 3, 20
Douglas 86
DownTown Music Hub 65
driftwood 65
Dromedarus 117
droplet treasure hunt *105*, *106*
drowning 181
dumping 41
Dunsmore, Stuart 9, 228
Dutch Royal House of Orange 86
dystopian 97, 98

E
EaeA **38**
EAEC **38**
EAF **38**
Eagle, Jane 224
Eastgate 94
ecology 18, 19, 37
economy x
EcoSeat *106*
ecosystem ix, 18, 28

ecotechnological 98
Edgeworth, Matt 75
Edo Empire 64
education 32
Eerste River 71, 79, 85
Eerste Waterval 72
effective impermeability 51, 56
effluent 115
EHEC **38**
EIEC **38**
electrical conductivity 42
electricity 200, 207, 208
Ellis Park 3
    eye of Jukskei 20
    lake 20
    proclaimed 20
    reservoirs 20
    wetlands 20
embodying 85
endemic species x
energy 64
ENT **38**
Enteroaggregative, *see* EAEC
Enterococci, *see* ENT
Enterohemolysin, *see* EaeA
Enterohemorrhagic, *see* EHEC
Enteroinvasive, *see* EIEC
Enteropathogenic, *see* EPEC
Enteropathogenic adherence factor, *see* EAF
environment 180, 185, 188, 195, 204
    changed 17
    devaluation x
    Johannesburg 99
    love for 25
    regulations 17
    remediation 223
    Suikerbosrand Nature Reserve 19
    value x
environmental drivers 18
environmentalist debates 89
EPEC **39**
Episode 1 70
Episode 2 70
Episode 3 70, *71*, 83
erosion 197
ERY **39**
Erythromycin, *see* ERY
estA **39**
Euclea crispa 19, **23**

235

Euro-African psychology 114
exhibition 66, 70, 73, 89
Exotically Divine *105*
experimentation 84, *84*
eye of Jukskei 20

F
faecal discourse 141
Fairall, Paul 222–223, 226
Falkof, Nicky 10, 229
farm murders 124
faulting 19
Fe **39**
fencing *107*
fieldnotes 168–177
Finding the eye of the Jukskei river beneath Joburg 88, 96, *97*
fines 32
fires 137, 210
Fischmann, Fernando 113
floods 186, 188, 200, 209, 210
    flash x, 53
    loss of life 1
    management 51
    mitigation 58
    reducing 54
    risk 215
    vulnerability 216
flora, *see* plants
fluvial art 75
FNB stadium 117–118
folklore 126
formations 75
For the One that Dances with Jiggling Brass 66
FOX **39**
freedom, *see* choice
frequencies 65
funding 198, 225

G
Ganges 5
Gauteng 28
GEN **39**
genocide 122, 124
Gentamicin, *see* GEN
geography 129
geology 18
geopolitics 91, 99
gifappeltjies 16

Gilloolly's 4
gold leaf 74
golf balls 192
golf course 183–184, 192
Gomorrah 81
Google Earth 202
governance 209, 211
grassland 6, 19
grazers 18
Greater Lanseria Masterplan 4
green corridor 226
groundwater 53, 56

H
Hammarskjöld, Dag 117
Harpo 130–134
Hartbeespoort Dam ix, 4, 40, 50, 130–131
healing 93, *105*
health 37, 45
Heat liable enterotoxin, *see* estA
Hennops river 16
herbivores 17
heritage 70, 197, 214
Heritage Precinct 170
Herzog, Dunja 10, 62, 229
Highveld 17, 18
Hillbrow 3
hippos ix, 130
Hlatshwayo, Lungile 10, 103, 146–147, 225, 226, 229
Hofmeyr, Steve 10, 121–122, 123, 124, 125, 126
holding dam 174
home 156
homelessness 153, 154–155, 161–164
Homeless Writers 156–157
Hoorzook, Kousar Banu 9, 116, 229
housing 111, 113, 163
Hughes, David McDermott 114
HUM 62, 63, 66, *67*

I
identity politics 123
iloqui 16
immersion 91
Immorality Act 118
incentives 53
Incidental Rift 74
income generation 163, 166, 196

INDEX

India 5
Indian Ocean 40
indigenous 115, 215
industrial discharges 41
inequality 94, 99
informality 91, 94
informal living 153–166
informal settlement 199–201, 207, 209
infrastructure 142, 200, 201
    Alexandra 40
    better 32
    breakdown 224
    green 217
    investment 58, 211
    lack 29
    local 57
    maintenance 94, 112
    programmes 210
    quality 28
    upgrading 94
injustice 139
installation 62, 66, *67*, 72–73
instruments 62, 63, 64, 65
interventions 76, 218
interviews 156–157, 199, 202–203
Invasion plasmid antigen H, *see* ipaH
invasive species 215
ipaH **39**
Iqani, Mehita 229
Iron, *see* Fe
Isitiya soLwazi 217–218
island 177
itunga 16

J
Jekyll, Gertrude 114
job creation 6
Joburg, *see* Johannesburg
Joburg's first beach 116
Joe Slovo Drive 20, 21
Johannesburg
    challenges 8, 47
    dome 18
    environment 99
    future 4
    gardens 114–115
    geography 2, 3
    geology 111
    history 4, 93

inequality 4
    literature on 2
    migration 157–158
    no major water source 1
    public space 165
    scholarship on 2
    and the sea 111, 113
    skyline 90
Johannesburg Water 115
Jukskei
    approaches 68
    bacterial contamination, *see* bacterial contamination
    barrier 140
    canal 20
    catchment 40
    conditions 77, 223–224
    confluence 30, 40
    course 40, 74, 148, 183, 215
    crisis 47–48
    dangerous 126
    degradation 141
    dirty river 125
    division between regions 2
    ecological benchmark 18
    eye 96
    floods 137
    game 1
    headwaters *104*
    healing 62, 66
    historical 16, 37
    history 91
    human relationships 98
    ignored 143
    interest 223
    its place in Johannesburg 2
    Johannesburg's river 3
    length 28
    map xii–xiii, 3
    microbiology 42–44
    multiple perspectives 9
    origin of name 1, 2
    partition 129
    perennial 2
    pollution 5, 94
    a presence 73
    profile *30*
    qualities 88, 89, 91
    rejuvenation 226

representations 88
significance 2
source ix, 21, 112, 224
as symbol 129
urban rivers 97, 98
views of 68–69
visibility 89
vital water source 46
Jukskei Derby 1
Jukskei Ghost 78
Jukskei River, *see* Jukskei

K
Kammakamma 71, 72
KAN **39**
Kanamycin, *see* KAN
Katse Dam 112
Kerzner, Sol 114
Khan, Gulshan 10, 88, 89–90, 92–93
kikuyu grass 16
'Kill the Boer' 121
King Solomon's Mines 114
Klein Jukskei Spruit 40
Klip river 88, 90–91, 112
Klipriviersberg Group 18
kloofs 19
Kombuis, Koos 114
Krige, Jamaine 10, 230
Kruger National Park 198
Kulick, Don 148
Kyalami 4, 29–30

L
lagoon 115–116
Lake Kariba 114
lakes 20
land 122, 123, 124, 125
landscapes 98, 124, 143, 214
Lanseria 4
Laserson, Marion 20
Latour, Bruno x
lava flows 19
LDPE, *see* Low-Density Polyethylene
Lead, *see* Pb
lechoe 16
Leeuwkop Prison 4
legacy 95
leisure 123
Lesotho 50, 112, 116

Leucosidea sericea **23**
Lévi-Strauss, Claude 182
Leye, Goddy 62
Li **39**
Liang, Olivia 71
Limpopo 216
Limpopo River 40
Lindu, Salifu 62
Linton, Jamie 69
Lippia javanica **24**
Listen 89–90, 91, 98
Listening Garden 146
Lithium, *see* Li
litter traps 180–181
lived experiences 10, 16
living conditions 153–166, 203, 206, 209
Locke, John 92
Lonehill 4
Lorentz, Simon 112, 224
Lorentzville 3, 18, 29, 66, *104*, 225
Low-Density Polyethylene 33–34

M
macroplastics 27
Mahlangu, Brian 136–137
Makandal, Io 3, 9, 146–147, 226, 230
Malema, Julius 121
malpitte 16
Maluleke, Paul 11, 180, 230
Mamlambo 168–177
management
    approaches 59
    cooperation 219
    decentralisation 53, 56–57
    floods 51
    land 123, 125
    stormflows 58
    targets 51
    urban rivers 11, 16, 215
    waste 32
    water catchment 10
    water quality 37
Manganese, *see* Mn
manillas 64
Maputo 219
marsh, *see* wetlands
mass production 83
Matake, Farai 65
Mavimbela, Daniel 135–136

INDEX

Maxwell, Keith 117
Mbembe, Achille 144
McKenzie, Paul 224
mediation 83
Merleau-Ponty, Maurice 190
Mertens, Alice 85
metals 45
Metro Police 160–161
Miami in Soweto 119
microplastics 27
migration 6
mining 41, 88, 96, 112
minority 122
Mkhondo 179
Mn **39**
Mntambo, Thembalezwe 65, 66
Modderfontein Spruit 40
Mogalakwena 217
monitoring x
Montecasino 115
monument 74
Morninghill 4
Morwalo wa Metla 76
mosaic 4, *109*
Mozambique 219, 222
mtuma 16
Munyaka 111, 113, 115, 116
museums 64, 69, 74
musicians 62, 65
myth 169, 174, 197
mythology 63, 124, 125, 126, 147
Mzangwe, Luyanada 117

N
NAL **39**
Nalidixic acid, *see* NAL
Namise, Refiloe 10, 68, 230
Nando's 222, 223, 225
nanoplastics 27
narrative 90
nature
    and Afrikaner identity 123
    in cities ix, 25
    colonial views 91
    and humans 93, 99, 125
    perceptions of ix
    polluted 90
    proximity 90
    purity 121

    and religious devotion 90
nature morte 93
Ndlovu, Cosmas 66
Ndlovu, Trust 223
neglect 3
Neimanis, Astrida 77
Nel, Ian 113–114
networks 158
news 1
Ngcobo,Grant *103*
Ngcobo, Sanele 223
Ni **39**
Nickel, *see* Ni
Nigeria 62, 63, 64, 65
nitrates 83–84
Nlangamandla, Siyabonga *106*
Noka ya Tsala 77, 78
Northern Transvaal 2
Northern Wastewater Treatment Works 115

O
occult 171
Olosun, Doyin Fani 63, 66
Omodamwen, Phil 63, 65, 66
On Breathing 73
open spaces 52, 53, *55*, 58
Ophidian's Promise 147
Orange River 69, 79, 86
Orange River Project 69
Oriental City China Mall 4
Osogbo 63
Ọṣun 62, 63, 64, 66
ozone plant 174

P
PA **39**
palms 114–115
palynology 17
parameters 42
park dwellers, *see* informal living
park land 160
partnerships 11
pastoral idealism 121
pathogens 27, 37
Pb **39**
PCR **39**
people x
perceptions 31
performances 76

permanence 203
pH 42
philosophers 182, 190, 191
photocopying 83
photographers 94
photographs 3, 81, 85, 88, 89, 90, 91, 92–93,
    97–98, 99
phytochemicals 23
Pierneef, J.H. 91–92, 93
Pikitup 94
planning 215–216
plants
    active ingredients **24**
    communities 19
    cover 19
    endemic x, 9
    grassland 6
    indigenous **22–23**, **24**
    invasive ix, 17, *107*
    magical 23
    medicinal 17, 23, **24**
    reintroduced 22, 25
    wetlands ix, 21
plastics
    categories 27
    micro 27
    nano 27
    not biodegradable 32
    number of items 33
    pollution 27
    single-use 27, 34
    sizes 34
    waste 27
    weight 34
plumbing 95
Poison Apple 16
policy 210, 211
politicians 204
politics 10, 11, 121, 123, 125, 129, 141, 196
pollution
    awareness 31, 33
    bacterial, *see* bacterial contamination
    characterising 28
    community perceptions 27, 28
    culpability 95
    diseases 27
    environmental impact 31–32, *32*
    fecal 94
    macroplastic 27

marine plastic debris 28
mining 96
natural 41
photographs 91
plastic 31, 92
quantifying 28, 31
reduction 32, 35, 58
sampling 31
solutions 32
sources 46, 88, 96
South Africa's ranking 28
ubiquity 28, 34
visible 96
Polymerase chain reaction, *see* PCR
Polypropylene 34
Polystyrene 34
Ponniah, Ujithra 10, 231
Ponte City 90
poverty 216
power dynamics 80
power relations 89
PP, *see* Polypropylene
praying churchgoers 90
Pretoria Rural 30
priorities x
property ownership 169
prophetic words 80
PS, *see* Polystyrene
Pseudomonas aeruginosa, *see* PA
public health, *see* health

R
racism x, 122
Raidoo, Renugan 11, 231
rain 56, 58
Rathebe, Dolly 118
Raubenheimer, Landi 10, 231
Real EYES Realize Real Lies 71
reclaimers 155, 162
recycled waste 64
recyclers *108*
red 76
Red Gold Import Export 63, 64
Red October 122, 125
referendum 122
rejuvenation 103
    botanical 22
    complex 6
    grounded in historical knowledge 22

investment 5
projects 6
revegetation 17
river 5, 11
religious dedication 90
relocation 203, 204, 206, 208
remediation 83
removal 201, 210
representations 98
research 8, 11, 27, 199, 202
reservoirs
    Ellis Park 20
    first 20
    storage 20
resilience 6–7, 48, 214
respondents 157, 158, 165
    awareness 31
    interaction with Jukskei 31
restitution 64
reterritorialization 87
retrofit 55, 56
Rhamnus prinoides 19
Rhodesia 114
Rhoicissus tridentata 19
Rhus pyroides, see Searcia pyroides
Ridder Thirst 71, *72*, 79, 81, 85
riparian
    citizens 8
    meaning 7
    zone 7
riparian urbanism
    definition 7
    history 8
    of Jukskei 7
    theoretical framework 1
    theorising 11
    work 11
Riparian Urbanism Symposium xi, 62, 66
risk 73
river banks x
riverine plastic pollution 27–28
rivers
    in art 62
    as artefacts 75
    as assets 5
    collaboration 75, 84
    contradictions 191
    dammed 80
    dangerous 179, 181, 187

divide 129
floods 80
health 58, 99
historical accounts 20
and human rights 5
impact 73
markers of time 80
meaning 186
metaphor 182
most polluted 28
origin of writing 71
pollution and healing 5, 93
relationship
as resources 5
riparian systems 21
storytelling 71
transformative 66
riverside living 153–166
river systems 5
Riverwork 75, 77
riverworkers 75
Roaring Lagoon 114
Rupert Museum 69

S
SA **39**
Salts 65
sampling 31, 33, 41, 72, 83, 112
San 17
Sandringham 4
Sandton 4
Sangweni, Sibusiso 11, 231
sanitation 201, 203–204
SANTA 117
Santner, Eric 142–143
Scabiosa columbaria **24**
Scadoxis puniceus **24**
Schadeberg, Jürgen 118
SciCOM xi
science
    abbreviations **38**
    acronyms **38**
    citizens *108*
    relevant 6
    vegetation 19
    water quality 38, 46
scientific evidence 9
scientists x
sculptures 65, 72, 76

Se **39**
Searcia pyroides **23**
security 210
sedimentary rocks 19
seepages 21
Segopotso 73, 76, 83
Segopotso sa Gomora – Open Studio 69
Selenium, *see* Se
Senegalia caffra **23**
service provision 203
sewage ix, 41, 51, 52, 98, 115–116, 141, 200, 205
sewerage, *see* sewage
Shareworld 117
Shinga toxin, *see* stx
Sibanda, Angel 134–136
Sibanda, Sbonisa 134, 135
Singh, Atheesha 9, 231
Sinthumule, Godfrey 136
Sjwetla 199–211
slave trade 64
snake 147, 171, 179, 181, 197
social connectivity 5
social divides 129
Social Impact Arts Prize 2022 69
social media 185
soils 18–19
Solanum species 16
solutions 49
Sontag, Susan 191
sound 64, 66, 83
source x, 3, 41
South Africa 129–130
South African Human Rights Commission 5
South African Institute for Maritime Research 117
South African Police Service 134
South African Research Chair in Science Communication, *see* SciCOM
Soweto 117
Soweto Beach Party 118
Soweto Highveld Grassland 6, 18
Spaza Gallery 4
species 19
spiritual change 198
spiritual world 64, 181
springs
    artesian 20
    definition 20

natural 3
stagnancy 84
Stander, Romy 11, 231
Staphylococcus aureus, *see* SA
Stellenbosch 85
Steyn City 4, 115–116, 133–134, 186
Steyn, Douw 115
still life 93
Stjwetla 136–140
    informal settlement 4
    living conditions 11
Stone Age 17
storage
    in soil 52
    subterranean 52
storms 53–54
stormwater harvesting 51
stormwater management 52, 53, 56–57, 58
stormwater runoff 41, 52, *55*, 56
streams, *see* rivers
Streams 81, *82*
strip map 3
studios 214
study area *29*
study methods 28
study results 31, 56
stx **39**
Subterranean Wavelength 65
suffering 93
Suikerbosrand 9, 21, **22–23**, 25
Suikerbosrand Nature Reserve 19
Sun City 114, 115
supernatural beings 148
surfaces 55
survey
    demographic groups 31
    Google Forms 29
    online 29
    participation 29
    respondents 31
    results 31
    sites 19, 29–30, 33–34
    units 19
sustainability 5, 57, *105*, 196, 214
sustainability manager 172–177
Sustainable Urban Drainage System 215
swimming 85, 179–180
symposium xi

INDEX

T
target sites 18
temperature 42
TET **39**
Tetracycline, *see* TET
Thamba, Joel 70, 76
Thamba, Ntate 73
Thames 3
The Blyde 113
Themeda triandra 19
theme park 117
The Point of Order 70
Theron, G.K. 19
Thsuma, Thabani 135
time *82*
toolmaking 17
total dissolved solids 42
totemism 182, 186–187
To the River 71
tourism 180, 196
townships 94, 100n12
Trachypogon spicatus 19
trails 184
training 225
translation 83
Transvaal 2
tree planting *106*
Troyeville 4
turbidity 42
Twitter 122

U
U2 121
ultra-low-budget living 154
umhlavuthwa 16
umthuma 16
underworld 98
unemployment x, 164
Union Buildings 126
Upper Jukskei Catchment Management Plan
 47
  challenges 53
  origin 49
  outcomes 58
  targets 51
urban designers x
urban development 214
urban drainage *106*
urban environment 8

urbanisation 215
urban landscaping 22
urban nature ix
urban planning 95
  apartheid 91
  colonial 91
  environmentally unsound 3
uses ix

V
Vaal barrage 112
Vaal Dam 50, 76–77, 79, 80, 83, 85, 112
Vaal River 5, 86
Vachelia karoo **23**
vadose zone 52–53, 56
VAN **39**
Vancomycin, *see* VAN
Van der Merwe, Hentie 85
Van Heyde, Kyle 9, 232
vanitas paintings 93
Van Wyk, Ernita 9, 232
Vaya 156
VC **39**
Ventersdorp Geological System 19
Ventersdorp Supergroup 18
Vibrio cholerae, see VC
victimhood 125
Victoria Yards 4, 29, 65, 66, *103, 104,* 222,
 223, 225
video 70, 77, 79, 85
violation 72
violence 124, 159, 210
Vladislavic, Ivan 117
voiceover 79
volk 123
volunteers 197

W
walking 84
Warburgia salutaris **24**
waste
  dumped 179–0
  interpretations 95
  meaning 93
  quantifying 95
  recyclers 94
  removal 93, 94, 95
  types *108*
water

243

in the body 77, 84
colour 90
commodification 168
elusive 87
and gold 75
healing 91
journey 116
nature 69, 87
needs 115
privatised 111
quality 28, 116
sample 83, 84
spirituality 91
watercourses 21
Waterfall City 168–177
Waterfall Estate 4, 115
Water for the Future xi, 4, 6, 16, 224
water quality
  analysis 37
  concerns 57–58
  implications **38**
  improving 51
  management 37
  measurements 41
  metals 45
  parameters 42
  science 46
  study 46, 96
water security 6
Watson, Patrick 114–115
wealth 123, 171–172, 192
weather station *107*
Webster, Jessica 10, 232
Wemmer Pan 116–117
Wenger, Susanne 63
WetHealth assessment method 18
wetlands 21
  built over 3
  fauna 21
  and grassland 1
  groundwater 20

integrity 18
plants ix, 21
systems 20–21
types 21
Weyers, Dave 188
WFTF, *see* Water for the Future
What is Water? 69
whiteness 121, 122, 126
white supremacy 71
Wicht, Hein 115
wilderness ix
wildlife 41
Windigo 143–144
witchcraft 179
witnessing 73
Witwatersrand
  Basin 18
  meaning 2
  Ridge 74
wood **22–23**, *107*
wooden spoon 76
work environments 222
Wouri River 62
writing 71

X
Xai Xai 219
xenophobia 159

Y
Yokeskei 2
Yoruba 62, 63

Z
Zambezi river 114
Zinc, *see* Zn
Zionists 90
Ziziphus muconata **23**
Zn **39**
Zuma, Jacob 121
Zylinska, Joanna 87